Group Workers at Work

Group Workers at Work

Theory and Practice in the '80s

EDITED BY
Paul H. Glasser and Nazneen S. Mayadas

Rowman & Littlefield
PUBLISHERS

ROWMAN & LITTLEFIELD

Published in the United States of America in 1986
by Rowman & Littlefield, Publishers
(a division of Littlefield, Adams & Company)
81 Adams Drive, Totowa, New Jersey 07512

All the articles herein were originally presented at the
Second Social Work with Groups Symposium,
The University of Texas at Arlington, November 1980.

Library of Congress Cataloging-in-Publication Data

Group workers at work.

    "All the articles herein were originally presented
at the Second Social Work with Groups symposium,
the University of Texas at Arlington, November 1980"
    Includes index.
    1. Social group work—United States—Congresses.
I. Glasser, Paul H.   II. Mayadas, Nazneen S.
(Nazneen Sada)   III. Symposium for the Advancement of
Social Work with Groups (2nd : 1980 : University of
Texas at Arlington)
HV45.G732   1986   361.4'0973   86–3862
ISBN 0-86598-160-4

88 87 86
10 9 8 7 6 5 4 3 2 1

Printed in the United States of America

Contents

Tables

Preface

From the beginning, social group work has been at the heart of the social work profession. Developed from the needs of the underprivileged and the poor in the settlement houses of our growing urban areas at the turn of the century, while its methodology has been work with small groups, its values, goals, and objectives have always been broadly conceived. The group is the means to such ends as participatory democracy, social action and social change as well as the maximization of individual growth and socialization, and resocialization of persons into the mainstream of American society. Social group work's dual emphasis on the individual and on his or her community continues as a central theme in social work.

The affluence that followed World War II was a significant factor in leading the profession to emphasize its *professionalism,* that is, its identity as a distinct vocation with its own methodology. In the process, the identity of social group work tended to get lost because the focus was on the generic curriculum and a basic set of methods and techniques for all practitioners. But the broader goals were not forgotten, as was illustrated during the 1960s and 1970, when social workers, including many group workers, stood at the forefront of the civil rights movement, the demand for peace, environmental change, and the war on poverty. As the number of practitioners rapidly grew and the profession became recognized in law by a majority of the states, social work became more secure. Method specialization came into fashion again, and with it social group work with its emphasis on the broader values and goals which social work has always sought. The journal *Social Work with Groups* began publication in 1978 and the first meeting of the Annual Symposium of Social Group Work was held in 1979.

We are in a new era as budget deficits and funds for the military threaten the continuation of many social programs. There is more reason than ever to give attention to participatory democracy, social action, and social change along with the more individualized goals of the group work method. And many social group workers are doing so. This volume is a reflection of their efforts as many of the papers reflect where we have been and the need to return to our roots. We hope it will stimulate and inspire not only social group workers but all social workers and other professionals interested in how groups can be the foundation for individual and social change.

We would like to thank each of the authors for their cooperation in revising their manuscripts to make this volume a reality. Special appreciation goes to Roberta Dotterer, who not only did much of the typing, but also coordinated work with the authors and assisted in the editing. We believe this book is another step in the pursuit of the goals of the social work profession and the unique position of social group work within it.

Paul Glasser
Nazneen Mayadas

Part I

Introduction

1

The Changing Nature of Social Group Work Practice

Nazneen S. Mayadas and Paul H. Glasser

Social group work has experienced many vicissitudes since its inception in the early settlement-house days at the turn of the century. Consistent with the historical development of social work, the group work method also emerged in response to human needs, particularly to those of immigrants in Chicago and other large urban areas. It started as a service methodology aimed at social change through the application of democratic norms and procedures in small groups to societal concerns. However, in the process of its development it went through a period when it took on the more narrow perspective of clinical intervention and psychotherapy. Today, group work is at the crossroads of a major decision—whether to maintain its uniqueness as a broad democratic approach that serves the community and society as well as individuals with special needs, or to merge with the burgeoning methodologies of sociopsychological and behavioral interventions in the field of group therapy. This may well be a survival decision, as illustrated by the concern and involvement of its proponent, the National Symposium on Social Work with Groups. It speaks to the awareness of its practitioners for the need of social group work to exist as a separate but necessary and vital entity in the overall profession of social work.

While sharing the ethical and philosophical base of social work, group work stands out as a distinct methodology, which derives its objectives, goals, and techniques partly from the practical experience of its pioneers and partly from the empirical studies in small-group research, group dynamics, and social psychology. In this approach the central focus of interventon is not the individual or the community but the small group. The purposes of intervention cover the spectrum from individual change through small groups to societal change through mobilization of

3

small groups for social action. The social group worker uses the small group as an entity to introduce change in whatever level of social phenomenon is targeted. Within this conceptual framework social group work subsumes both the preventive and the rehabilitative model in determining its plan of action. It is this dual thrust that distinguishes social group work from other group modalities, treatments, and therapies. Groups in social work are used not only as the means and context of change but also as the vehicle for mutual growth and development of the individual, the community, and society. For schematic purposes, the intervention strategies used in social group work may be separated into those that focus on change and growth in the individual per se and those that are used for change in the social milieu that affects the life space of the group, its individual members, and others in the environment.

A concern that has plagued the profession since the days of the Milford Conference in 1922 is the struggle between "generic and specific." Social group work has not been immune to this swing of the pendulum. Having received its initial impetus for growth from the demonstrated needs of the settlement movement, and being committed to participatory democracy, social group work entered the field of social work with a rich assemblage of programming skills and practice experience, which added a new and hitherto unknown dimension to the profession—that of reciprocal responsibility, client participation in decision making, and member–worker-initiated plans of interventive actions. While this merger of social group work with the profession contributed to the expansion of social work knowledge, it also served as the death knell of group work as a unique methodology.

The 1940s and 1950s saw the emergence of the generic emphasis, when educators and practitioners alike were immersed in the search for a common body of knowledge—the swing of the pendulum to the generic side. Social group work submerged into this phase and concentrated its efforts extrapolating commonalities with the field of social work in order to establish its integrity within the profession. By the end of the 1960s the trend was once again to the "specific." Group work flowed with the tide, after spending two decades trying to establish a generic stance within the profession, and the change stimulated renewed efforts to reestablish an exclusively identifiable position. This preoccupation with finding its identity led social group work to associate itself with group-therapy methodologies, just as casework had done with the psychoanalytical school of treatment in the 1940s. During this period social group work allowed itself to become almost too closely affiliated with group psychotherapy, thus running the danger of losing its uniqueness.

This was understandable in light of the tremendous growth and interest in group psychotherapy during the recuperation phase of the post–World War II years. Time and cost considerations, along with the increasing alienation of the individual from his or her social environment and the traumatic impact of the personal devastation caused by the war years, all led to underscore that a one-to-one treatment approach no longer was sufficient to solve the complexity of problems in an organizationally oriented society. Groups were seen as the panacea for freeing the individual from loneliness and alienation, a substitute for lost familial ties and the simple communal lifestyle of the small-town agrarian society of the past. Group work joined the bandwagon of the "in-group." About 1960, social group work went through a phase where professional activities were primarily associated with therapeutic interventions. Some group workers fought shy of professing any interest in preventive, community oriented activities and, to some extent, disclaimed the proud heritage of their settlement-house origin. "Programming" and "recreational activities" became less important, and many group workers looked down at their professional peers who still dared to claim affinity with preventive group activities. (A repeat of this denial of its professional heritage is seen in more recent times, where social workers are enamored of the behavioral psychologists and once again are contorting their image to fit into a mold that is not necessarily designed for them.) Social change was to be left to the community organizers. This phase lasted for almost two decades, until the late 1970s, when group work woke up to the realization that under a different guise and therapeutic nomenclature its preventive/program orientation was being usurped by various other professionals and "new" orientations, such as expressive art therapies, simulations, and modeling therapies.

At this juncture, since the latter half of the 1970s, group work has made a concerted effort to revert back to its original stance of serving both the individual and society through multiple techniques and interventions that embrace both the therapeutic and program/preventive dimensions. Having survived the pressure to assimilate with group psychotherapy, group work and group workers are once again conscious of their special heritage and are keen to expand the specific nature of group process to include more generic strategies in order to cater to a much wider clientele with varying service dimensions. In other words, there is a growing recognition in the field that generic and specific are not necessarily diametrically opposed concepts. The terms complement each other in the applied sciences through multiple service technologies. For example, using the group as the unit of intervention is specific to social group work; however, the group approach itself becomes generic when applied in service to groups of diverse populations with varying purposes, goals, and objectives. Hence, the controversy between generic and specific in social group work becomes irrelevant so long as the group worker is convinced of his or her own identity and unique contribution to the larger field of social work. The possibilities for new applications of methodologies to ever-growing areas of social needs are unlimited; it is left to the workers in the field to innovate and affect societal developments with techniques and strategies of social group work that has at its base the philosophy of collective responsibility and the underpinnings of democracy. Groups are a microcosm of society and the natural habitat of the human race; as such, it is only logical that this slice of life be used in a planned, systematic way to influence individuals and society.

Social group work and group workers have not been idle in the past decade. There is an upsurge to revive the holistic nature of group work as it had been originally conceptualized by the pioneers in the 1930s and 1940s, to incorporate the psychotherapeutic dimension of the 1950s and the 1960s, and emphasize the scientific component of accountability and evaluation, which are products of the last two decades. The synthesis of the past with the emerging new trends toward assessment of outcomes and effectiveness of service has widened the horizon of social group work to include interventions for populations hitherto not recognized as vulnerable groups in need of specialized services. The literature is now becoming prolific with studies related to ethnic minorities, women, children, and other socially or politically oppressed groups. Moreover, there is a move away from bland statements of theory and descriptive data toward a more critical analysis of information in an effort to determine and isolate those factors that have a significant effect on processes in groups and that the worker can manipulate toward desired outcomes. No longer are group workers satisfied with platitudes and arm-chair theories; they are now asking for empirical evidence to document the effectiveness of their interventions. Practice wisdom no longer suffices to compete with the demands of society for accountability in service. Skills, in order to have credence, must now be derived from theoretical bases that are supported by empirical research. This trend permeates all aspects of social services, and social group work is not immune to it. Social group work has not only come around full circle; it also has spiraled to a more sophisticated level of expertise, where the practice wisdom of yesteryear is gradually being substantiated by the documented empirical knowledge of today. This reinforces the practice behaviors of the group worker, which are not only governed by pragmatic humanitarian considerations, but are based on tested knowledge of effectiveness of selected interventions.

The inclusion of the empirical dimension in social group work has expanded its application to techniques and methods in management training in industry and the corporate world. In fact, there are few areas of training, education, social and industrial programming, and human services left that do not rely on the knowledge base of small group research, group dynamics, social psychology, and social group work in planning and implementing their projects. Services are rendered both through task and socioemotional groups. It is hard to conceptualize a task activity without conjuring up the image of a committee at work or a meeting in process. Social planning and administration, community organizational, and community development all utilize the group as the basic unit of organization and the organ through which they discharge their respective activities. The democratic principles of group work permeate not only social welfare administration but also large-scale industry and commercial management, where use of committees for decision making has become an expected and integral part of conducting daily business. Likewise, group approaches have been incorporated in treatment modalities that originally relied heavily on one-to-one approaches. Implicit in this range of activities and services is the awareness that to manage such complex, multifaceted tasks there has to be a high level of discrimination to determine *what* techniques apply to *which* populations under *what* specified conditions in *which* particular settings, and toward accomplishment of *which* objective. Thus, under the overall umbrella of the generic term *social group work*, innumerable specific theories, techniques, and strategies of intervention have emerged that must be acknowledged if this professional method is to keep its identity and stand abreast of other, related human services.

This book is a product of just such a concern. As a result, some four hundred social group workers came together to share ideas and present formal papers and issues at the Second Annual Symposium of Social Group Work held in Arlington, Texas. The selection of papers for the book was based on four considerations:

1. To provide a consistent conceptual framework for the assessment of social group work as a method based on the interrelated processes of: (a) identification of phenomenon of concern; (b) intervention design; and (c) outcome evaluation. Such a broad general framework should provide explanations that can be applied across the board to a diverse range of group work activities with varying populations and special groups.

2. To highlight a sequential trend depicting the developments in social group work, from its historical inception to its current stage of searching for a firm scientific base.

3. To illustrate how social group work services can be applied to special populations in society. Basically, this relates to: (a) groups whose members share a common problem but not necessarily similar personal characteristics, such as alcoholics and mental patients; (b) groups whose members share common personal characteristics, such as street corner gangs and youth groups; and (c) vulnerable groups whose members are socially, economically, or politically oppressed, such as the handicapped, migrant workers, and ethnic minorities.

4. To analyze critically and evaluate social group work education and its effects on the preparation of students for the profession. Here attention is concentrated on teaching methodologies that identify linkages between theoretical formulations and intervention techniques used by group work-

ers, as well as focusing on the progressive recognition given by group work professionals to empirically tested practice behaviors.

Based on these considerations, the book is broadly organized into five sections. The first section consists of papers dealing with historical perspectives of social group work and the challenges the profession faces in the 1980s. The second section is oriented toward the development of conceptual frameworks for analyzing various processes of social group work. These designs are theoretical explanations posited by the various authors that can be tested and further developed through empirical research. The papers in this section were selected to illustrate how theory is linked to practice and how the group worker derives his or her interventive strategies from conceptual understanding and theoretical formulations of group phenomena.

The third section concentrates on illustrations of direct practice with special groups; the similarity and differences in strategies vis-à-vis specific groups and their effect on selected group and particular client outcomes. The articles here deal with such vulnerable groups as the elderly, children of divorced parents, and alcoholics. In addition, they address strategies for the application of special program techniques in social group work.

The fourth section continues the emphasis of the previous section but concentrates exclusively on social group work with ethnic minorities. Emphasis here is on education, treatment, and social-action elements in group work interventions related to special services for minority groups.

The last section deals with current trends in education and research in the field of social group work. It highlights the growing awareness on the part of the profession of the need to validate theoretical formulations with empirical data and underscores the attempts made by practitioners and educators to apply research methodology to various dimensions of social work practice.

The authors hope that this book will serve as an incentive to social group workers to continue their endeavors toward enriching the field with empirical knowledge and theoretical frameworks, which are the bedrock of any applied social science and service-oriented profession. The content of this book can serve as a springboard for additional creative techniques for work with diverse populations and the education of professionals, which in turn, will augment the knowledge base of the profession.

If the trends of the past and the indications of the present are any predictors of the future, social group work stands on solid ground as an integral part of professional social work, with a well-defined identity of its own that owes its allegiance to both the individual and society.

Part II

From the Past into the Future

Social group work traces its origin to the aftermath of World War I, when its protagonists advocated the use of the small group to deal with a gamut of activities, ranging from social change to the development of the individual within the group context. The chapters in this section concentrate on the vicissitudes in the historical development of social group work and project its status within the profession of social work for the 1980s. A common theme that runs through all the chapters is the original broad emphasis of group work, which encompassed the relationship between "group processes" and "group outcomes," and pioneered the use of groups both to teach democratic functioning and to make democratic decisions. Thus, there is a place for group workesr in a variety of settings to serve in administrative and community organization leadership roles, as well as in clinical positions.

Chapter 2, "Old Themes for a New World," focuses on the evolution of social group work and the likely directions it will take in the future. Social group work essentially sprang from a health model, concentrating on growth and the stimulation of human potential for citizen participation. Its emphasis was on providing a developmental model for identity affirmation and character building. However, this focus gradually changed in the 1950s as social group work was incorporated into professional social work and acquired a problem-solving character. The author believes these two historical trends will be amalgamated and services will be provided at a much more comprehensive level. She suggests service strategies and program typologies required for a rapidly changing social structure.

9

Chapter 3, "Group Work with Work Groups: A Case of Arrested Development," stresses the indispensability of work groups to tasks of daily management. Historically, work groups were recognized in the social groupwork literature as the basis of democratic functioning. Unfortunately, over the years, this focus has receded. As social group work merged into social work, it lost its identity as the pioneer of participatory democracy. Once again we need to produce competent social workers who can conduct effective and efficient task groups; that is, demonstrate administrative and leadership skills. The author provides strategies on how all three aspects of social work—practice, education, and research—can remobilize their efforts in this direction.

Chapter 4, "Group Work Method and the Inquiry," traces the origin of group work to the period following World War I, with special emphasis on the struggle to establish an identity within the profession of social work. The author describes the social-educational focus of groups on democratic functioning as preparation for and promotion to the democratic way of life. This influential status of group work was undermined as its focus narrowed. The author advocates that with a historical heritage as rich as that of social group work, the profession once again needs to concentrate explicitly on its tasks of social reform, work group orientation, and group therapy, all of which comprise an integral part of social group work.

Chapter 5, "Social Group Work: Concerns and Challenges for the '80s," deals with the identity of the profession, its accountability to society, and its ability to articulate and define its values, knowledge base, and skills so as not to become diffused within a maze of other professions. To achieve these goals, the authors discuss the role social group workers must assume in practice and the systematic methodologies that must be incorporated into their professional stance to ensure efficient and ethical delivery of service. The chapter delineates guidelines necessary for accomplishing these tasks.

2

Old Themes for a New World

Ruby B. Pernell

There has been a continuing chorus of voices all through the last two decades telling us that we are in a time of change, that society is being reshaped in its social, political, and economic dimensions, resulting in new power equations, new national priorities, and new lifestyles. There have been technological changes, increasing leisure, changes in social structure, changes in ideologies, intensification of life's developmental crisis periods, and changing institutions and lifestyles. And the pace of change itself has speeded up in striking, even spectacular ways.

Toffler in *Future Shock* (1970) identified three characterstics of the changes society faces today: transience, novelty, and diversity. He looked at the effect of the acceleration of change on the individual's ability to cope with life, forcing him to "live faster," and postulated that the people of the future will live in "a condition in which the duration of relationships is cut short. . . . In their lives, things, places, people, ideas and organizational structures all get 'used up' more quickly" (p. 44). In interpersonal relationships, duration and depth become increasingly limited, and "much of the social activity today can be described as search behavior — a relentless process of social discovery in which one seeks out new friends to replace those who are either no longer present or who no longer share the same interests" (p. 107). There is also a search for a sense of belonging, a kind of social connection that confers some sense of identity. Accompanying this is a bewildering diversity of values, with fast turnover and no stabilizing consensus of core American values. The situation of overchoice and freedom is somehow terrifying. Toffler says a "flood of newness" confronts individuals with unfamiliar institutions and first-time situations.

This chapter is a revised version of "Social Group Work" in *Goals for Social Welfare, 1973-1993*, Harleigh Trecker, ed. (New York: Associated Press, 1973).

Reaching deep into our personal lives the enormous changes ahead will transfer traditional family structures and sexual attitudes. They will smash conventional relationships between old and young. They will overthrow our values with respect to money and success. They will alter work, play and education beyond recognition. And they will do all this in a context of spectacular, elegant, yet frightening scientific advance. (p. 166)

The pace of social change that was accelerated by the confrontations and experiments of the 1960s has slowed, and the resistances to change have surfaced in organizations devoted to pushing things back into place; but the effects Toffler characterizes remain with us.

Against this characterization, let us examine one small professional effort: social group work. What are its dynamic and enduring elements that should be nurtured for their utility and meaning in a changed and changing society? What service designs shall carry its content to which sets of "new society" problems? And how are we to conceptualize it for purposes of identifying its place in social work education in order to sustain it in practice?

Alfred Kahn pointed out in a future-oriented paper in 1959 that as social workers we had tended to narrow our horizons to what could be conceptualized. "The institution of social work as depicted through the resultant efforts in the major social work methods of group work and casework is narrower in responsibility, potentiality and scope than what is possible, desirable, or actually observable!" (p. 34). So far as group work is concerned, the narrowing process was a gradual one in which historic circumstances, crucial decisions by the professional association, definition and status needs of social group work within the profession and of the social work profession itself, and the ebb and flow of currents of thought and practice in the field all played a part. This fact of a narrowing of scope that has marked the more recent past impels me to move backward in time to search for a better take-off point for moving ahead in the future. In Henry David's (1967) words, "strong roots and a sense of history are major sources of a profession's strength. . . . But what matters enormously is the purposefulness and intensity of its forward glance" (p. 11). It is this connection between the roots of social group work and future directed growth that will be examined.

Social group work, as Clara Kaiser (1959) has pointed out, has no exact birth date, "nor is there full agreement of its progenitors." It evolved out of the recognition of common interests and concerns of a number of persons who were working with groups in a variety of educational, recreational, and social service agencies; and it was shaped significantly by a number of philosophical and scientific systems of thought.

Through its history its practitioners have been defining and redefining it (Hartford, 1964), and in both definition and practice they have tended toward narrowing and specializing its scope. It started out as a method firmly committed to the growth and development of healthy individuals through interaction with others around program interests and activities within a group and agency context in which social responsibility and democratic participation were valued and actively promoted.

In the 1920s and 1930s three major strands of emphasis were repeated in the various definitions being attempted: (1) individual growth and adjustment through the group; (2) group development toward specified ends; (3) social action, social change, or change of society through group experience.

Through the ensuing years, each of these elements was reworked and reworded in various ways, but with a discernible trend toward an increasing focus on the malfunctioning individual and decreasing emphasis on the social action, social change, and education for the citizenship component. In the 1950s social group workers made a historic decision about their identification and affiliation with social work and let go the identifiable bonds with recreation and informal education. The problem orientation grew, especially as social workers moved in increasing numbers into problem-oriented settings and away from the earlier "leisure time" services.

Between 1959 and 1963 the National Group Work Practice Committee of the National Association of Social Workers formulated a "Frame of Reference for Social Group Work," which listed five purposes for which the social group work method was used: "corrective purposes, preventive purposes, facilitating normal social growth, personal enhancement, and citizenship responsibility and participation." In the ensuing discussion across the country strong voices were heard for letting go the "personal enhancement" and "citizenship participation" purposes, and there was some doubt that "normal social growth" was an appropriate target for professional services that were in scarce supply. Many variations of the statment of purpose, the relative priorities and emphases, or the comprehensiveness of the definition were offered then and later; but the fact was that the weight had shifted toward the therapeutic or corrective purposes as a result of a number of historical circumstances, including the search for status within the social work profession itself. The subsequent narrowing of focus and lessened attention to the earlier purposes of personal enhancement and development of citizenship participaton and social responsibility and the neglect of program content other than problem-focused discussion was reflective of the general interest and milieu of the period.

In 1964, commenting on this shift of attention, I wrote, "Our present practice developed out of the formulations of concepts about the experiences of normal groups, rather than around the abnormal; and while other professions are moving in the direction of understanding the meaning of health, and directing services and resources towards its maintenance, we may be moving away from identification with such concerns." And regarding services to normal groups, "There are growth needs among members of some of these so-called 'adequate' groups which we are still fumbling in our efforts to skillfully effect." The loss or confusion of meaningful values, the denial of rights to others, the anxieties and strivings for relatedness to others are some of the needs which persist. Interestingly enough, the social changes and federally funded programs of the 1960s brought about a renewed activity in the area of citizenship participation and social responsibility; and something called "community group work" began to appear in the literature, reflecting a reawakening of professional interest in this area. However, to quote the White Queen in *Through the Looking Glass*, "It's a poor sort of memory that only works backwards." Although our history is engaging in its own right, the purpose of this backward look is only to indicate the roots and shoots of social group work, which carry the genes for significant growth into the future.

A number of powerful and distinctive concepts derive from the early development of social group work that seem to have important potential for today and tomorrow and that were different from the more common concepts of the dominant social casework of the earlier period. These are:

"member"	versus	"client"
doing with	versus	doing for
doing	versus	talking about doing
activity and others as primary agents in the helping process	versus	worker alone as agent
personal and social development and social contribution as legitimate professional foci	versus	remedial, palliative,
health and strength	versus	sickness and breakdown

The key words of the earlier period were *democracy* (as a way of life, not just a political concept), *responsible citizenship, social growth,* and *character development.* The agency context and the worker's purpose were value-laden, and the individual was viewed within society and in interaction with it; and, though "social adjustment" may have meant conformity to some, to the leading group workers of the period it was closer in meaning to Grace Coyle's (1936) comprehensive definition as "training in cooperative relations for common ends, increasing capacity for social contacts, development and enrichment of personality through activity, and training for world responsibility." The fact that the interlocking socialization institutions of the period presented little of the value discontinuities so prevalent today gave the concept a quality of conformity. However, the concepts themselves are equally adaptable and of even greater importance in today's changing world. Most of them have persisted in some form or in some areas of practice; some have already reemerged into prominent positions, modified and adapted to the present-day milieu. The shifting perception and nomenclature of client groups as "consumers," the development of peer-group conceptions of worker and group engagement, particularly at the community level, a renewed concern with explicit value orientations of agencies and groups, with growth and health, and with citizenship participation in community development efforts are all indications of the living, growing quality of these ideas.

In the brave new world of the 1980s these are the concepts that have the potential for keeping the vitality in social work and for addressing some of the problems. Rather than radical and spectacular changes occurring in the provision of social work services sparked by technological changes, the real effect on practice will continue to take place from just such changing perceptions of client groups, of the professional worker's position in the helping relationship, of broadening perceptions of needs and professional purposes, and of recognition of the human potential for action in behalf of self and others.

Moving forward to a renewed concern with growth and maintenance of health of individuals throughout their life cycle and in their interactions with the shifting social milieu, we see a special place for social group work practice. In a world characterized by transience, diversity, and novelty, the "normal" process of growth and development becomes highly problematic. Life's developmental crisis periods intensify their demands on individuals for successful resolution. The rapid-fire presentation of self to new, shifting groups, coping with novel situations and moving in and out of occupational and social relationships, makes the everyday life of each individual a hazardous journey. The achievement of a stable identity, a consistent set of core values, a sense of self-actualizing direction, and a capacity for intimacy that reaches beneath the superficial level of transient social relationships may require special social services beyond the institutional arrangements of family, church, and school. Tropp (1969) points out that the concept of "optimum functioning" has not yet taken full hold in any field dealing with man's well-being. Yet in the future world we visualize ordinary coping will require optimum functioning. There will have to be social provision of experiences over time that help stabilize the personality, giving it depth and meaning; short-term experiences that help with the task of change; and "common goal" endeavors that help individuals together to cope with the forces of change. The personal capacities will have to be enriched and, to quote Tropp, "group work, is, in effect, the primary social work practice in a position to meet people at the point of average functioning, and the primary one with the structure and method to undertake the task" (p. 17A). To this can be added Clara Kaiser's (1959) words: "social group work has its major contribution to make in focusing on building ego strengths of individuals and on the social health of groups."

As social group workers, we will probably have to give renewed attention to social group experiences of children. Will the child who is constantly stimulated by fast-moving, novel situations, prodded by change-ridden and changing parents, and growing faster in practically every aspect of his and her development, have the time needed to "grow up" in self-knowledge, interpersonal competence, and social responsibility? Will there be time and place to achieve for the pleasure rather than the necessity of achievement, to experience friendship in more than transient terms? And will there be opportunities for the kinds of peer-group activities that contribute to the development of values through experiences that are beyond self-seeking, opportunistic conformities? Given novelty and diversity as features of the new society, we can expect an increasing array of groups and values presented for individual choice. If, together with this, transience in family relations means shorter marriages and changing marital partners, the potential value discontinuities for the growing child can be a threat to the development of a stable value core for the personality. The wholeness and autonomy of the person who is to survive in a rapidly changing world will need to be compounded not only of skills that permit mastery of the environment but also of a morality that informs and directs the exercise of mastery.

We may need to revitalize the youth-serving agencies whose "character building" function has embodied value premises that, though often laughed at or derided as "middle class," have been concerned with self-actualizing behavior and social-responsibility goals. Perhaps these older agencies and new ones to come need to take on a stability-building or "shock absorbing" function. For example, they could be closely related to schools, be organized in new ways to serve the child over several years' span, and might take over some parental functions, possibly offering residential group living services, somewhat on a camping model, for short- or long-term periods, but during the school year. Such organizations might differ in their ideologies and/or program emphases, offering choice according to individual tastes within a given geographical community; but intergroup emphasis would be on cooperative rather than competitive activities, on understanding instead of unwillingness to understand, and on equality rather than elitism. They would be communities in which real tasks and decisions would be made with "a deliberate sharing of power and responsibility as the growing competence of the child enables him to use it" (Smith, 1968, p. 315), and a value milieu based on reciprocal obligations and respect for others in child-adult as well as peer social interactions and transactions. They might be deliberately organized as heterogenous communities, providing a real-life experience for their members.

A social group worker would bring to such services the combination of knowledge about the socialization needs of childhood, specially the role and meaning of the peer group, the humanitarian values of social work, the understanding of group process, the skill in effecting it to create a growth-inducing environment, and creative knowledge about programming to facilitate the acquisition of values and skills through experience. The changing structure of the profession and changing roles and functions of the M.S.W.-level worker should mean a renewal of an earlier emphasis on the program design, training, supervisory and administrative skills of the Master's degree holder, with the direct service function carried by the BSW, aides, volunteers, or others.

For adolescents, the importance of the peer group is well recognized as a medium through which the young person seeks to gain separation from his parents and develop and confirm his identity and movement into adult status in the society. Clausen (1968) writes:

> By adolescence, the nature of the socialization process has markedly changed. The child has become far more active in defining his own goals and in seeking the kind of socialization that will help him achieve them. . . . He is likely to be much more au courant (than his parents) with changes occurring in social patterns and moral norms. . . . If the child alone is aware of the contradiction in norms that are presented to him in various settings . . . the whole task of resolution and synthesis remains with him to accomplish without assistance. In the last analysis, of course, only he can achieve such resolution, but this is a place where skilled socialization agents can offer guidance and enhance understanding. (pp. 172, 174)

Any social group worker who has worked with adolescents knows the uses made of the nonparent, mature, understanding, helpfully disposed adult who is availabe to them. Yet, if the rapidly changing social norms widen the gaps in understanding between generations, then the peer group becomes increasingly important to its members and the exclusion of adults is more likely to occur. With this increased utility of the peer group to its members, and with the smorgasbord of behaviors and norms characteristic of various groups to choose among, along with the importance of a peer relationship as the objective of affiliation, inevitably many young people misplaced in a group become displaced. They experience enormous conflict in conforming to group norms for the sake of acceptance, and they often want and need an understanding adult to relate to for help to find their way through their dilemmas of relationships, personal morality, and social development. We already see the formation of highly attractive groups that offer opportunity for personally destructive and socially unproductive behavior. Unlike gangs, which have a central core of activity and high degree of structure, many of these groups are loosely structured and provide media for being "spaced out" in ways that are self-alienating. Along with this have come a number of creative programs by youth-serving agencies to provide helpful resources for those youth who wish to use them. These new type of services may be prototypes for program designs for the years ahead, when the services of professional workers, or those under professional guidance, are made available to youth groups and individuals for assistance in finding their ways out of dilemmas: "Pathfinder" services, we might call them.

In discussing adult socialization, Brim (1968) points out that "the socialization experience in childhood is not enough to meet the demands of later years. . . . In these rapidly changing societies (e.g. the United States) . . . the younger adults must find new models, or develop new styles of life without them; meanwhile, the older adults try to adjust to the conflicts created by the rapid rate of ideological and technological change" (p. 184). In the ordinary course of life, the average nondeviant adult must change and must be socialized into new roles; he must meet the demands for change made by others and the demands he makes on himself. He has many self-initiated ideas and role prescriptions for his own personality and behavior change. Again, considering Toffler's projections of transience in jobs, home, communities, family relationships, and social groups, the problems of changing roles and meeting one's own and other's role expectations can be expected to increase beyond today's experience. Given the tendency toward self-initiated socialization, which Brim (1968) speculated "may already be on the increase because of greater affluence of the average adult and the greater leisure for experimenting in new areas of life" (p. 189), perhaps there is another cue here for program design in which groups become key media.

Job orientation and training seminars will undoubtedly continue and multiply and a variety of adult education and retraining courses be available on a self-selection basis through educational institutions. But beyond occupational role adaptations lie a number of other challenges to the adult self: marriage, stages of parenting, divorce and remarriage, retirement, various citizenship and social group roles, and interpersonal relationships. The transience, diversity, and novelty of many of these experiences pressure the adult into seeking new ideas for ways of dealing with the demands; but also, as Brim says, "new ideal states for the individual's personality evolve . . . ; thus the individual directs himself toward these new ends" (p. 191). The women's movement is an excellent example of this.

Toffler suggests that a variety of short-term groups will be needed in the new society through which individuals will seek solutions to specific types of problems that face them. Brim and Wheeler (1966) support this in their observations on the use of informal, primary-group relationships by adults to test out, compare, and socialize each other in relation to new interests and roles. And indeed we are seeing this. The group and its members may actively assist the individual with the change he seeks or may merely provide the conditions within which his own developmental purposes can be pursued. Aside from the growth in entrepeneur or self-organized groups, provisions of group services to meet adult socialization or resocialization needs is already a feature of many social agencies. Offerings to their actual or potential clientele range across the remedial, supportive, preventive, and developmental purposes, from young adults to the aged, in institutions and out, and focus on a host of special problems and concerns and social roles. There is no reason to assume that in this decade there will be any lessened need for such services, although the content of the group experience and the target groups may change. In all these groups, however, the supportive interpersonal relationships are the key elements, and the direct or consultative services of the social group worker are pertinent.

While the demands of role performance in handling day-to-day tasks are important, a continuing thread of concern is the deepening meaning of one's self in interaction with others, the reaching for intimacy in human relationships, the eliciting of response from others that confirms the reality of the self. In the rock musical *Godspell*, there comes a moment when the clownlike characters who have romped their ways through a fun-and-games interpretation of the New Testament parables turn to each other and in a tender, caring way wipe the grease-painted clown faces off one another. From this point, real selves revealed, the action takes on seriousness and depth. In a way, the world we live in makes it possible to move through life with surface presentations of self, while the need for deeper investment and revelation of self may be sought through experiences that promise "instant intimacy." Personal-growth labs and their variants, offering therapeutic group experience for "normal" individuals, have sprung up. For some individuals, this may be a genuine seeking of release from the isolation and impersonality of machine culture; for others, the appeal may be in the novelty, or in the manipulative, contrived experience (consistent with a machine culture) in which one experiences one's self or takes apart others and is taken apart by them and hopefully put back together again in a way that runs better.

There is no doubt that the need for primary-group experience in which one can find and become one's real self will be a continuing one. It is also probable that the short-term, controlled and manipulated media for this experience will continue to develop. This is the direction in which knowledge and commerce move us.

The stream of practice developed around use of groups for treatment purposes will continue to grow, for the individual casualties of a fast-paced, changing society are heavy and the group treatment milieu has great utility. The incidence of persons handicapped by emotional disturbances in our large cities has been estimated as 20 to 25 percent of the population. Their distress handicaps them in their work, their personal relationships, their family life. In various ways they are experiencing an inability to cope with life's problems. Not only will tomorrow's world create new problems of stress, but new services are already being designed to extend help to greater numbers of those experiencing problems of coping than in the past. The usefulness of the group as a treatment form does not have to be debated here, but various aspects of the present-day organization and use of groups may need to be examined, experimented with, and reconceptualized. Henry Maier (1970), for example, suggests that homogeneity as a basis for group composition—persons in similar functional dilemmas—may not be as advisable or clinically necessary in the contemporary world as heterogeneity: "A group has to bring together a wide spectrum of age ranges and persons of different segments of life because living with diversity, coping with the predictably predictable, and finding a personal integrity amidst many others are the challenges of today."[1]

Historically, the core content of social group work has enabled its practitioners to move with professional ease into activities centered around a wide range of purposes, acquiring the additional appropriate education as needed. With the expansion of knowledge, trends to specialization, and new patterns of curriculum organization in schools of social work, we must be watchful that we not further widen the distance between the personal and social purposes.

Toffler's *Future Shock* is only one book that provides predictions for the coming years. There is also Orwell's *1984*. Recent political events and the activities and pronouncements of various far-right groups, together with the increasing ability to control and manipulate opinion through sophisticated technology, makes the damages of his predictions very real in today's world. This compels us to look again at our roots and to find ways of fitting an explicit value stance back into our services and practice. As social workers and as group workers, we must guard against retreat into the confines of "safe" activities.

In sickness and in health, for self-centered needs of individuals and for expression of their social responsibilities, for maintenance of stability and for creative forms of engagement with change, for self and social development, the group has meaning and utility. It was the particular genius of social group work to bring together into one concept, into one group, and sometimes into one action the concerns for the individual, concern for the group, and concern for the society, and to do this through activities that range from play to social action.

The group is a bridging concept in social work between our business with individuals and our business with communities. It has content and values distinctly its own, applicable and different emphases to the various purposes and tasks of social work, and important enough to have its unique context preserved and developed for continued enrichment of professional practice as a whole.

References

Brim, Jr., Orville G. "Adult Socialization." In J. A. Clausen, ed. *Socialization and Society*. Boston: Little, Brown, 1986, p. 184.

Brim, Jr., Orville G., and Wheeler, S. *Socialization After Childhood: Two Essays*. New York: John Wiley and Sons, 1966.

Clausen, John. Perspective in Childhood Socialization. In J. A. Clausen, ed., *Socialization and Society*. Boston: Little, Brown, 1968, pp. 172–74.

Coyle, Grace, "Group Work Agencies in Relation to Community Forces." Minnesota Conference of Social Work, September 1936 (mimeo).

David, Henry. "Education for the Professions: Common Issues, Problems and Prospects." *Journal of Education for Social Work*, Spring 1967, 3, no. 1, 5–12.

Hartford, Margaret. "Social Group Work 1930–1960: The Search for a Definition." In M. Hartford, ed., *Working Papers Toward a Frame of Reference for Social Group Work*. New York: NASW, 1964.

Kahn, Alfred, J. "The Function of Social Work in the Modern World." In A. J. Kahn, ed., *Issues in American Social Work*. New York: Columbia Press, 1959, pp. 3–38.

Kaiser, Clara. The Social Group Work Method in Social Work Education. New York: Council on Social Work Education, 1959, pp. 115–28.

Maier, Henry. "A Sidewards Look at Change." Seattle: University of Washington, 1970 (mimeo).

Pernell, Ruby B. "Implications of the Statement: A Frame of Reference for Social Group Work Practice." In M. Hartford, ed., *Working Papers Toward a Frame of Reference for Social Group Work*. New York: NASW, 1964.

Smith, Brewster. "Competence and Socialization." In John A. Clausen, ed., *Socialization and Society*. Boston: Little, Brown, 1968.

Toffler, Alan. *Future Shock*. New York: Random House, 1970.

Tropp, Emmanuel. "Group Intent and Group Structure: Essential Criteria for Group Work Practice." In *A Humanistic Foundation for Group Work Practice*. New York, Associated Education Service Corporation, 1969.

Note

1. Maier (1970) gives an example of this connection in his suggestion that social action by means of client activation, group confrontation, and advocacy efforts become legitimate and essential features of the clinical approach: "The focus is upon vitalizing the client's own competence in effectively entering into the change effort of his changing society. . . . The stress is upon the client's competence in effecting change rather than upon societal change per se."

3

Group Work with Work Groups: A Case of Arrested Development

Paul H. Ephross

Suppose that an inhabitant of a newly discovered civilization on one of the moons of another plant were to encounter a social worker for the first time. Because the visitor would be free of complicated conceptions of professional practice, he or she might be free to ask questions that we cannot, and might therefore obtain answers that we cannot. Such an observer might ask a question like, "What do social workers do?" If he has been taught to value naturalistic observation, the interplanetary visitor might decide to answer the question by observing social workers in their daily practice. Using a pencil made of extraterrestrial stuff, he would then note how much time social workers spend engaging in various activities that are parts of their working lives. The visitor might have been informed of the existence of a small but influential subtribe of earthlings, sociologists who call themselves "symbolic interactionists." These people insist that interpersonal life on earth is entirely dependent on a system of meanings that humans attribute to events and experiences. Learning of this point of view, the visitor might then inquire of social workers what meanings they give to various work activities.

Were such a study to be done, one would find that a large number of professionals' working hours are spent participating in work groups such as staffs, committees, subcommittees, task forces, boards, commissions, and subunits of these bodies. Some social workers, especially those who hold jobs with large administrative, planning, policy-formulating, or research components, may spend a majority of their working hours as part of such groups.[1] As to the meaning that participation in such groups has for members, it seems logical to hypothesize further that some of the events that have the most meaning to social workers take place within the arena of such work groups. Points of view are accepted and rejected. Decisions are reached that enable and support or frustrate and disparage the

deepest purposes of the profession, organizations, and individual workers. Agencies, services, and projects are funded or ended. Particular targets of service are selected. Criteria for future decisions are chosen.
Learnings take place or do not. Judgments are made, hirings and firings
confirmed, influence strategies adopted, rewards and sanctions distributed—all within the context of work groups in which social workers are
members, chairs, staff, or sometimes all three.

Community development, community organization, and social planning are carried on almost entirely within a context of work groups.
Funds are raised and allocated, whether in the voluntary or public sec-
tors, largely by groups that exist for those purposes. Administration, as
Trecker (1947) reminded us so many years ago, contains a heavy and
meaningful component of group leadership. Clinical practitioners, particularly as their careers progress, find themselves spending a good deal
of time in work groups such as committees.

Work groups are as important in the lives of many lay people as they
are for social workers. Our visitor, were he to replicate his naturalistic observation with ordinary citizens, would find not only that task groups occupy a great deal of time in the lives of a broad spectrum of people, but
also that what goes on in such groups makes a great deal of difference
both to the inner lives of participants and to various institutions and processes in society at large. The fabric of social living for many adults is
woven of experiences in the union local and the trade association, the
charitable organization, the church group, the community council, the
political club, the sports team, the church choir, and the ethnic organization, each with its omnipresent committees and subunits.

If work groups are so important, it might be expected that social work
as a profession and social work education programs would pay them attention. One might expect that the skills required both for effective participation and effective leadership of such groups would be widely taught
and that the processes of task groups would be widely studied both
through formal research and informal means as well. This is certainly not
the case at present, despite the fact that work groups attracted the attention of many of the pioneers of group work. Why work in and with these
groups has fallen into neglect and how the neglect might be remedied is
the subject of this chapter.

Task Groups and the Sociology of Group Work Knowledge

The immediate stimulus for this consideration of group work with work
groups was a slightly wistful musing of Northen's and Roberts'. Having
produced their useful reader, they point out:

> Although Glasser and Garvin, Hartford, and Somers give considerable atten-
> tion to purpose of social change, it is only the problem-solving approach that

describes a process whereby small-group participation is seen as teaching skills and attitudes necessary for competent and active participation in a democratic government, and states the conviction that both personal and social goals are germane and omnipresent in small-group activities. Somers goes on to add, however, that for the last two decades scholars have emphasized aspects of small-group problem-solving relating to personal growth and change: "The social goals aspect has not been worked on to the same extent, nor has it been as precisely developed and operationalized . . . as has the personal goals dimension of problem-solving." The reasons for this, despite an increase in political and social action within the profession, are not clear. (1976, p. 385)

Indeed, the observation by Somers on which Roberts and Northen muse is an accurate one. The "classical" group work texts of the period from 1948 to 1972 were clear on two points.[2] All group work practice was viewed as having social content, sometimes implicit and sometimes explicit. The ultimate purpose of practice was viewed as contributing to the development of a better, more just, more equitable, more humanistic society. Equally important, group work skills were presented as applicable to a wide gamut of types of groups, including the work group. It is useful to remember that Wilson and Ryland in their great green book not only devoted a chapter to administrative processes, and used the NAACP Youth Group as an example of practice,[3] but they also prefaced the book with a quotation from Mary Parker Follett's *The New State:* "The group process contains the secret of collective life, it is the key to democracy, it is the master lesson for every individual to learn, it is our chief hope for the political, the social, the international life of the future" (1949, frontispiece).

What happened to this essential element in the social group work tradition, the emphasis on contributing to society-building with its corollary emphases on the importance of democratic group participation and the importance of group workers developing skills in working with citizens' groups? Why has group work neglected one of the major types of groups in which its identity was formed?

Retrospect is useful for several reasons, not only to understand what has happened but also to learn about our present dilemmas and possibly to enable us to influence the future of group work practice. It seems that just when group work was establishing itself clearly as a major part of social work, some of the concepts that were being used contained within themselves the seeds of neglect of what had been until then a fertile field for the development of group work practice; namely, work in and with work groups. Phenomena in the social work profession and developments in the broader society helped make it possible to inhibit important understandings of the human condition and promising beginnings in the development of practice skills.

As far back as the 1940s at least, major figures in group work had been calling for greater clarity in definition as to whether group work is a process, a method, or a functional field of practice (AAGW, 1947). At the same time, a debate raged with an intensity of which we can now only hear echoes as to whether group work was education, recreation, social work, or a unique combination of the three. Group work became defined as a method in social work, and group processes and group work processss both became topics of major interest. A good deal of the connotative weight of the term *group work*, however, became identified with a field of practice, a field that was not to be highly valued either within or without social work during the late 1960s and the 1970s. These were the years during which deviance was glorified and ordinariness decried, the decades of the scream, the shock, the exposé, the rejection of history, the times when ever more radical rhetoric concealed an increasing lack of substantive concern with social change. In such an atmosphere, what "sex appeal" could be found in the leisure-time settings such as community centers and neighborhood houses and summer camps and the rest in which the skills of democratic participation and problem-solving could be learned and taught? What was happening in society was reflected within social work as well. Settlement and neighborhood-house staffs neglected their established means of producing patient incrementalists in favor of an all-too-short-lived dream of generating massive, instant social change. Interpersonal and group skills were sometimes—but not always—overlooked in favor of talk of grand strategies, forgetting that these strategies demanded highly sophisticated group task-accomplishment or they would become empty rhetoric.

The other side of the coin, the clinicalization of much of group work, is familiar. One should by no means minimize the enormous contribution that group work theory and practice have made and are making to the practice of clinical social work in general, though sometimes one is tempted to wish that more of the exchange between group work and therapy were reciprocal, so that the reflected light of the psychiatric and the medical settings would not be so blinding. The point is that by unavowedly and sometimes avowedly allowing group work to be defined as a field, the basis was laid for the bifurcation of social work into treatment, on the one hand, and direct social change effort, on the other, leaving group work, or "mezzo studies" as some have called it, rather more *mezzopiano* than *mezzoforte*.

Group processes have an impact on people's lives in all settings and at all times. Only a small proportion of the population has ever been involved in purposeful group experience within so-called group work agencies. A much larger proportion, of course, is involved in groups on the job or in neighborhood organizations or churches. To have influence on large numbers of people, group workers need to develop the skills needed to work with naturally occurring groups of adults. Most of these groups exist in order to achieve purposes that are important to them. For most of them, their work is not experienced as program, as a means to an end, but as an important end in itself. There is no contradiction in most cases between the objectives and values of group work and the ends they seek, but achieving those ends must be given full weight and respect by the worker.

The very term *group work agency* has always been a misnomer. Virtually no agency or service has ever been established or maintained in order to practice group work. Rather, agencies and services exist in order to meet particular social needs, to alleviate particular social problems, to serve specific populations, or to serve as expressions of social conscience and concern for a voluntary or governmental body. Group work is method—a useful, creative, humanistic, life-affirming, educationally valuable one—by which services can be rendered and purposes such as those just listed can be attained. However, practicing group work is not an end in itself, nor is an opportunity to practice this method a reason for establishing a service. Nor should group work be viewed as a field in and of itself. For example, leisure-time recreational services are a field of practice, and an important one; group work is not. A corollary that flows from this view is one that is often misunderstood, especially by beginning professional workers; namely, that the values and objectives for which agencies and services are established need to be viewed as legitimate by group workers. Of course, each group worker needs to exercise informed choice as to which kinds of auspices and which kinds of agencies' purposes fit one's view of one's own career and are consonant with the contribution one wishes to make. But the notion that citizens, members of the society, establish agencies and services for the "wrong" reasons is sophomorish and misunderstands the whole point of social work as well as the historical roots of social group work.

Another concept in the group work tradition that has had some unfortunate results is "program." Making this statement causes considerable discomfort. Questioning the concept of program is sacriligious for anyone who values the group work tradition. Further, for many years the contribution of participation in group activities to individual and group development has been an interest of the writer's. We have taught and believe deeply that group work, by understanding that there are many other ways to advance interpersonal closeness and to produce change in interpersonal relationships besides sitting and talking, has held a major insight into the helping process that the rest of social work has frequently ignored. Both the opportunities to experience various roles that activity media make available and the educational, artistic, and physical experiences that the media themselves provide can and do have great value for the development of groups and their members. In fact, we agree with Middleman (1980) and others that group work's view of people as doers, as able to accomplish and able to contribute to group accomplishments, comes largely from the concept of program. Why, then, argue that the concept as it has been used in group work has had unintended negative consequences?

The major problem with the concept of program is its potential for trivialization of the activities, the tasks, the *work* of a group. It is all well and good to point out that when a group of children makes wooden boats, for example, technical excellence in boat-building is less important than the interpersonal learning that the process of boat-building facilitates. However, such a view of the work of a group becomes patronizing and trivializing when it is applied to a committee of neighborhood residents concerned about a common problem, or a staff committee that is working on a task with which it has been charged. For the neighborhood committee's members, their task is not just a means to further growth, but a piece of work whose accomplishment is important in and of itself. Not only the group's development but its very survival may be entirely dependent upon successful completion of their task. For the staff committee, not only are the members being paid in order to accomplish the work, but important outcomes such as continued existence of an agency's service may depend upon accomplishing their task. In a sense, as soon as one views what a group is doing as program, or as group content, to use another traditional term, one has created a need for a different frame of reference for groups that are doing work that is important for its own sake. Phrased differently, so long as concern with process takes precedence over concern with product, the place of work groups in group work will be skewed.

One can argue that this is exactly what happened historically and that the new frames of reference created became known as "new style" community organization, social planning, and administration, respectively. The view of group work held by some social work administrators, for example, though somewhat stereotypical and reflective of long-standing biases, contains a kernal of accuracy. Administrators see the work in which groups within organizations are involved as serious in itself, and those whose experience of group work is a course in graduate (or undergraduate) school perceive a lack of fit between such a view of the work of groups and that implicit in the concept of program. The purpose here is not to advance a sort of group work imperialism, but rather to point out that group processes are, if anything, more complex, the meaning of group participation for members, if anything, heightened, the social objectives of group work, if anything, better served, when the work of a group is serious and purposeful. One can find little, if any, evidence that groups that do "real" work affect members less intensely than do groups that do "make believe" work; in fact, the evidence is almost entirely in the other direction.

This discussion began by mentioning the importance of groups composed of social workers as members. What applies to groups composed of lay citizens applies as well to groups within organizations populated by social workers. Group experience in many service-delivery organizations reflects the same dehumanizing and destructive processes and norms as does much group experience in the broader society. Social work education and practice share a responsibility to teach effective participation skills as well as effective performance in the specialized role we call worker. Performing effectively in the role of chair while advancing the values and objectives of the profession requires skills of some sophistication—skills rarely taught and rarely learned in the course of professional education. Yet, member and chair are roles that social workers of all sorts, not only those identified as group workers, are called on to perform frequently and consistently. Why leave such important skills to be learned haphazardly?

Not teaching effectiveness in the roles of member and chair feeds a fantasy that can have some dangerous effects. Not teaching how to work in and with groups and how to direct them leaves the field clear for a perception that such roles are better left to those trained in generic management. The specter of the all-purpose manager, the manager who is ignorant of the substantive activities of the service-delivery organization, is raised by such a perception. Despite several noteworthy recent failures by all-purpose managers, despite scores of attempts to rationalize social services by bringing in all-purpose managers, the fantasy persists. We may not be able to eradicate it, but we should not feed it by producing social workers ignorant of the basic interpersonal tools of management.

The Consistency of Human Needs

Who needs it? Why at this time should one be concerned with returning attention to group work within social work and to group work with work groups within group work? There are many reasons, chief among them are that the concerns and objectives of group work are increasingly identified by various observers as crucial within our society. In order to understand this, it is necessary to recast our vocabulary, as Pernell (1973), among others, has pointed out.

Primary prevention of mental illness is identified as a concept and a direction "whose time has come" (Klein and Goldston, 1977). The popularity of this concept and its adoption as a program focus by some very unlikely institutions should have great meaning for group workers. For by primary prevention is meant the sort of supports and skill provision for dealing with life's stresses that the group work pioneers had in mind. It is even noteworthy that some of the attention in primary prevention has emphasized interpersonal experiences in childhood and adolescence. The ability to obtain satisfaction from interpersonal experience and the development of social competence are objectives stated both in the classical group work materials and in the newest materials put forth by organizations such as the National Institute of Mental Health. Once one makes the translation from "character education" and "citizenship training" to "primary prevention" and "quality of life," it becomes clear that the objectives are the same.

What was once primarily the concern of a small minority of group workers within social work is now being stated as national health policy. *Anomie* is not only a household word but a favorite term of some newspaper columnists. It would be travesty if those who first identified the reduction of anomie through small-group experience as a societal goal forgot their interest in and knowledge of ways of doing this just when other social institutions discovered a position that group workers have argued for decades.

Within service-delivery organizations, "burnout" is a popular concept; in fact, it is showing signs of becoming a fad, if one is to judge from the recent and sudden outpouring of literature on the subject (such as Edelwich, 1980) and the proliferation of programs, seminars, and institutes designed to prevent and combat it. Often, one is reminded of Blumer's (1971) speculations about why social problems are identified as problems at particular times when they have existed for many years. Burnout is caused in large part by a lack of a sense of support and positive valuation by colleagues and administrators. How inappropriate it would be if group workers, who have argued since the 1930s that administrative skills should include skill in group leadership and skill in promoting healthy group life on the job, should not recognize that here again our society is recognizing the validity of a phenomenon that we have known for decades. The need for translation is obvious: One simply substitutes the term *burnout* for earlier terms that denote the same phenomenon.

Ecological concerns and worry about overconsumption of finite supplies of resources have brought home to society at large the need to be concerned with the small, the local, the intimate, and interpersonal sources of life satisfaction. The minimal technology movement leads to perspectives with which group workers can feel comfortable, because it suggests a complementary and congenial view of ecology. To take just one such perspective, the idea that leisure-time pursuits need to reflect more and more things that people and communities can do for themselves and less and less of the mindless overconsumption of the past few decades is one that can easily be found in the group work literature.

The "ethnic revival" of the past decade provides another example of old concepts in new labels. Glazer and Moynihan (1975) and many others (Naparstek and Collias, 1975; Novak, Mindel, and Habenstein, 1976; Fandetti, 1978) have documented the renewed sense of ethnic community in America. Further, they have pointed out the implications of this revival for service-delivery systems. Locally developed and locally controlled institutions, they argue, sensitive to the needs of local, often ethnically self-defined populations, can produce a better and more satisfying fit between service provider and consumer than can huge, bureaucratic structures, which by their very nature have to view a variegated population uniformly. These points of view should by no means be taken lightly. However, some of the research and polemic on the subjects of ethnicity does have an ironic ring to someone who is part of the group work tradition. One expects that any day now someone will invent a new social institution – the neighborhood center. In fact, it has already been reinvented, though various names are used for it. The idea of a "one-portal" multiservice-delivery center, accountable to a representative board heavily weighted with service consumers and other local citizens, is hardly shattering in its novelty. No one knows more about the skills required to develop such institutions and to deliver their services than do group workers, not that all is known by any means. We have a choice of participating in their development or sitting by while others reinvent a wheel whose earlier version we kept rolling years ago.

Many other examples can be cited of services and roles whose adaptation requires just simple translation. The aggressive outreach or street gang work of the 1950s and early '60s now provides one of the few effective models for programs designed for the primary and secondary prevention of drug and alcohol abuse among adolescents. The role of group work or group-process consultant goes under many names now, among them "management consultant" and "organization development consultant."

It would be a mistake simply to take the examples presented here as proof that "we knew it all years ago." To some extent we, or our professional ancestors, did. To that extent, group work deserves credit for prescience. But having congratulated ourselves and those who came before us, we need to get to work on at least three tasks that lie ahead if the sketchy analysis that has been presented is to have the desired impact of remobilizing group work and group workers to pay attention to work groups.

Implications for the Future

The review presented here is far from definitive. One intention in presenting it is to stimulate further consideration of the issues discussed. Tentatively, however, let us proceed to draw the implications of what has been presented for an agenda for practice, for social work education, and, perhaps most important of all, for research.

The agenda for practice is clearest. Group workers need to extend their range of vision again so as to include several kinds of groups now neglected. Much more attention needs to be given to citizens' groups and to staff who work with such groups. Greater attention needs to be paid to legitimating the value of work with such groups. Greater attention to sharpening practitioners' skills in this demanding work is needed as well. Work with agency boards and their committees and with citizen's groups needs to be redefined as an important and rewarded part of group work practice.

For social work education as it begins to recast itself to meet the needs of the last two decades, what is implied is a re-recognition of the place of group work in the curriculum. The profession and the world continue to need a social worker whose particular field of expertise lies in the delivery of services to groups, in training paraprofessionals and other social workers in the skills involved in such service delivery, in consultation on group services, and in carrying on practice based in group work. Further, curricula need to provide basic skills in work with groups for all students, both at the undergraduate and graduate levels. Basic-skill teaching means, as it has always meant, classroom teachers who are willing to "get their hands dirty" and teach practice behaviors as well as concepts (Ephross and Balgopal, 1978), and making sure that field instruction processes and objectives accurately reflect the importance of providing opportunities to try out and deepen the skills that need to be learned. Among the basic skills in work with groups that all social workers need are skills in working with work groups. Fortunately, a new generation of instructional texts for such teaching is emerging. One should note especially Tropman, Johnson, and Tropman's (1980) book on working with committees, which is the first book written from a social work perspective to address this important element of practice in a long time. Also, one should note a new textbook on group work by Garvin (1980), who seeks to reflect the breadth of group work's origins, concerns, and applications.

The agenda for research is an important and demanding one. Despite the proliferation of what purports to be research into group processes, most of it is simply not useful for practitioners, and even less of it is useful for practitioners concerned with work groups. There are two major reasons for this lack of usefulness. First, most of what purports to be group research is really nongroup research. The collectivities studied, such as the stereotypical *ad hoc* aggregates of college students, are simply not groups. They do not engage in group processes as do groups in their development. Thus, no matter what the statistical and methodological sophistication of the studies, the findings are not useful for practice because the "animal" being studied, though possibly of the correct *genus,* is not of the proper species. Second, there is abundant evidence throughout social work research that intimates familiarity with the phenomena of interest that is required in order for research to be useful. Researchers from other professions and disciplines are not going to accomplish our research agenda. We will have to undertake a sizeable and sustained program of research ourselves.

The majority, if not all, of the research needed into the processes of work groups and the group work process with work groups needs to be done *in vivo* rather than *in vitro*. It is virtually impossible to duplicate most groups in any kind of laboratory setting. Work groups need to be studied "in the wild" and, in addition, need to be studied with methodologies that are capable not only of counting but also of understanding meanings in depth. Naturalistic observation, the construction and testing of typologies, content analysis, and participation observation are the kinds of methodologies that may yield the most fruitful results. The need for research is urgent and pervasive.

A great deal of review and reflection about group work's historical roots has been presented and written during the past few years.[4] It is time to create some more group work history so that future practitioners and scholars will have more history to look back on and feel good about. It is also time to refocus attention on the importance of skilled, sophisticated, conceptually guided group work with work groups.

References

American Association of Group Workers. *Towards Professional Standards*. New York: Association Press, 1947.

Blumer, H. "Social Problems as Collective Behavior." *Social Problems*, 1971, *18*, 298–306.

Edelwich, J., and Brodsky, A. *Burn-Out: Stages of Disillusionment in the Helping Professions*. New York: Human Sciences Press, 1980.

Ephross, P. H., and Balgopal, P. R. "Educating Students for the Practice of Creative Group." *Journal of Education for Social Work*, 1978, *14* (3).

Fandetti, D. V. "Ethnicity and Neighborhood Services." In D. Thursz and J. Vigilante (eds.), *Reaching People: An International Annual, Vol. III*. Beverly Hills, CA: Sage Publications, 1978.

Garvin, C. *Contemporary Group Work*. Englewood Cliffs, NJ: Prentice-Hall, 1980.

Glazer, D., and Moynihan, D. P. (eds.). *Ethnicity: Theory and Practice*. Cambridge, MA: Harvard University Press, 1975.

Klein, D. C., and Goldston, S. E. (eds.). *Primary Prevention: An Idea Whose Time Has Come*. Washington, DC: Government Printing Office, DHEW Publication ADM 77-447, 1977.

Middleman, R. R. "Program Activities: A Review and Update." *Social Work With Groups*, 1980, *3*, (2).

Mindel, C., and Habenstein, R. W. (eds.). *Ethnic Families in America: Patterns and Varieties.* New York: Elsevier, 1976.

Naparstek, A., and Collias, K. "The Ethnic and Class Dimensions in Neighborhoods: A Means for the Reorganization of Human Service Delivery Systems." *Journal of Sociology and Social Welfare*, 1975, 2, (3).

Novak, M. *The Rise of The Unmeltable Ethics.* New York: Macmillan, 1972.

Pernell, R. "Social Group Work." In H. B. Trecker (ed.), *Social Policy Goals for 1973–1993.* New York: Association Press, 1973.

Roberts, R. W., and Northen, H. (eds.). *Theories of Social Work with Groups.* New York: Columbia University Press, 1976.

Trecker, H. B. *Group Process in Administration.* New York: Association Press, 1947.

Tropman, J. E., Johnson, H. R., and Tropman, E. *The Essentials of Committee Management.* Chicago: Nelson-Hall, 1979.

Wilson, G., & Ryland, G. *Social Group Work Practice.* Cambridge, MA: Houghton Mifflin, 1949.

Notes

1. Technically, of course, only some of these so-called groups are groups. Others are collectivities, or aggregations, or whichever term one chooses to use for them.

2. This term is used here to refer to a body of literature that began approximately with Grace Coyle, *Group Work with American Youth* (New York: Harper & Row, 1948) and ended with Alan F. Klein, *Effective Groupwork* (New York: Association Press, 1972). Included are books by Wilson and Ryland, three by Trecker, three by Konopka, two edited by Saul Bernstein, two additional books by Klein, texts by Sullivan, Tropp, Northen, and many other writings. It does not include many valuable writings that define group work or social group work more narrowly or in a more specialized framework.

3. Despite the misperceptions of an ahistorical era, group work discovered and pointed to the social costs of inequality long before the 1960s. It is sometimes useful to remind ourselves how contemporary some of the concerns of group work's past sound today. Contemporary social work educators are referred, for example, to Gertrude Wilson, "Trends in Professional Education in Group Work" (AAGW: 1947). Wilson's questions are as current as a school's last curriculum committee meeting.

4. Note, for example, the Annual Symposia on Social Work with Groups in Cleveland in 1979, in Arlington in 1980, and in Hartford in 1981, as well as the emergence of *Social Work with Groups* as a professional journal.

4

Group Work Method and The Inquiry

Max Soporin

In this chapter, we embark upon an excursion into history. We will consider some historical facts that are of importance in understanding our heritage and our historical identity as social workers. Mainly, tis is a "once-upon-a-time" story about a fabled olden time, when heroic people were fired by a golden dream and an ideal vision about democratic group life. These heroic figures made some wonderful discoveries, some of which largely have been forgotten and need to be rediscovered. They created an exciting social movement, which they called "group work." It is particularly their kind of work with groups, as part of social work as a social movement, that needs to be advanced.

Some of these people and some of their discoveries, will be described in terms of salient ideas about group membership and experience. This paper will consider what happened to that movement and then will attempt to draw some possible lessons to determine how these older insights may be applied in social work practice and in social work education in order to meet current social needs.

The Inquiry

This is a presentation of some little known facts about a group of people and an organization called "The Inquiry."[1] The concern here is not with the history of this organization, but with its influence on social work practice. The Inquiry had a lively and productive existence from 1923 to 1933. Its members brought into being a form of study and helping that they called "group work." This association represented a coalescence of people and interests active in the social settlements, in the new national

---

This chapter is a revision of the paper presented at the Symposium, entitled "Group Membership and Experience: Older Insights and Current Needs."

movements for adult education, progressive education, recreation, and in the youth-serving agencies and programs under religious and secular auspices. Following the effort in World War I to "save democracy," the social-reformist impulses and ideals of the Progressive Era found renewed expression in a new cause. This was to develop small-group life and to use small-group processes, as well as group educational and discussion methods, to further community and societal integration, the personal and social adjustment of people, and their development as enlightened, actively participating citizens. In this way, the members of The Inquiry hoped to advance social change and to help build democratic communities and a better society.

The organization that became The Inquiry was established initially in 1918, under the auspices of the Federal Council of Churches of Christ in America, and named the National Conference on the Christian Way of Life. It took on its new title and a more expanded and secular character as The Inquiry in 1923. Founding members were such youth-service agency officials as E. C. Carter, A. J. Gregg, and Harrison S. Elliott of the YMCA and Rhoda McCulloch of the YWCA, also with a particular interest in developing group discussion and educational methods for use in club and recreation work with youngsters.[2] A major founder was Edward Lindeman, who published his influential book *The Community* in 1921, in which he reported on the importance of vital-interest groups in generating community processes and activities. He later came to be considered the "father" of adult education, and he was a seminal leader in the development of group work and community work in social work. He also became a teacher-philosopher in social work as a long-time faculty member of the New York School of Social Work. Another early leader was Alfred Dwight Sheffield, an English instructor and later Professor of Group Leadership at Wellesley College. He published a pamphlet in 1922 entitled "The Way of Group Discussion" for the Conference on the Christian Way of Life and one entitled "Joining in Group Discussion" for the Worker's Education Bureau; he also served on the Executive Committee of The Inquiry. Representatives of the settlement houses and community centers were quickly involved, such as Bruno Lasker of the Henry Street Settlement and then an editor at *Survey* magazine. He became the editor and later the secretary of The Inquiry and was a driving force during the life of the organization. Mary K. Simkhovitch, head of Greenwich House, was a long-time member of the Executive Committee, and her participation was influential for this organization, for her own work with groups and also in her later study, *Group Life* (1940).

Mary Parker Follett, who came out of the Boston settlement scene, published her highly esteemed *The New State* in 1918, in which she wrote about small community groups as "the key to democracy" (1920, p. 23). As a friend of Alfred Sheffield and his wife, Ada Sheffield, a Boston social worker, Follett was quickly, though briefly, drawn into this new circle. She was much influenced by the Sheffields and by Lindeman, and she proposed to Lindeman that they co-author a book about the group process.[3] However, they wrote separate books, both of which were published in 1924, Follett's *Creative Experience* and Lindeman's *Social Discovery*, in which each paid tribute to the other and also to Alfred Sheffield.

Also drawn into The Inquiry circle were a number of educators from Columbia University. John Dewey, who was associated with Hull House in Chicago and with Greenwich House and The Henry Street Settlement in New York City, was an inspiring force and an active member of this group. Robert MacIver, the already eminent sociologist, who published his major text *The Community* in 1924, was a strong ally of social workers and became an active member. Dewey's disciple, William Heard Kilpatrick, noted for his work on learning and teaching methods and on character development, quickly assumed a leading role in the association. Other Columbia educators were Goodwin Watson and F. Ernest Johnson, the latter serving on the Executive Committee. As a result of these people, The Inquiry formed a close identification with Teacher's College at Columbia, which became a university base for many of its activities.

A number of young social workers soon were deeply involved in the organization's programs. For example, Joseph McCaskill and Henry M. Busch of the YMCA, and Margaretta Williamson, Grace Loucks Elliott, and Grace Coyle of the YWCA, consciously sought to apply some of the new ideas about group process in leading club groups. They taught at the New York School of Social Work and trained group leaders in the agencies.[4] Busch (1934), Gregg (1924 and 1928), Williamson (1929), and McCaskill (1930) wrote the first textbooks on group work. Coyle, who was employed part-time by The Inquiry, did her research on groups for her doctoral dissertation at Columbia, in which she was assisted by MacIver and Sheffield, and this dissertation became the seminal *Social Process in Organized Groups* (1930). Mary van Kleeck, a prominent social worker with the Russell Sage Foundation, later served on the Executive Committee.

The Inquiry was active in promoting social-action causes and in developing adult education and discussion groups to further them. There were four working commissions—on race, industrial relations, immigration, and religion—that drew prominent and influential community leaders from New York and nationally into these projects. The members, particularly Lasker, Lindeman, Sheffield, and Elliott, traveled around the country preaching the new gospel and training leaders for this work. The Inquiry sponsored or directly published a series of highly useful papers, pamphlets, and books for such purposes.[5] Basic publications were on the methods of group discussion, conference, resolution of community and intergroup conflicts, and group leadership. Elliott's *The Process of Group*

Thinking (1929), Sheffield's *Creative Discussion* (1926) and *Training for Group Experience* (1929), Follett's *Creative Experience* (1924), Lindeman's *Social Discovery* (1924), *The Meaning of Adult Education* (1926), *Social Education* (1933), and *Dynamic Social Research*, with John J. Hader (1933), Fuller and Mayer's *Community Conflict* (1929) were among the more important books generated by The Inquiry's chemical leavening.

In addition, there were pamphlets on alien registration, religious prejudice, business ethics, recognition of unions, the right to strike, married women in industry, and international relations. A particular concern was for improving race relations. Lindeman and Lasker were active on the Race Commission, which was chaired by James H. Dillard. A number of publications were addressed to this aim: *And Who Is My Neighbor?* provided a casebook and study outline; *All Colors* was a study outline for women; *Race Attitudes in Children* was written by Lasker, and he did the draft for what was completed by Herman Feldman as *Racial Factors in American Industry* (1931).

Social workers were thought to have a particular responsibility to help improve interracial understanding and to increase the provision of welfare services to Negro community residents. Such social-action endeavors undoubtedly contributed to a more liberal national climate and to the later acceptance of the New Deal reforms.

Contributions of The Inquiry

In addition to its influences for liberal social action, The Inquiry made important contributions to the development of theory about small groups and of the method of "group work." It stimulated interest and research in small groups and in group-functioning processes. The members encouraged researchers in the field and helped develop a new body of facts and theory about the social psychology of small groups. Of particular interest is the research on small groups in relation to group work by Coyle (1930), Kaiser (1930), and Newstetter (1938).

Along with this development of behavior theory about small groups came a theoretical conceptualization and formulation of a technical helping method called "group work." Also, there emerged a body of useful knowledge about how to teach this method to group leaders. The term *group work* already had come into use in social work several years earlier. For example, in a 1915 National Conference paper, Zilpha Smith said that "the kinds of social work are few that do not require both the family and the group work method." Mary Follett also referred to group work in her *The New State* (1918, p. 364). However, neither the settlement house nor youth-agency workers had any clear theoretical understanding of group structure or process or of how to influence them. It was The Inquiry members and the new breed of "group workers" who helped to formulate its particular form and character. It is noteworthy the The Inquiry talks, classes, and workshops were frequently given to social workers at the Ys, settlement houses, community centers, and at state and national social work conferences, so there was a good deal of reciprocal give-and-take in this developmental process. Social workers quickly adopted the new knowledge and techniques of study, discussion, and leadership and melded them into activity programs for work with youth and adult community groups.

In developing this method of group work, The Inquiry identified and began to formulate a social philosophy upon which the method was based and which it came to express. This is a humanistic, democratic philosophy, with a respect for individual differences, rights, and responsibilities, as well as a recognition of the necessary complementarity and interdependence of individual, family, and community development and well-being. It also presented a commitment to racial and cultural pluralism and to social experimentalism. It expressed a high regard for rational group discussion and social consensus, and for progressive educational processes, as ways of resolving problems of and between individuals, groups, communities, and nations.

The Inquiry also gave to this new "method" an organizational and institutional identity. It helped crystallize a convergence of various trends during the 1920s and early 1930s that led to the development of this new method and field of practice within social work. Several Inquiry members enthusiastically formed a New York Conference on Group Work, which by 1934 had come to meet with group workers from other parts of the country to organize the section on group work at the National Conference on Social Work in 1935 (Wilson, 1976, pp. 16–19). This led to the establishment of the American Association for the Study of Group Work in 1936.

In their 1935 National Conference papers, Coyle and Newstetter defined group work as an educational, helping method and process, and also as a social work method and field of practice. Other group workers, such as Bowman (1935) and Kilpatrick (1940), opposed the identification with social work. It was Coyle, in 1946, who led and justified the shift to a professional social work organization, established as the American Association of Group Workers. Several persons who were primarily associated with the field of adult education continued to be associated with the AAGW and contributed to its journal, *The Group*. However, in 1947 they founded the National Training Laboratory, developed their own small-group theory as "group dynamics," and their own form of group work as the "T Group Laboratory," "sensitivity training," and then as the "Laboratory Method" (Benne et al., 1975, pp. 3–10). Other members of the AAGW, led by S. R. Slavson, broke away to form the new group psychotherapy association (Wilson, 1976, p. 31). But group work found a firm and congruent identity within social work, and in 1956 the group workers became part of the new National Association of Social Workers.

The Inquiry continued to be active until 1933, when the lack of funds during the Depression became severe, and many of its members became heavily involved in the New Deal programs. It was in many of these new programs that the work of The Inquiry for community development and the use of small groups were applied. There was much hope (Chambers, 1962, pp. 253–67) that the ideals and social-reform projects of the kind that The Inquiry stood for would be realized in the great changes that were about to take place.

The Small Group and Its Functions

We turn now to consider what these pioneers in group work thought about the small group, their conceptions of group membership and process, and how these could be used to further their reformist purposes. There is no need here to summarize the historical development of small-group and group work theories and their varied strands, including the influences of progressive education, the new social psychology, psychoanalysis, the mental-hygiene movement, group dynamics, and psychodrama. Rather, let's discuss certain salient themes and ideas collectively emphasized by the members of The Inquiry circle, which became influential in shaping group work methodology and characterized group work practice in social work for the next few decades.

As Coyle (1930, p. 12) took pains to explain, the organized small group assumed great significance within modern urban, industrial (and impersonal) society because it provided the basis for new types of "psychological neighborhoods." Such groups have important functions in supporting individual identity and self-esteem and in furthering the realization of common interests. Lindeman (1924) pointed out that it was in terms of the vital interests and wants of individuals that small groups evolved and established social and psychological bonds in order to further those interests as shared ones in and through community activities; such action groups thus constituted local communities. The processes of reciprocal interaction and relationships were thus viewed as powerful, influential forces for learning, for individual, group, and community development and problem-solving, and for social change.

The small group and its processes also were recognized as a powerful influence for personality and character development and for learning new behavior, especially the attitudes of self- and social responsibility, knowledge of social issues, and the skills of an educated, responsible citizenship. Also valued was the learning of attitudes and skills: for social adjustment and functioning in the relation of the individual and the environment, and for social and community integration among community members, as well as for the social contribution by each member to community functioning and advancement. It is through such social functioning, integration, and contribution that people also attain self-realization. Lindeman (1933, pp. XV and 187) stated: "Social education is a process and a goal. . . . Social situations may be rendered flexible and thereby resolvable by means which give assurance that participants derive education from the process of social problem-solving. In other words, social education is not merely a preparation for social experience but also a derivative of such experience."

Another important set of functions of small organized groups is its influence for group and community development and for social problem-solving, as Somers (1976) has noted. Through study and discussion processes, there is an interweaving, conciliation, and coordination of interests, desires, and values that enable people to cope better with common problems in social living and with intergroup conflicts in the community. Conflicts of interest and values, as well as social issues and problems, can thus be studied and resolved and people led toward harmony, unification, and integration in cooperative living. The transmutation of the power and wills of individuals into a new collective power makes for a profoundly educational and "creative" experience for its members. Follett (1924, p. 126) spoke of this "circular" transactional group process as "the deepest truth of life."

It is this great power of the small-group process that these leaders sought to harness for social goals and societal betterment in a democratic, pluralistic, just society. Thus, Sheffield (1926, p. 37) believed that "the energy created from within a fellowship in spiritual striving and . . . the power bred with and between people is a dynamic surpassing" any nondemocratic kinds of power. Coyle (1947, pp. 146–47 and 165) emphasized that group work provides an "experience in democratic participation," is a "schooling in democracy," and is a mode of social action "in the creating of a better society by orderly and democratic methods" of social change. Follett, Lindeman, and Lasker, in particular, were interested in a worldwide dissemination of these ideas and in the use of group work for peaceful, communal, and democratic international relations.

We should note that such aims and the specific social-action programs mounted by The Inquiry were neither presented nor declared to be "political" or "radical" in nature. While recognizing their aims to influence political and legislative processes, these programs were presented in a nonpolitical or politically nonpartisan way. Partisanship, according to Lindeman (1933, pp. 177 and 184), may be necessary to preserve one's integrity, but it should be ethical rather than political in nature.

The conceptions, philosophy, methods, and processes of group work were relatively new discoveries for that time. They were enthusiastically applied in an amazing variety of settings and with many types of groups. These were found in the youth-service agencies, settlement houses and community centers, religious organizations, community clubs, fraternal organizations, unions and industrial firms, educational classes, and various conferences and committees. As a social movement, group work proliferated across the country. The accounts of group work and of the helping activities of the group leaders as they operated during the 1920s and the 1930s are impressive in demonstrating the realization of stated objectives and ideals. This is evident, for example, in the accounts of group educational and social-action projects described by Gaynell Hawkins (1937; 1940), as well as in the issues of *The Group*. There did not appear to be a real separation of "social goal" and "reciprocal" approaches in the group work practice of that period, as compared to what Papell and Rothman (1962) asserted to be evident at a later time.

Group Thinking and Discussion

Certain aspects of group process and group leadership were particularly prominent in groups that were oriented more to youth-activity programs, as well as in those that were oriented to adult educational and social-action concerns. A tremendous amount of emphasis was given to group discussion, thinking, and problem-solving, and to a "situational approach" that anchored the group process in a real-life, social-situational context. Almost all of The Inquiry associates wrote books, or chapters of books, that dealt with group thinking and discussion. There was an enthusiastic fascination with these processes as the royal road to an Utopian ideal. The development of these theories, principles, and procedures continued to evolve and reached a remarkable point of maturation, as reflected in the work published after 1933—by Coyle (1948), Lasker (1949), and particularly by Sheffield (1951).

Group discussion and the leadership of group discussion for learning and problem-solving were conceived by Follett (1920, p. 23) as a "methodology for democracy," and by Lindeman (1933, pp. 6 and 9) as a "technique of inquiry and art of reconciliation," in which people reeducate themselves through participation and also risk themselves in the arena of social conflict. The discussion process was seen to meet individual needs, expand personal perspectives, and enable personality redirection and reintegration. Discussion also provides a way of integrating and transforming individual interests, goals, and wills into common ones. It provides a way of arriving at necessary group decisions as a basis for collective problem-solving action and for group cohesion and self-government. The synthesis of interests optimally results in collective feeling and thought and in the formation of gestalt wholes, or what today we call a "holistic system." This social integration fosters an identity of individual and group wants, so that individual and collective action becomes beneficial to both, in what is now called "synergistic" culture and action. As Lasker (1948, p. 463) said, "A democratic solution is one that enlists the group both in the common cause and in a plan for its realization." Follett (1920, p. 208) thus believed that integrated neighborhoods could be created by "learning and practicing a genuine discussion, that is a discussion which will bring the group will of the neighborhood to bear directly on city problems."

This discussion process also was viewed as constituting a dynamic and creative experience in group thinking, in which the members could "interthink" as a group (Sheffield, 1929, p. 84). The reciprocal communication and transactional relationships that develop should lead to a creative and synergistic emergence of new values, forms, and qualities of individual and social welfare. Here there was a common acceptance of Dewey's conception of the thinking process for problem-solving purposes, but it was adapted to their own situational approach. The thinking process was seen to include a joint "willing and purposing" in relating the individual and situation (Follett, 1924, p. 85). Much attention was given to clarifying the duties and tasks of the group leader as a discussion leader, in organizing, focusing, and progressively moving the learning and integrative thinking processes. Care was taken to provide a structure of program content, including carefully selected case examples, as in the book *Community Conflict* by Fuller and Mayers (1929).

As Lasker (1949, pp. 172 and 178) explained, this discussion process involves a "dialogue" and a "dialectic" in a reorientation of individual thought, a "joint search" and "thinking together" to understand a problem so as to arrive at common meanings and a larger, more meaningful knowledge. Lindeman emphasized the importance of opening the group to an expression and confrontation of differences and of conflicting interests. He spoke of this as "making a creative use of difference" (1933, p. 186) and "transforming the battle of interests from warfare into creative conflict" (1926, p. 97) by minimizing the "conflict mindset," recognizing and creating common interests and purposes and enabling mutual adjustments and consensual solutions to life problems. In a major study, Hader and Lindeman (1933) suggested that a combination of research and conference methods be used in labor-management committees to resolve conflicts in industry.

Alfred Sheffield, in a highly unusual, difficult, and creative work, *The Mind of a "Member"* (1951), further explored the "group adjustive" process that takes place between group members. Here he made use of the material and ideas that he had developed with his wife, Ada. He described this process as involving an "appreciative awareness" of a social situation, with social insight into its values and symbolic meanings, its differentiated and multicasual aspects, its structure of role, communication, and authority patterns, and its dynamic-process qualities. Also involved is an "adjustive thinking" by members that enriches the "culture-conscious" quality of their selves and "grouphood." These in turn lead to reciprocal "group adjustive responses," in which there is a spread of democratic participation and interaction; a transformation of values, roles, and relationships; mutual helping in a resolution of conflicts and problems; and a group fulfillment and maturation.

Sheffield was interested in identifying important qualities of the "mind of a member" and the competencies needed by a member for creative group experience. Such competencies, he thought, consist of capacities for "situational thinking" and for situational analysis, redefinition, and transformation, as well as capacities to help fellow members do the same. He illustrated the application and helpfulness of these processes and procedures in aiding both factory work groups and family groups. The social worker was thought to be especially well suited to lead these kinds of group processes, both in industiral counseling and in family casework.

Another striking feature of the work of Follett, Lindeman, Lasker, and Sheffield was their use of a "situational approach" in understanding and dealing with group behavior, interaction, and problem-solving. Situation theory and the "situational approach" had been imaginatively developed and applied to casework by Ada Sheffield (1937).[6] In this approach, individual and group behavior was understood, for example, by Follett (1920, pp. 72 and 187) as "not a function of environment, but as a function between self and environment"; the adjustment of such a relation generates a new gestalt, a release of energy and power, and a "will of the total situation" for creative personal and community experience. Lindeman (1924, pp. 191–200) suggested that the group leader in the role of "participant observer" could best understand the group's "real" situation. A commonly held conception of the problem-solving process gave emphasis to the primary stages of the perception and analysis of the situation. These were then followed by problem definition, clarification of issues, conflict confrontation, consideration of values, analysis of data and solution alternatives, then agreement and joint action. The group leader, according to Sheffield (1951, p. 196), helps members make an "adjustment of a situation" and thus a change in both person and environment, rather than to adjust to some norm. All of this kind of person-situation conceptualization occurred long before the recent development of ecological-systems theory.

We observe here the other worldly quality of these kinds of ideas compared to the present cultural climate and *weltanschauung*. We cannot help but be stirred and moved by the force of this social and moral vision and by these democratic, altruistic ideals. The importance accorded to verbal group discussion and to rational, logical thinking is very discrepant from the current emphasis on personal, subjective feelings, self-expression, and individualistic self-fulfillment. Today, a critic may find fault with the relative lack of priority given to the emotional aspects of intragroup relation or to subjective personal experience. "The interplay of personalities," said Lasker (1948, p. 37), "makes for rational sympathy" with others. Lindeman (1926, p. 98) held that the "social process is essentially a contact between minds," and he also believed that learning is also experiencing, and that "true learning is always insight or understanding derived from the interpenetration of facts with feelings" (1933, p. 197). It is in this way that they viewed group work as a situational, experiential process, always close to the real-life experience of human beings.

The Decline and Possible Revival of Group Work

Those early days of group work and of The Inquiry represent a time that is easy to romanticize. We need such images of shining hours and of heroic people who fought the dragons of discrimination and injustice for a democratic way of life. We need these images and figures especially during the dispiriting times that face us today. But these were real people. Their ideals and accomplishments are part of our heritage, and part of social work as a cause and social movement in our society.

Since that time, much progress has been made in reducing discrimination and poverty, and we do live in a more democratic, egalitarian society. But our communities are fragmented, and there continues to be much social conflict, endemic feelings of alienation and apathy, and a loss of purpose and meaning in our national, public life. This is not a total picture because there are areas of hopefulness and constructive effort. We do have a better understanding of social groups, their dynamics, and their normative and pathological functioning. We are more cognizant of the major functions of small groups and how essential they are to the development and well-being of individuals, families, and communities. Yet we do not seem to be able to make optimal use of this knowledge to foster the social and community integration that is so badly needed today. Many of the relevant insights and discoveries of The Inquiry that could help in this regard have been forgotten or cast aside.

It is true that many of the The Inquiry contributions have been deepened and elaborated by group work theorists and practitioners since then. For example, Schwartz (1976), Shulman (1979), and Tropp (1976) have attempted to further our understanding of the developmental and "group adjustive" mutual-aid processes that take place within helping groups. Hans Falck (1978; 1980) has done admirable work in furthering our understanding of group membership in terms of the individuality and "groupness" of the individual, and of how each member is a significant part of each other. For Falck, group work thus deals with changes in membership, and a group leader is an influential member of the "group situation," who is able thereby to accomplish behavior and personality change.

But it is the social-reformist, educational, and altruistic goals, the group discussion and thinking processes, that effect socially oriented learnings and community development. These Inquiry ideals and emphases are not prominent in recent or current conceptions of social work with groups. Social group work has become "social work with groups" and a generic aspect of social work practice. Yet, in this process group work has narrowed its concern mostly to corrective, therapeutic purposes and seems to consist largely of group therapy. Goroff (1979) and Pernell (1970) have well described this shift. Let us observe also that during the social-reform era and the civil rights movement of the 1960s and early 1970s many social workers aided the social- and community-action trends that fought for special interests and for a win-lose conflict ideology, to the detriment of common interests and community integration.

Most social workers continue to be committed to a liberal political and social philosophy and also to social reform. It is this ideological meaning of the early group work that remains so appealing and that many of us would like to see regained. It is this concern that seems to activate Tropp's (1976) arguments for a separate and distinctive social group work method. These same considerations are what Ruth Middleman (1978) seems to have in mind when she advocates putting the group process back into group work. It is these same impulses that led Beulah Rothman and Katy Papell to found Social Work with Groups. And it is these same impulses that have led so many people to attend annual symposiums "for the advancement of social work with groups."

To help realize these desires and this cause, one must make several suggestions and ask several questions. First, it would not seem helpful to try to revive group work as a field of practice and attempt to reestablish a separate identity on such a basis. Social work with groups now is a basic method in all of social work, and that is a mark of its success. It is not a "method" in the sense of contrasting it with casework or community organization as "methods." There is, however, a question and a task as to how social work with groups can be further developed as a generic "method" and also provide a basis for a valid specialization in social work. Should group therapy be considered part of such a specialization? Should there be an effort to accredit a specialization on the basis of a methodological orientation? Many social workers want their expertise in group thearpy to be recognized and accredited within social work. How is this to be done?

Another task that seems important is how to bring the practice of "group therapy" closer to social work perspectives and purposes. This is a task the profession faces also in regard to individual psychotherapy and to family therapy. It may be better to "join" social work therapists and attempt to bring their "therapy" back into social work. Thus I emphasize to students the importance of learning the role and skills of group discussion leadership with all kinds of groups—in helping individuals, in family therapy, and in organizational and community development. At the same time, there is a need to consider where this therapy business is taking us. There are questions to be asked concerning the widespread "therapeutic culture" in which so many people now live, with social worker encouragement, and also there are questions about the increasing medicalizations of social problems, as well as well as of social work practice itself. In dealing with such questions it may be helpful to consider the usefulness of the older group work model of social education and character development, of learning for responsible citizenship and democratic, consensual problem-solving in and through community group membership and experience.

There is a need to give much more attention than we do at present in social work practice and in social work education to work with task groups. Students must recognize the needs and values of working with task groups in community development, in industrial social work, senior-citizen centers, and neighborhood associations, and with self-help groups, and in nontraditional settings, such as in urban and rural communes. Rothman (1979) has pointed to the tremendous potential for social work functions in community programs with these and other groups. An important aspect of this situation is that there now are institutionalized, legal, federal, and state mandates for citizen participation in planning and decision-making in regard to a great many community projects, with funding for such group work services. Many of these community groups need social work guidance and expertise, as well as training for volunteers in group leadership, discussion, and problem-solving.

Conclusion

We have examined a relatively unknown chapter of social work history, dealing with the development of group work as a helping method and as a social-reform movement, led by the members of The Inquiry. A number of their insights and discoveries merit further study and application in social work practice with groups. These may help us with current societal and professional tasks. We face a conservative tide that may be as severe as the conservative period of the 1920s, when The Inquiry members publicly stood and worked for social reform. To help us with our tasks we can try to emulate the heroic, courageous, and creative early group workers who formed The Inquiry.

References

Benne, K. D., et al. (eds.). *The Laboratory Method of Changing and Learning.* Palo Alto: Science and Behavior Books, 1975, pp. 3–10.

Bowman, L. E. "Dictatorship, Democracy and Group Work." Proceedings of the National Conference of Social Work, 1935, Chicago: University of Chicago Press, 1935, pp. 382–92.

Busch, H. M. *Leadership in Group Work*. New York: Association Press, 1934.

Chambers, C. A. *Seedtime of Reform*. Minneapolis: University of Minnesota Press, 1963.

Coyle, G. L. *Social Process in Organized Groups*. New York: Smith, 1930.

_____ *Group Experience and Democratic Values*. New York: The Woman's Press, 1947.

_____ *Group Work with American Youth*. New York: Harper, 1948.

Elliott, H. S. *The Process of Group Thinking*. New York: Association Press, 1932.

Falck, H. S. "The Individuality-Groupness Effect." *Social Thought*, 1978, 4,, no. 3, 29–39.

_____ "Aspects of Membership." *Social Thought*, 1980, 6, no. 1, 13–26.

Feldman, H. *Racial Factors in American Industry*. New York: Harper, 1931.

Follett, M. P. *The New State*. New York: Longmans, Green, 1920. (This is a reprint with a new introduction of the book published in 1918.)

_____ *Creative Experience*. New York: Longmans, Green, 1924.

Fuller, R. G., and Mayers, H. *Community Conflict*. New York: The Inquiry, 1929.

Goroff, N. N. "Social Group Work Within a Political and Social Context." Presented at First Symposium of Social Work with Groups, Cleveland, 1979.

Gregg, A. J. *Group Leaders and Boy Character*. New York: Association Press, 1924.

_____ *The Organization of Supervision*. New York: Appleton, 1928.

Hader, J. J., and Lindeman, E. C. *Dynamic Social Research*. New York: Harcourt, 1933.

Hawkins, G. *Educational Experiments in Social Settlements*. New York: American Association for Adult Education, 1937.

_____ *Education for Social Understanding*. New York: American Association for Adult Education, 1940.

Kaiser, C., (ed.). *The Group Records for Four Clubs at the University Neighborhood Centers*. Cleveland: School of Applied Social Sciences, Western Reserve University, 1930.

Kilpatrick, W. H. *Group Education for a Democracy*. New York: Association Press, 1940, p. vii.

Lasker, B. *Democracy Through Discussion*. New York: Wilson, 1949.

Lindeman, E. C. *The Community*. New York: Association Press, 1921.

_____ *Social Discovery*. New York: Republic Publishing, 1924.

_____ *The Meaning of Adult Education*. New York: New Republic, 1926.

_____ *Social Education: An Interpretation of the Principles and Methods Developed by The Inquiry During the Years 1923–1933*. New York: New Republic, 1933.

MacIver, R. W. *Community*. New York: Macmillan, 1924.

McCaskill, J. C. *Theory and Practice of Group Work*. New York: Association Press, 1930.

Middleman, R. R. Returning Group Process to Group Work. *Social Work with Groups*, 1978, 1, no. 1, 15–26.

Newstetter, W. I. "What is Social Group Work?" Proceedings, National Conference of Social Work, 1935. Chicago: University of Chicago Press, 1935, pp. 291–99.

Newstetter, W. I., Feldstein, M. J., and Newcomb, T. M. *Group Adjustment.* Cleveland: School of Applied Sciences, Case Western Reserve University, 1938.

Papell, C., and Rothman, B. "Social Group Work Models: Possessions and Heritage." *Journal of Education for Social Work,* 1962, 2, no. 2, 66–77.

Pernell, Ruby B. *"Purpose in Social Group Work: A Life Model."* Cleveland: School of Applied Social Science, Case Western Reserve University, 1979 (mimeo).

Rothman, J. "Macro Social Work in a Tightening Economy." *Social Work,* 1979, 24, 274–81.

Schulman, L. *The Skills of Helping.* Itasca: Peacock, 1979.

Schwartz, W. "The Interactionist Approach." In J. B. Turner et al. (eds.). *Encyclopedia of Social Work.* Washington, DC: National Association of Social Workers, 1977, pp. 1321–38.

Sheffield, Ada. *Social Insight in Case Situations.* New York: Appleton-Century, 1937.

Sheffield, A. D. *The Way of Group Discussion.* New York: National COnference on the Christian Way of Life, 1922.

_____ *Joining in Group Discussion.* New York: Doran, 1922.

_____ *Creative Discussion.* New York: Association Press, 1926.

_____ *Training for Group Experience.* New York: Association Press, 1929.

_____ *The Mind of a 'Member'.* New York: Exposition Press, 1951.

Simkovitch, M. K. *Group Life.* New York: Association Press, 1940.

Siporin, Max. "Situational Assessment and Intervention." *Social Casework,* 1972, 53, 91–109.

Smith, Z. D. "Field Work." Proceedings of the National Conference on Charities and Corrections, 1915. Chicago: Hillman, 1915, pp. 622–26.

Somers, M. L. "Problem-Solving in Small Groups." In R. R. Roberts and H. Northen (eds.). *Theories of Social Work with Groups.* New York: Columbia University Press, 1976, pp. 331–67.

Tropp, E. "A Developmental Theory." In Roberts and Northen (eds.). *Theories of Social Work with Groups,* 1976, pp. 198–237.

Williamson, M. *The Social Worker in Group Work.* New York: Harper, 1929.

Wilson, G. "From Practice to Theory: a Personalized History." In Roberts and Northen (eds.). *Theories of Social Work with Groups,* 1976, pp. 1–41.

Notes

1. The primary historical data source for this paper is the Bruno Lasker papers, particularly the three-volume *Reminiscences and the Working Notebooks* (31 vols., vols 1–12, 1923–35) in the Columbia University Rare Book Library. From 1923 to 1933, Lasker was an editor for the National Conference of the Christian Way of Life and its successor, The Inquiry, both initially sponsored by the National Council of Churches of Christ in America. He was the editor and also served as secretary (1930–33) for The Inquiry and was secretary of its Race Commission. His notebooks contain detailed letters, memoranda, and minutes of committee meetings regarding the Race Commission and The Inquiry organization. The

other primary source used here is Edward Lindeman's quasi-historical book on The Inquiry, *Social Education: An Interpretation of the Principles and Methods Developed by the Inquiry During the Years 1923–1933,* published in 1933. Lasker wrote two lengthy critiques of the manuscript, which are included in his notebooks. A full history of The Inquiry is very much needed.

2. E. C. Carter was associate general secretary of the YMCA and served as secretary (1923–30) and chairman (1930–33) of The Inquiry. Elliott served for many years as chairman of the Boys Work Department of the YMCA and also taught at Columbia Teachers College and at the Union Theological Seminary. Rhoda McCulloch was a YWCA worker and official who also served as an editor for the YWCA's Woman's Press; Lasker gave her name as "McCulloch," and Lindeman referred to her as "McCullough."

3. This is reported by Mary Follett (1924, p. xviii).

4. It is noteworthy that Gusch, Williamson, and Coyle served on the faculty and taught group work in Cleveland at Western Reserve University. Grace Loucks Elliott was married to Harrison Elliott.

5. Lindeman (1933, pp. 207–33) lists 194 "Inquiry publications."

6. For a discussion of Ada Sheffield's contribution to situational theory, see Siporin (1972).

5

Social Group Work: Concerns and Challenges for the '80s

Janice H. Schopler and Maeda J. Galinsky

Examining the future of social group work in the '80s impels us to share our concerns about group work in the next decade and to enumerate the challenges we face as group workers. Because group workers have never been in total agreement about group work methodology, we don't expect consensus about the future of group work. In fact, we hope our predictions will stimulate debate and the development of ideas about what the future direction of group work should be.

The best of group work traditions requires beginning with the positives. Negatives can be identified and social group work can be criticized because of the solid base of group work practice and theory. Group workers can rely on a series of sound theoretical frameworks to guide their practice. They are supported by the practice wisdom and dedication of the group workers who serve a wide variety of groups. Further, the continued efforts to build and expand group work methodology are encouraging. Thus, our criticisms should be viewed within the context of our conviction that social group work is a vital and dynamic method of social work practice.

As social group work moves through the '80s, three interconnected concerns must be addressed: *identity* within the profession; *accountability* to clients, the profession, the community, and ourselves; and ability to *transmit the knowledge and skills needed* to meet the demands of the next decade.

Concerns

Identity

With the proliferation of models and approaches to working with groups, there is confusion about what social group work *is* and what it *should be*. There are theories to guide group work practice, and group workers draw

50

on the theoretical formulations developed by other helping professionals. Group work theories, however, tend to be general formulations that
can be applied to the broad range of situations that social workers face.
Since the days of the settlement houses, group workers have been
committed to working with those most in need and to dealing with whatever individual, social, and organizational problems clients present. To
carry out this commitment, group workers could not be restricted to a
particular model or approach of group work because no single framework
would meet the needs of their varied clientele.

Social workers are involved in all varieties of group psychotherapy:
T-groups and encounter groups, marathon weekends focusing on everything from total body awareness to mind encounters, behavioral approaches and cognitive behavioral approaches, assertion training,
problem-solving efforts, counseling and support groups, parent-effectiveness training, positive peer counseling, consciousness-raising, self-
help, leadership analysis, and grief work. Social workers also assume
leadership and consultative roles with task forces, organizational groups,
policy-making bodies, and legislative committees. Where does social
group work fit? Do social work methods of working with groups differ
from those of other professionals? Can group workers continue to incorporate theory and techniques from other models and retain a firm
identity?

In the 1940s and '50s group workers fought to have group work recognized as something more than "fun and games." They realized they had
something to offer and demanded that group work be included within
the social work profession. By the 1960s social group work had arrived
and was considered an effective approach to resolving individual, organization, and community problems and a way of providing support and education. Perhaps social workers oversold the group method because in
the 1970s it was assumed that anyone could work with groups, and did.

In all facets of human services, groups are now considered essential.
Groups are viewed as a viable approach to solving the problems of individuals, organizations, and communities; as an important means of support in a society that is becoming increasingly complex and impersonal;
as an educational method; as a vehicle for promoting causes and social action; and as a way to get the work done. Thus, group skills are basic for
social work clinicians, administrators, policy makers, and organizers.
Yet, where do social workers acquire their group skills?

Although some students learn about social group work through organized group work courses and supervised field practice, this happens
all too rarely. Many social workers now learn about groups and how to
work with them on the job, in workshops, in personal encounter groups,
through trial and error, or possibly through one or two undergraduate social work courses, where the focus is often generic, with attention directed more toward work with individuals or families. The instructors

and trainers are not necessarily social workers; they may also be psychiatrists, psychologists, psychiatric nurses, counselors, or ministers. Unfortunately, when these instructors come from other professional backgrounds, they may have no knowledge or understanding of social group work models, methods, principles, or ethics.

There should be concern about the identity of social group work in this confusing maze of group developments. Can social workers articulate their own contributions to group work practice? Can they define the essential group skills and knowledge that are required of all social work practitioners, whether or not they specialize in work with groups? Group workers promoted social group work as a necessary part of social work education, but they are not meeting the current need for training. They promoted social group work as a method for meeting diverse purposes, but they need to reaffirm the core of social group work and to identify the particular knowledge and skills necessary to accomplish specific purposes. Unless social group workers promote the basic knowledge, values, and skills necessary for any group approach and define specialized skills, social workers will turn to other professions, other programs, for their training.

Thus, group workers should be concerned about the identity of social group work because they have knowledge, skills, and values that are vital to the profession, but they have not paid enough attention to promoting or developing these offerings. With the focus on the development of a generic base and support of creative applications of group skills, social group workers have been too accepting, too broadminded, and they have done a disservice to the profession of social work and the special contribution group work has to offer.

Social workers should recognize the strengths of social group work and should place the contributions of other professionals within this perspective. Social group work provides a broad framework for practice and is unique in its attention to individual, group, and social system levels. To remain relevant through the next decade social group workers must affirm their values, beliefs, and theoretical base; and they must develop and promote social group work frameworks.

Accountability

The second concern that emerges in the current group work scene has to do with accountability. If social group work is to continue as a vital part of the profession, social group workers must demonstrate in every group endeavor that they are accountable to their clients, to the profession, to the public, and to themselves. The piles of paperwork so frequently required by bureaucrats whose definition of accountability is limited to detailed "accounting" of time and dollars spent on services are frustrating. However, as conscientious practitioners and educators, group workers must accept accountability in a broader sense as a basic professional responsibility.

Accountability to clients is not ensured when social workers practicing with groups have scattered training and diverse methods that may not incorporate social work values and ethics. Group workers are not accountable to clients when they do not routinely evaluate the effectiveness of their service. Nor are social group workers accountable when they fail to provide safeguards necessary to protect members from harmful group experiences.

Currently, groups conducted by social workers, and by other professionals as well, are too seldom evaluated in a systematic way. True, there are impressionistic assessments of group work with clients, and usually clients are engaged in the process; but evaluations must be more exacting and goal formulations more precise so that it is possible to examine the outcome of group efforts. Only then can practice be improved. Lip service has been given to evaluation, but, too often, rigorous assessment of practice has not been required. Assessment procedures have not been developed, nor has the single cell design been applied to group work. This emphasis on evaluation must be prominent in the '80s.

In recent years, the large number of social workers who have led, observed, or been members of groups where individuals have been negatively affected by participation is disturbing. Many social workers describe negative group experiences, and the few social workers who report that no one is ever harmed in the groups they serve cause particular concern. Group forces can be very potent. To ensure accountability to clients, social workers who work with groups must adhere to professional ethics, have skills in leadership and the development of protective norms, and must constantly evaluate the group's effectiveness as well as the impact of the group on individual members. Clients and other consumers of group services have a right to expect their group experience to be helpful, not harmful.

Social group workers should also be accountable to the profession and the public. A social worker employing group techniques should be governed not only by the ethics and values of the profession but should also *perform* according to professional standards. The competencies required for the practice of social group work must be defined. The type and degree of knowledge and training for various forms of group intervention must be determined.

A vital consideration, however, is with personal accountability. Conscientious recording, supervision, and consultation provided generations of practitioners with the opportunity to examine their practice and opportunity for professional development. Unfortunately, a review of group work practice today indicates that there is no consistent pattern of recording, and that supervision and consultation for group work are available only sporadically and often provided by members of other professions. There must be regular, informed examination of group practice to assure that social group workers are accountable for what happens in their groups and for the development of their skills.

Relationships with other professionals interested in groups and the development of new techniques must be encouraged. Without the stimulation of novel viewpoints and different approaches, social group work would stagnate. Creativity must, however, emerge from a base of professional integrity if social group workers are to be accountable for their work with groups.

Transmission of Knowledge and Skills

A third area of concern relates to the transmission of knowledge and skills needed for effective work with groups. In the practice arena there is a virtual explosion of knowledge and theory related to groups. Practitioners may choose from a range of models, depending on the needs of clients and preferences of the workers. Nontheless, particular gaps in theory should be noted.

Group assessment has been a neglected area in the social group work literature. Few firm guidelines exist to assess systematically group functioning and malfunctioning. While group dimensions such as norms, cohesion, structure, and goals are regarded as important, there is no clear means to evaluate their contribution to the performance of a particular group. There are numerous group development frameworks, but for the most part these have not been directed specifically to developmental phases of open-ended or short-term groups which are in frequent use. Theory related to ethnic and minority content has only begun to be developed. Furthermore, few guidelines exist for judging the effectiveness of group work. Instruments are needed that can aid not only in the evaluation of individual achievement but also of group progress.

At this point, practice is clearly ahead of theoretical development. Social workers are responding to client and consumer needs. In groups throughout the country social workers apply networking concepts, develop support systems for the elderly, adapt to the varied communication patterns of different ethnic and cultural groups, provide training in assertion, advocacy, and social action, and organize self-help groups. Practitioners are varying the "traditional group worker's role" to meet current needs; they are orienting, consulting, training, administering, and leading groups. They are also using a variety of patterns to accomplish members' goals: one-session waiting-room groups and marathon weekends, short-term and long-term, closed and open-ended. This creativity is worthy of applause, but chaos will result if these diverse activities are not codified.

Students and practitioners wishing to work with groups need some guidelines so they will know when and why a particular approach, technique, or role is needed. Social group workers have a responsibility to develop the theory necessary to support practice. If group work continues to lag behind, social workers will no longer look to social group work as a base for their practice. This means the development of models, not just for treatment, but for consultation with self-help and consciousness-raising groups, models for advocacy and social action, and models for staff and problem-solving groups. Further, the base of social group work must be reaffirmed and the particular roles and techniques that are compatible with that base must be identified.

Not only must theory be expanded and developed, but the theory that is currently available to social workers must be organized and evaluated. A system is needed for codifying this material so that it will be readily accessible to social workers. In addition, criteria to guide our selection of theoretical material must be stated. These criteria must include some reference to social work values, clarity of conceptualization, relevance to current practice issues, and empirical support.

Unless social group workers press forward in the development of group work theory, they will do little more than mark time in the '80s. At present, the knowledge base is too often narrowly related to treatment in traditional settings. Social group workers have a responsibility to reaffirm the foundations of social group work, to conceptualize and codify current practice, to fill in the gaps in theory, and to define new knowledge and skills. If group workers do not respond, they m ay find their usefulness and relevance again challenged in 1990.

These concerns about group work as it moves through the next decade relate to its confused identity, its limited accountability, and the lag in theoretical development. This statement of concerns could well be construed as a death knell for group work. However, this is not intended. Defining the problem is merely the first step. Group work is indeed a vital method, and these concerns can become the challenges of the next decade.

Challenges

Identity

Major concerns with group work's identity lie in the multiplicity of roles and approaches used by social group workers, the loosening of ties to social work, and the inadequate group training of many social workers. While it is true that social workers may be following divergent paths and using an array of models in their group work, recent developments or interests are not cause for despair. Over the years, social group work has inspired and fulfilled some of the best traditions of social work: democratic procedures, basic respect for human dignity, a concern with the social environment, and an attention to the welfare of those most in need. These traditions are evident in the new roles that group workers are assuming today and in the variety of approaches that are being developed to meet new needs.

Group workers are responding to the needs of such populations as the elderly, refugees, violent or disrupted families, the unemployed, ethnic and racial minorities, and the handicapped. They are developing more sophisticated techniques for serving those with emotional difficulties and for addressing community problems. They are finding ways to use knowledge about groups to make institutions more responsive and effective. Practitioners are also recognizing that social group workers can't directly address every need, and, through new roles as organizers and consultants, they are supporting the development of self-help and community groups whose purposes range from support in dealing with grief and loss to advocacy and action. These group developments, including the emphasis on values, advocacy, and ethnicity variables, indicate that the basis for a strong identity is present.

Although diversity poses problems, social group work cannot depend on just a few select models. The field is too young and the needs are too broad to expect certainty and dogma. The challenge in the next decade is to strengthen group work foundations so that they can support diversity. Group workers need to continue to reaffirm the importance of values and traditions so that they will provide a base for practice with groups. The focus on the group as a whole and its properties, and the concern with the social environment not only as a context, but as a vital source of influence, are unique contributions and should continue to direct our work with groups. Social group work models stress three levels of analysis and interventon—the individual, the group, and the social system—and group workers must press for recognition of these not only from social workers but also from other professionals as well.

To strengthen group work's foundations, social group workers must do more than reaffirm the old; they must also provide a framework for incorporating the new. If social group work is to remain an identifiable part of the profession, a theoretical structure must be developed that will support and provide direction for practitioners' efforts and experimentation in the field. This structure needs to be compatible with the mission and values of the profession as a whole. It must provide general theories that take account of the breadth of interest but be specific enough to point to particular interventions for identified situations. Social group workers must begin to categorize and consolidate what is being done and provide guidelines for the practitioner's choice of models. If group workers cannot provide a viable and flexible structure, social workers will turn to other professions, and other group orientations, to find a base for their practice with groups.

Group work training must be part of every social worker's preparation and education. Social group work courses must be taught as a regular part of the master's curriculum and must be required of all students, not just as part of a generic base. The '80s must be a time of renewed respect for the singular contributions of social group work. Group workers have been content in the '70s to let their method merge with social work practice in general, but it is difficult to project a strong, forceful image unless group workers insist on the inclusion of social group work as a dynamic and important aspect of training.

Concerns about the identity of social group work can be considered as a challenge. Social group work's identity will expand in the next decade with the definition of the multiple roles that group workers can serve and with the development of the models and technology to serve a variety of functions. Practitioners may be leading the way, but their innovations have pointed to the vast potential of group work. By 1990 there will be more clarity about what social group work is and greater respect for what it has to offer.

Accountability

Despite the concerns, social group workers should be confident about their ability to respond to the challenge of accountability. Social workers may not consistently evaluate the effectiveness of their practice with groups, but they are invested in the kind and quality of service they offer clients. Workers must do more than attempt to evaluate group efforts; the '80s must be a time when standardized and systematic means of evaluation are used. The introduction of behavior approaches to groups has heightened our awareness that it is not only desirable but also possible to assess objectively group outcomes. Whether group efforts are accounted for in qualitative or quantitative terms, there must be support for the development of measurement tools. Only in this way can group workers inform their clients, themselves, and the public about the results of social group work practice.

The measures devised must be ones that are possible for busy practitioners to use, but social group workers must lead the way in insisting that some evaluative measures be employed. They can no longer afford merely to tell others that they believe groups are effective. They must be prepared to buttress those beliefs with hard data. The tradition of detailed record keeping, supervised practice, and attention to clear and realistic goals will be assets in this evaluative process. While these evaluations must be more than impressionistic, they need not be based on rigorous experimental designs. There must be a middle ground whereby practitioners doing the day-to-day delivery of service can account for their group outcomes. This middle ground must be based on practitioner- and client-inspired criteria related to the agreed-upon goals for service. The measurements may be crude at first, but social group workers must take steps that begin to provide the information required. Imposed accountability has often turned into meaningless paper work with criteria that are irrelevant to the purpose of service. To prevent this, group workers must develop their own means of proving themselves accountable.

Evaluative measures should be designed that will give information on the contributions of group work methods to the outcomes. Social group workers need to know not only the success or failure of their efforts but also how their actions with individuals, the group itself, and related social systems influence the results. This kind of information will be eminently useful to the practitioner and can serve as a motivating force for carrying out the sometimes onerous task of evaluation.

Evaluation in group work is more complex than in work with individuals. Not only must individual members be assessed for positive and negative progress, but there must also be some measurement of the overall impact of the group itself. This awesome task is difficult but not impossible. The combination of societal clamor for proven efficacy and social group workers' desire to prove and improve their interventions will make the '80s a time of productive attention to accountability.

In the course of evaluating group work services, it is likely that negative effect will be noted. Social workers are aware and concerned about the harmful effects that occur in groups. Practitioners can point to a lack in their skills as well as gaps in group theory that lead to negative effects. They attempt to address problematic functioning by seeking consultation and training and by drawing on the practice wisdom gained from bitter experience. They must be provided with the theory and evaluative tools they need and want to ensure the protection of their clients.

The challenge to become more accountable is clear. It can be met by developing procedures for evaluation that are applicable for different types of groups, by filling in the theoretical gaps, and by providing the skills training practitioners are demanding. This is possible, but it will require creativity and hard work.

Transmission of Knowledge and Skills

The identity and the accountability of social group workers rests on their success in meeting the challenge to transmit the knowledge and skills needed to address the group needs of the 1980s. To meet this challenge in the next decade, group workers must consolidate and integrate yet continue the expansion of their methodology and techniques. They must identify the basic competencies for working with groups needed by any social worker and must define more specialized skills. They must find ways to monitor and evaluate the impact of groups on individuals and the environment and develop the techniques necessary to optimize their effectiveness.

As a first task, the current group approaches that are useful to social workers must be categorized. The techniques developed in encounter groups, transactional analysis, gestalt, grief work, and countless other modes are applicable to social work practice, and the effectiveness of these approaches can be enhanced when practitioners apply them within the context of values, knowledge, and skills of social group work. Because there are so many group approaches, students and practitioners need a "catalog" of what is available and what works for different purposes. Furthermore, a means for assessing the appropriateness of different group techniques and activities and for integrating them into social group work methodology must be provided.

Social group work theories have provided broad frameworks for practice. Since social workers serve such a diversity of clients, no single model or framework will suffice. Social workers should continue to have a variety of options so they can select the approach most compatible with their own philosophical and theoretical orientations. Group workers should, however, have empirical data to guide the selection of the most effective approach for a particular group. Group workers must continue to develop and sharpen social group work models and, within these boundaries, identify specific practice principles applicable to the particular populations served by social group workers. As group workers begin to catalog and codify group approaches from the literature and practice, the '80s should produce coherent diagnostic and treatment typologies for social group work.

A special strength of social group work since its inception has been its attention to programming techniques. Social workers have always been interested in verbal and nonverbal activities, and they have been creative and ingenious in devising means to help individuals and groups reach their goals. For a time this focus lost some of its dominance, but recently there has been a revival of interest in programming and group workers should capitalize on this in the '80s. The prodding of other professionals, such as the encounter and T-group leaders, who use exercises, and the behaviorists and family therapists, who promote role-playing, seems to have reminded group workers that programming is an integral part of social group work practice. Programming concepts can be used to examine and evaluate the activities that are currently so popullar and that have been so much a part of our heritage. Specific guidelines can be developed for practitioners so they can select the group technique or the verbal or nonverbal exercise or activity that willl meet their particular needs.

Categorizing current group approaches and developing the framework for group work programming is onlly a first step toward meeting the challenge of providing needed knowledge and skillls. Social group workers must also face the continuing task of developing theory and sellecting theory from the sociall sciences to ensure that all social workers have a solid base for work with groups no matter what their role or purpose. Social group work must continue to utilize concepts and data from psychology, sociology, s should have, whether they are intending to be direct-service practitioners wid social systems in group work practice. Social workers cannot, however, rely solely on social scientists. They must continue to identify what is lacking in their models of practice and supply the theory to fill the gaps, whether they borrow knowledge from other disciplines or draw on the research and practice of social workers themselves.

Social group workers must identify the basic group knowledge and skills all social workers should have, whether they are intending to be direct-service practitioners with individuals, families, and small groups, community organizers, consultants, administrators, policy makers, or educators. Every social work student should be expected to learn group principles and to develop skills in group work. It is not enough to be a generic social worker. One mut also have the specific competencies required to work with groups. Even the student who never intends to lead or work with a group must be prepared to function as an effective member of teams, committees, and work groups. Group work has become an auxiliary method in some schools. Its primary status must be advocated in social work in the '80s.

Group workers also need to develop the knowledge and define the skills necessary to deal with other specialized areas of group practice. Social group work has traditionally been geared to preventive, socialization, and rehabilitative purposes of direct-service practitioners. Community organizers, administrators, and social workers on legislative committees need to have assessment skills, as well as principles to guide their interventions, skill in achieving their purposes, and ways to evaluate their effectiveness.

In addition, social workers in direct practice have for too long dealt with situations for which there are few well-developed models. Social workers need practice guidelines directed toward open-ended and short-term groups. Practitioners often apologize that they do not have any "real groups" because they serve clients only on a short-term basis or have a changing membership. Current theoretical models do not completely address the needs they face. At the very least, group development frameworks and composition criteria should be related to these special group types.

Social group work should also expand its theoretical base for consultation in a variety of areas. Self-help groups are no longer a passing fancy.

They are a necessary support in a complex society; yet, they often run into trouble. The members need freedom to determine their own goals and do not want a worker "leading" them, but they often welcome consultation. Social workers should also be prepared to offer consultation and assistance around such current group concerns as resettlement of refugees, industrial relations, and the mediation of grievances. Social workers have always responded to the needs of people as they have arisen. This continues to be a distinguishing characteristic of social group work, and our theory must keep pace with our practice.

New ways must be found to transmit knowledge and skills. There probably will not be enough social group workers to meet the expanding training needs, nor will there be enough skilled group workers to offer the supervision we have relied on for professional development and accountability. Thus, laboratories must be designed for training and clinics must be held for on-going skill development. Using new technology, students and practitionrs can obtain self-instruction, immediate feedback, and programmed learning packages to meed deficits in their training or add new skills; and hotlines can be installed so they can dial for consultation when they run into group problems. The efforts to categorize, integrate, build, and expand have already begun. The challenge is to continue these efforts and to develop and maintain standards for competent and effective group work practice.

Conclusions

The concerns of group work and the challenges they pose cause us to view the next decade with guarded optimism. The new directions for the '80s lie not so much in new practice arenas but in a strengthening of the directions we have taken. By 1990 one can expect that social group work will have a more coherent and visible identity; that there will be more precise standards to measure performance and more effective means to ensure accountability; and that there will emerge a clearer picture of the basic and specialized knowledge and skills social workers need to practice with groups. With concern and commitment, social group workers can meet the challenge of the next decade.

Part III

Putting Theory to Work

Part III. "Putting Theory to Work," presents selected conceptualizations as they relate to social group work, and then analyzes them in the context of their applicability to actual small-group processes and dynamics. The techniques and strategies of intervention discussed in this section are derived from the literature on small-group theory and practice.

In Chapter 6, "Play Is More Than a Four-Letter Word," the author takes on an ingenious posture in making play and playfulness a central part of daily management. He artfully traces play in various facets of life and gives numerous examples of its liberating effects on human interaction. Sanctions given through play and liberties taken in play are placed in a therapeutic context for social group work. The article provides the reader with an understanding of the usefulness of play in combating tension, ennui, and a range of other physical or psychological stress situations. It opens up a variety of techniques and skills, limited only by the worker's imagination, which can be applied in work with groups.

Chapter 7, "Loneliness in the Group: An Element of Treatment," is as highly analytical and sensitive study of an area of practice seldom encountered in group work literature. The author outlines the dynamics surrounding the phenomenon of loneliness, differentiating it from other related states, such as depression, anomie, and aloneness. The paper goes on to present a model for combating loneliness and describes its application within treatment groups by a schema of diagnostic assessment that demonstrates how overt manifestations of loneliness are associated with group development stages. Further, worker strategies are outlined relative to three factors: the stage of group development, the intensity and experience of loneliness, and the personality structures of individuals in the group. The article recognizes the demands and stresses such a group places on the worker and discusses the use of co-therapists as a supportive measure in the concurrent interest of workers and the group.

Chapter 8, "Consensus As a Form of Decision Making," reviews the literature on consensus from a range of empirical and theoretical as well as field situations. The discussion is enriched by examples and the procedural steps involved in making use of this particular model of decision making. Further, the chapter discusses the advantages of consensus over other models of decision making, outlines clear-cut guidelines to achieve effective outcomes, and shows how they can be applied in a conscious, deliberate way to social work groups.

"Assessment and Change of Group Conditions in Social Work Practice" deals with a range of techniques that the group worker can use in modifying group conditions. Group conditions are analyzed from three perspectives: group structure, group process, and shared member cognitions. Each analytic category is illustrated with specific examples of empirical phenomena that are identifiable and distinguish categories from each other. Special attention is given to the behaviors of the worker in each category so that group conditions can be explicated, modified, and manipulated to achieve the desired group goals. Emphasis is placed on criteria for measuring varying levels of activities within the group and the interrelationship of group process, group conditions, and member outcomes on group functioning.

"The Uses and Abuses of Role-Playing" traces the historical development of role-playing and analyzes its functional and dysfunctional applications within group situations. Role-playing is viewed as a desirable prerequisite to behavior change and skills acquisition, and its failure is seen more as a function of poor management of techniques rather than as a shortcoming in its use. The chapter spells out the procedures and steps involved in the various modes of role-playing that are frequently incorporated in group activity programs.

6

Play Is More Than a Four-Letter Word: Play and Playfulness in the Interaction of People

Henry W. Maier

Everyone plays; it is part of life. Just recall the last time you ate an ice-cream cone or tried to put spilled salt back into a saltshaker; or you clicked the end of a ballpoint pen during an endless staff meeting. It is difficult *not* to be playful in these situations. Play, with its quality of playfulness, is an energizing force in everyday life (Czikszentmihalyi, 1976, pp. 7–8). Conversely, people lacking playfulness in their daily activities are decisively limited in their repertoire for managing everyday events (Bower, 1974).

A New Perspective on Play

Play and Playfulness

We seem to be short of words to describe the vast variety of "play" activities. We speak of "play" in describing a wide range of activities. Some play falls within the realm of leisure, such as playing baseball; some falls within the category of a vocation, and playing baseball can qualify as a vocation as well. Then there are such activities as skipping rope, constructing sandcastles, joining in a game of hide-and-seek, as well as such hard-to-define nonproductive activities as "playing hard to get," tossing of a frisbee for no particular purpose at all, or "just playing around." In short, in all of these activities the very heart of play is playfulness.

Human play is a developmental phenomenon, similar to digesting, reasoning, or bonding (Vygotsky, 1978, p. 92). Edward Norbeck defines it as "voluntary, somehow pleasurable, distinct temporarily from other behavior, and distinct in having a make-believe or transendental quality" (Norbeck, 1974, p. 1).

Of the many facets of play, this article focuses on the attributes of *playfulness* in various pleasurable activities. In playfulness, means and ends are one. Play outcome and play process are intimately intertwined; the *experience* of playfulness is central rather than the actual outcome. For example, basketball viewed for its playfulness involves running, blocking, jumping, dribbling, and getting the ball through the hoop. In the *game* of basketball the outcome dominates and basically defines the impetus. Playing playfully draws from experience that is divorced from outcome. A lucky twist of the arm before shooting the ball creates a momentary sense of mastery and control. This is playfulness set apart from the rules and outcome of the game. It is a highly personalized game within the game, and in such moments of playfulness a person feels a head taller (Czikszentmahalyi, 1979a, p. 268).

Focusing on playfulness requires a shift from preoccupation with overt behavior to experiential components inherent in play. Playfulness has less to do with the behavioral events of running around, moving of the checkers, or making weird noises than with the *experience* involved in being included, connecting with others, being surprised or alert, acting younger or older, exhibiting one's skills, or being glorified for trying, however awkward the performance.

"Playfulness," as Mihaly Czikszentmihalyi (1979-a, p. 261) observes, "is a flow state. It's like flowing; it's like being carried away and yet being in control of the direction of the flow." Playfulness spurs our creativity. While throwing frisbees, people playfully tend to reach wider, higher, and speedier; in square dancing or disco dancing, dancers become more agile, free, and flirtatious. Playfulness encourages people to stretch beyond their usual capacity, beyond their usual concepts of themselves. Frequently in social group work sessions, in moments of playfulness, clients find an added capacity to deal with heretofore apparently unmanageable events. Usually, tense group members, for example, will begin to relax during moments of fun in batting at balloons or when daring each other in a playful water-squirting match. Even fearful youngsters can find themselves daring and momentarily in control.

Playful situations can be facilitative in moments of tension and futility. Playfulness actually enhances progress in ordinary life by providing "a breath of fresh air" and new momentum for continuing beyond a momentarily hopeless situation. A writer who crumples and throws unsatisfactory pages at a wastebasket is engaging in an act of playfulness. The act of playful crumpling and throwing is actually a process instrumental in freeing the writer for moving ahead.

In many ways, playfulness takes people away from their immediate life situations while allowing them to maintain a place on their respective life stages. As in a Shakespearean drama, the play within the play moves to center stage. Play is noteworthy for its physical activities in contrast to mere mental fantasy or daydreaming. In fantasy or daydreaming a person is solitary and not actively engaged in her or his social environment. In contrast, playfulness always involves interactions with the environment and invites others to join in. Players and others are aware of entering a temporary differentiated play reality that has its own verifiable and clearly delineated social context.

While play is an essential feature of everyday living, it is important to note that we are the *least* able to play when we need playfulness the most. At crisis moments, in periods of stress, at points of social isolation, we find it most difficult to be playful. Yet at these moments playfulness could actually ease the situation. There is a challenge here for all of us to use playfulness as an added resource in our helping repertoire.

Play Viewed Within a Contextual, Nonlinear Perspective

Play viewed from an interactive rather than a behavioral or analytic perspective requires contextual (that is, ecological or nonlinear) thinking. Let's return to the example of the use of balloons at a group meeting. Balloons are benign objects, easily obtainable, and usually associated with festive activities. The group session is presumably also an ordinary event, readily accessible, and usually associated with rather sedate activities. In fact, these two ordinary experiences are usually not joined, and together they create an unfamiliar event. If one adds a balloon to a group or committee meeting, lively interactions occur; those present tend to respond as if involved in a novel experience. Balloons, as all physical objects, follow the laws of gravity. They also follow the less apparent laws of air resistance and air currents, so we are surprised and enticed by their unpredictability. "Inevitability and surprises are necessary correctives to each other. If everything is inevitable we are turned to stone, rigid, and inflexible. If everything is surprising, we live in a [mad] world of chaos. We have to keep a foot in each world" (Miller, 1974, p. 50). In many ways we are tempted to do something foolish every so often, and play is a ready vehicle for this. The desire for respite and temporary frivolity are reflected in the refreshing lines of A. A. Milne:

"Hello, Rabbit," said Pooh, "Is that you?"
"Let's pretend it isn't," said Rabbit, "and see what happens"
(Miller, 1974, p. 46).

Playfulness creates the possibility for living momentarily within two realities. In playful play, individuals manage to integrate *predictable unpredictability* and *unpredictable predictability*. Two different apparently opposing realities are reconciled in play. Playfulness includes "affective, cognitive, cultural as well as behavioral components" (Czikszentmihalyi, 1976, p. 8). Concern with behavioral activities alone shifts the focus to single cause-and-effect behavioral units, a linear perspective. The concern is then essentially with control, efficiency, vesting energy into personal success, or avoiding failure. By contrast, within a nonlinear contextual framework, interconnectedness, alternate ways of doing things, and the feedback of the experience are all tied into the same events (Beker and Maier, 1981). The difference between a linear and contextual perspective of play is analogous to the evaluation of applause in the midst of an opera, which rewards linearly the aria performance while it denies the contextual experience of the opera. An opera, after all, is enjoyed for its musical pageantry, rather than for any single musical phrase, just as phay is enjoyed for the stimulation it provides, rather than for any of its many inherernt actions.

Conceptual Framework and the Use Of Play While Working with People

In the following pages, the focus shifts to practice considerations in the use of play, particularly in the utilization of playfulness in the interaction of people in groups. Conceptual and empirical material will be applied directly to social-work-practice concerns.

Rhythmicity

Rhythmic interactions are a central component of human interactions, including playful transactions. Recent research findings hint at the likelihood that basic rhythmic units between people are instrumental in establishing intimate linkages (Byers, 1973; Condon, 1975). These rhythmic connections may be akin to the popular saying of "getting each other's vibes."

Rhythmicity tends to be a salient feature in play. Much of early childhood play entails rhythmic experience; for example, rattling a rattle or playing peek-a-boo. Other familiar activities include the give-and-take of patty-cake or action on a teeter-totter. For older children and throughout life, the *joint* rhythmic experiences of walking together, singing, dancing, breathing, or clapping together, or volleying at table tennis create a genuine sense of togetherness through mutual rhythmic experience (Maier, 1979, pp. 167–68). In working with people, introducing rhythmic play activity, such as tossing around a few beanbags at the beginning of a group session or staff meeting, can help members gain a sense of togetherness.[1]

Rituals are the social counterpart to interpersonal rhythmicity. They represent a confirmation of sound cultural rhythmic practice; the applause after moments of success in a game, the chants of cheerleaders, or the established practice for determining who has the first turn. Whatever the ritual, each expression assures mutual involvement and togetherness at crucial moments of potential discord: They serve to solidify the group. In working with groups, one may want to develop group-specific rituals if one wishes to build group rapport (Maier, 1974, p. 168).

Play: A Resource for Trial-and-Error Learning

In early childhood most learning occurs through *trial-and-error learning*. Making things move, fitting objects into corresponding spaces, and controlling objects or persons emerge out of trial-and-error experimentations and the inherent feedback in these transactions. Later in life (most likely from the time it takes two numbers to specify one's age), children, adolescents, and adults primarily use inductive and deductive reasoning. As people get smarter and use more complex modes of reasoning, they also become less apt to take on novel situations where typically a trial-and-error approach would be used. This void makes play with its trial-and-error predominance a rich additional learning resource.

In play, trial-and-error thinking, and subsequent rich feedback, we are provided with opportunities to rely upon these little-used thinking processes. The Boeing Corporation is a case in point. When the engineers find themselves struggling with apparently unsolvable problems, the company schedules a retreat for the expressed purpose *of playing* with the complexity, to find new resolutions by means of trial-and-error activities. Such an approach is akin to the one Watson and Crick used when they made a breakthrough in their search for the structure of DNA. They played with sticks for an entire night, eventually landing upon the idea that DNA consists of a double-helix structure (Watson, 1968, pp. 123–26). We can also point to Einstein, who explained that his major scientific findings could be traced to his play with blocks (Clark, 1972, pp. 27–28). Research in a variety of fields indicates that learning becomes more pervasive when individuals play in a trial-and-error fashion with the ideas, materials, or skills to be mastered (Brunner, 1976, pp. 244–56). On close examination we find that in play inductive and deductive reasoning is augmented by trial-and-error thinking, the most fundamental learning-discovery process: *Playful play is to invent, and to invent is to learn.*

As an illustration of trial-and-error learning, let us envisage ourselves working with a group of adults who have considerable difficulty expressing their anger or joy. The introduction of a few *filled* water pistols may herald a change. Little has to be said, taught, or modeled: accessible water pistols speak for themselves. A playful period of squirting will bring into the participants' lives new experiences of expressiveness. People are apt to find that they can survive attacks and can also find pleasure in expressing themselves aggressively. The importance of the experience is not the catharsis of having expressed anger or fear, but rather the experience of successfully prevailing with a high-energy level and experiencing full engagement with others.

In trial-and-error play, it is interesting to note that extrinsic reward or punishment formulas seem to be inoperative. A number of research findings suggest that when children or adults are rewarded in the midst of their play for their efforts or accomplishments, their play behavior tends to drop instead of being reinforced (Czikszentmihalyi, 1976, pp. 5–6).

Play: To Make the Strange Familiar and the Familiar Strange

The Piagetian Formula of the Human Adaptation holds that cognition proceeds by *making the strange familiar and the familiar strange.*[2] In everyday life, new requirements, crises, or encounters are conceived within one's existing framework of understanding. The strange is familiarized in terms of one's present range of comprehension; the new experience actually becomes a familiar reality. With the discovery of new ramifications and possibilities, however, the former familiar experience suddenly emerges as strange. The once-familiar becomes valued for its margin of strangeness. In working with groups, we frequently witness that group members become excited over similarities they share. Later, as a next step, they develop enthusiasm in discovering variations about each other. (Folk wisdom informs us that the "best friendships or marriages are the ones that are filled with surprises.")

Play can help to make the familiar strange and intriguing, and thus it invites further explorations. For instance, in *playing out*[3] puzzling dilemmas or painful, frustrating, or personal dead-end events, these persistently haunting events might be experienced anew through play as novel or strange "wrinkles." The old familiar scene can possibly be seen with an added perspective that offers a hopeful glimmer. For example, in Alcoholics Anonymous meetings, members tend to talk over their dilemmas. If, in contrast, they were to *play out* their experience, they could find enjoyment and challenges, however trivial, irrational, or foolish the incidents may be The challenge is "to explore alternative ideas (and ways) and alternative concepts of behavioral consistency" (March and Olson, 1976, p. 77). The familiar and old "heavies" offer potential new rays of life. New, strange variations can be explored in order to become familiar. *Playfulness does open new ways.*

Play As a Risk-Free Venture

Human beings, like other animals, need time out from the weight of everyday behavior; they require time-in for "duty-free" expressions. Humans and animals continuously reach for moments where life activities are "in neutral" and they can idle, roar, or putter away. It is a way of life generously granted any motor-driven vehicle. Play actually affords not periods of idleness, but rather busy moments of unaccountable accountability. In Jerome Brunner's terms: "Play is buffered from normal consequences" (Garvey, 1977, p. 6).

In fact, many essential life skills are learned in moments of play that parents, teachers, or social workers are unprepared to teach. To bluff, to plot, to cheat without being caught, to give up with contentment, to be in the center unashamed, or to perform better than one's place in everyday life allows — all these skills are rarely practiced except in play. In fact, playful play engages people in those very aspects of life that are often denied or forbidden in everyday life. Much of play makes inoperative the facts of time, space, gravity, and moral judgment. In play, time can be reversed or altered, and a person can be part of any time span, require any space, or deny all laws of gravity. It seems that whatever is forbidden by the Ten Commandments or by other cultural taboos is allowed and sanctioned in play. To lie, to steal, to kill, to commit adultery, are common challenges within the spheres of play. It is in play that the impossible, unpermissable, or intolerable is ventured and temporarily accepted for reality.

It is no wonder that John Calvin called play the "devil's dish." If the serf, farmer, spouse, child, and ordinary citizen are to be kept in their place, they must not play lest playfulness allow experimentation with a temporary relaxation of rules. They might then explore alternatives in orientation and alternative ways of doing things (Marsh and Olson, 1976, p. 77). This possibility may also operate in our mission to assist others as they search for alternatives to their dilemmas. In playing "for fun" rather than "for keeps," we can help others to risk and to experiment with different behaviors, ideas, and, possibly, values. In a (group) counseling, session, real-life situations are taken up as playful events. A few possibilities:

> Play "all is afoul." In a strife-torn, very verbal family, a worker might introduce a playful period of providing a spiced-up make-believe situation where all participating family members are plagued with a sore throat and are capable of speaking only in a whisper. Anyone talking above a whisper has presumedly aggravated his or her difficulties and has to lie down on the floor and simulate being "sick in bed." Such a playful interaction can be instrumental in helping this family slow down temporarily, relate to their strains in less tragic ways, and experience each other differently. Here playing is "for fun" and serves to induce learning "for keeps."

> Take a make-believe trip to the planet Neptune with a group of teenagers for the purpose of setting up a new civilization. This may challenge the participants to struggle with old value issues within a new context.

> In a group where daring to reach out to contemporaries is difficult for the group members, emulate "Knights of King Arthur's Roundtable." Plan new exploits and play them out in order to induce new perceptions, behaviors,

and fresh affectiveness for the participants. Participants may suddenly find themselves interacting with the exultant feeling: "I did it!"

When group members are learning to take on new steps for themselves and their interactive capabilities are at stake, first play and later rehearse such learnings. Opportunities for playing and rehearsing are potent steps toward new learning for affecting one's environment.

In these examples emphasis is upon playing with the risky or marginally forbidden. In play, group members are challenged to play out what they want to do and to be. They are thus able to experience what they have not dared to do yet in their lives.

The notion of helping people to risk may also have to be extended to play itself. Many persons in search of a change in their life situation need assistance with the very process of *risking to play*. For some, it may be an enrichment of their everyday lifes; for others; it may be essential for maintaining a sense of selfhood within their spheres of work. We have learned from a broad range of studies that people at the assembly line maintain their sense of sanity by choosing to play while pursuing the assigned tedious tasks. They engage in such playful activities as giving "juicy" names to tedious operations, making up songs or stories, or adapting work to a sport or carnival event. They have learned to incorporate play in work (Mergen, 1977, pp. 187–200; Terkel, 1974). In bureaucratic situations playfulness can also assist in rendering tedious or awkward routines into more bearable events. Possibilities include how one might be appropriately playful while standing in line, filling out forms, and so on. Inserting playfulness into bureaucratic existence does not spell disorder. It merely involves a temporary reordering of order, or helping people create new variations in their orderly, stultified routines of living. Playfulness mobilizes energy and synergizes a work situation. In short, playfulness adds to the quality of life.

Conclusion

It is not play per se, but the particular content and focus of play that can be an energizing agent. It is the exploratory experience, the activities of play rather than behaviors themselves, that facilitates learning (Hutt, 1970). In the therapeutic use of play, recent research findings suggest that the use of generalized play has yielded little success except when the use of play *and* training a person to play were combined around specific play objectives. This was especially true when play involved risking and when it occurred with companionship of others—that is, within a group (Williams, 1980).

We are reminded by Tom Robbins that "humanity has advanced, when it has advanced, not because it has been sober, responsible, and cautious, but because it has been playful, rebellious, and immature"

(Robbins, 1980, p. 19). In this vein, Eli Bower's observation challenges us that "learning to play [and to be playful] may be even more critical and significant to the human species—that is us—than playing to learn" (Bower, 1974, p. 3).

References

Beker, J., and Maier, H. W. (1981). "Emerging Issues in Child and Youth Care Education: A Platform for Planning." *Child Care Quarterly, 10,*(3) 1981, 200–09.

Bower, E. M. *Learning to Play—Playing to Learn.* New York: Human Science Press, 1974.

Brunner, J. S., Jolly, A. and Sylva, K. (eds.). *Play: Its Role in Development and Evolution.* New York: Basic Books, 1976.

Byers, P. "From Biological Rhythm to Cultural Pattern: A Study of Minimal Units." Ph.D. diss., Columbia University, 1972.

Clark, W. *Einstein: The Life and Times.* New York: Avon, 1972.

Condon, William. "Speech Makes Babies Move." In R. Lewin (ed.), *Child Alive.* New York: Doubleday, 1975, pp. 75–85.

Czikszentmihalyi, Mihaly. What Play Says About Behavior. *The Ontario Psychologist,* 1976, *8* (2), pp. 5–11.

_____ (1979-a). "The Concept of Flow." In Brian Sutton-Smith (ed.), *Play and Learning.* New York: Gardner Press, 1979a, pp. 257–74.

_____ (1979-b). "Some Paradoxes in the Definition of Play." Fifth Annual Meeting of the Association for the Anthropological Study of Play, Henniker, New Hampshire (unpublished keynote address), 1979b.

Garvey, Catherine. *Play.* Cambridge, MA: Harvard University Press, 1977.

Hallow, Harry, and Mears, C. "The Power and Passion of Play." *New Scientist,* February 10, 1977, pp. 336–38.

Hutt, Corine. "Specific and Diverse Exploration." *Advanced Child Development Behavior, 5,* 1970, 119–80.

Maier, Henry W. "Human Functioning as an Inter-Personal Whole: The Dimensions of Affect, Behavior, and Cognition." In CSWE, *Teaching for Competence in the Delivery of Direct Services.* New York: Council of Social Work Education, 1976, pp. 60–72.

_____ *Three Theories of Child Development,* New York: Harper and Row, 1978a.

_____ (1978-b). "Piagetian Principles Applied to the Beginning Phase of Professional Helping." In *Theory and the Helping Professions,* chap. 1., Los Angeles: University of Southern California Press, 1978b, pp. 1–13.

_____ "The Core of Care." *Child Care Quarterly, 8* (3), 1979, 161–73.

_____ Play in the University Classroom. *Social Work with Groups, 3,* (1), Spring, 1980, 7–16.

March, James G., and J. P. Olsen. "Play and Reason." In *Ambiguity and Choice in Organization.* Bergen, Norway: Universitets Forlaget, 1976, pp. 76–81.

Mergen, Bernhard (1977). "Work and Play in American Subculture: American Shipyard Workers, 1917–1977." In Michael A. Salter (ed.), *Play: Anthropological Perspective.* West Point, N.Y.: The Leisure Press, pp. 187–200.

Miller, Stephen N. "The Playful, the Crazy, and the Nature of Pretense." in E. Norbeck, *The Anthropological Study of Human Play*. Houston, Tex.: Rice University Studies, vol. 60, no. 3, Summer, 1974, pp. 31–51.

Norbeck, Edward. *The Anthropological Study of Human Play*. Houston, Tex.: Rice University Studies, vol. 60, no. 3, Summer, 1974.

Robbins, Tom. *Still Life with Woodpecker*. New York: Bantam, 1980.

Sutton-Smith, Brian. Editorial. *Newsletter: The Association for Anthropological Study of Play*, *6*, (4), Spring, 1980, 1–3.

Terkel, Studs. *Working*. New York: Avon Press, 1974.

Vygotsky, L. S. (Cole, Michael, V. J. Steiner, et al., eds.) *Mind in Society*. Cambridge, Mass: Harvard University Press, 1978.

Watson, J. D. *The Double Helix*. New York: Signet Books, 1968.

Williams, Rosalind. "Symbolic Play in Young Language Handicapped and Normal Speaking Children." In *Piagetian Theory and the Helping Professions*. Los Angeles: University of Southern California Press, 1980.

Notes

1. In this connection we can also employ some of the "touchy-feely" encounter-group exercises. Many of them had heavy components of rhythmicity with a real potential for fostering togetherness (such as waving together, arms intertwined, in a closed circle; rocking in pairs; or rubbing each other's back).

2. This statement is a popularization of Piaget's concept of the human processes of *adaptation* with its two interacting subprocesses of *assimilation* and *accommodation* (Maier, 1978, pp. 22–23).

3. Playing out rather than acting is the essence. Acting out requires replication. Playing out challenges the parties involved to reach out beyond the reachable.

7

Loneliness in the Group: An Element of Treatment

James A. Garland

Loneliness is an essential aspect of the human condition. It has existed as a conscious preoccupation or as a lurking spector in all ages and in all cultures. It is sought after by the artist, the poet, the mystic. It is imposed on the stigmatized, the powerless, the minority. It is denied and displaced by the conformist. It is the partner and counterpoint of fusion throughout the life stages of each woman and man. It is the core and essence of emotional illness and yet is intolerable to the emotionally troubled. It is endured for cause by the prophet, the cultural hybrid, the social reformer. It is in the small group a recurring theme, the counterface of the coin of cohesion. It may be the constant companion and instrumentality of the interpersonal broker, the group worker.

This chapter investigates the phenomenon of loneliness as a social, interpersonal, and existential fact and describes its natural and predictable emergence in the life cycle of the small group. The special influence of social fragmentation in contemporary life in encouraging the use of supportive group intervention will be noted, as well as some cautions concerning possible sacrifice of individual autonomy in the process. The technical and ethical issues involved in the therapeutic exploitation of the recurring cycle of separation and cohesion in the group will be the central focus. Of special significance to group workers will be the evocation of counter-transference reactions in the worker, which are perhaps related among other things to separation-individuation phases of early childhood. A basic thesis of the chapter is that the experiencing of loneliness in the group may be of significant value in the resolution of problems of autonomy and the exploration of life losses. The manner and the extent to

A briefer version of this chapter was published in *Social Work with Groups*, 4, (3), Fall/Winter 1981, 95–110.

which loneliness can be faced and resolved are seen to be functions of personality structure.

A Word on Where We Have Been

Frieda Fromm-Reichmann noted in 1959 and Joseph Hartog in 1980, thirty-one years later, that psychoanalysts and psychotherapists in general have shied away from the systematic study of loneliness. Social group work, despite its long-standing commitment to helping people to build social relationships, has viewed loneliness primarily as something to be cured by group involvement. One could hardly disagree with such a humane goal; neither could one deny that both in theory and practice group workers have been sensitive to respecting individual rights and boundaries. For the most part, however, the preoccupation has been with the affiliative dimension of human affairs. Distance between persons and the potential benefits for the client of the unhurried experiencing and examination of that interstice have been of cursory interest. My colleagues and I (Garland, Jones, and Kolodny, 1965; 1976) emphasized closeness as the driving force and central theme of the evolving group process. We urged moderation in the pacing of the affiliation process, emphasizing the need for cautious initial exploration of the group situation and identified the evocation of personal-loss issues during the termination phase. We did not (nor have others since) elaborated on the possibility that other aspects of group development, embodying both symbiotic and individuating symbolism, might provide for the exploration of both distance and closeness, or that out of the anguish of nonfulfillment might come ego-enriching growth.

A combination of factors, including astute observations made by students concerning their personal reactions in our experiential group-dynamics course, the increasing awareness in the popular press and in scientific writings of social loneliness, the continuing developments in object-relations theories and further reflection on past and present client groups, not to mention the losses and gains occasioned by my own passage into mid-life, have resulted in this renewed look at the topic.

The Faces of Loneliness

A Generic Definition

Sadler and Johnson describe loneliness as "an experience involving a total and often acute feeling that constitutes a distinct form of self-awareness signaling a break in the basic network of relational reality of self-world" (1980, p. 39); a cosmic view nevertheless applicable to the small-group setting. Melanie Klein emphasizes its presence even in the context of intimate relationships when she says, "By the sense of loneliness I am referring not to the objective situation of being deprived of external companionship. I am referring to the inner sense of loneliness—the sense of being alone regardless of external circumstances, of feeling lonely even when among friends or receiving love" (1963, p. 1). Hartog emphasizes the conditions of disconnectedness and longing as essential elements in loneliness (1980, p. 2). Klein further described the feeling as being "the result of an ubiquitous yearning for an unattainable perfect internal state" (1963, p. 1). All of these definitions have in common the idea that loneliness has to do with a cognitive and affective sense of longing and discomfort about one's sense of being and one's apartness from places, states of life, or communion with others. Or to put it perhaps too simply: "I am not where I ought to be, and it doesn't feel good."

To delineate what loneliness is about, it is useful to indicate how it is related to, but different from, some familiar psychosocial states with which it is often intertwined. It seems to be distinguishable, for example, from *depression*, in that depression has more specifically to do with the affective state of pain and energy depletion and inversion associated with the loss of an ideal state or object. It is different from *anomia* because anomia suggests a sense of rootlessness that has drifted into a loss of identity. Similarly, it is not the same as *alienation*, a condition that connotes a separation from, even an aversion to, something. It is also important to distinguish loneliness from *aloneness*, or that state of relative comfort that a person may attain when he or she is apart from familiar persons, places, or frames of reference. It speaks to the capacity of a person to maintain identity, self-esteem, and quiet contentment in the face of temporary or prolonged isolation and is closely related to the development of cognitive, instrumental, and psychic autonomy. Many ego psychologists and most of the writers on loneliness conceive of the state as emerging from the creative coming to terms with loneliness, and the evolution is observable in the small group.[1]

A Central Issue of the Human Life Cycle

The human animal, perhaps the only earthly species to have the capacity for self-observation and reflection, is occupied from birth to death with thought and action that revolve around the process of merging and separating. From an existential point of view, homo sapien is profoundly and eternally alone and at the same time most fiercely attached to and defined by his or her fellows. This individuated and symbiotic duality is expressed in an often wrenching ambivalence regarding ongoing one-to-one and collective relationships and in the alternating flux of evolution and growth. The very conception of the human infant is the result of the pairing and merging of parental gametes, cells that are distinct and yet incomplete. The cycle of blissful intrauterine envelopment proceeding to the literal tearing apart of childbirth, the establishment of independent breathing and body rhythms, and the symbiotic reattachment between mother and baby in the early hours of life is destined to be replicated symbolically in action and in concept throughout the lifespan. Milestones such as the separation-individuation process of early childhood (as described by Mahler, 1975), the emergence of the school-age child from the family cocoon and subsequent (sometimes slavish) adherence to the latency peer group, the adolescent tearing away from parental values and identifications, and the somewhat more autonomous attachments, individual and collective, to the loves and loyalties of youth culture (Blos [1967] speaks here of the second individuation process), the lonely odyssey of youth culminating in fidelity to a loved one and to oneself (Erickson, 1968) are familiar to practitioners. Increasingly we are aware, through the work of Levinson (1974), Sheehy (1974), Lowy (1980), and others, of the affiliations and separations unique to the adult years, as evidenced in events such as marriage and divorce; work and career commitment and career change and retirement; child rearing, empty nest, and renewal; mid-life reemergence of fraternities and sororities; and disengagement, reminiscence, and transcedence in old age, to name a few.

In all of these transitions we note the move from structure to relative amorphousness and back. We note the firming and fragmenting of identities, identifications, and affiliations. We note stabilization and security on the one hand and destabilization and insecurity on the other. We note communality and individuality. And of course we can read into all of these swings and polarities the desolation of being apart and the joy of reunification, the thrill of independence, and the stultification of conformity.

Culture

There is not space to review in detail cross-cultural variations in the communal-individual dimension as it affects the life cycle. When considered from the group perspective, however, a few tentative observations may be made. First, it appears that in highly group-centered societies, individual identity and awareness are not so sharply defined as in individualistic societies. Second, in these communally oriented settings there is, nevertheless, careful, often intricately organized attention given to the need for personal boundaries and to periodic relief from social and interpersonal overstimulation. Note the exquisitely orchestrated greeting and communication rituals of the Japanese and their capacity for organization and demarcation of limited living space. Note also the *rites de passage* of Native Americans, wherein the youth in the process of entering manhood goes through a symbolic death and rebirth as he experiences a period of social, interpersonal, and physical isolation and loneliness so severe as to induce a transitory psychotic state complete with hallucinations.

Third, it seems that fairly long periods of solitude, as are common in some hunting societies, are endurable partly because they are sanctioned as vital to the survival of the group and partly because the cultural framework or reference point within which they occur is secure and stable. Both those who leave and those who wait at home see them clearly as time-limited. Is there an urban counterpart in the long-distance, corporate nomad-commuter? Fourth, the risk that is endured by the communal societies is that when the cultural structure is ruptured, either as a result of radical ecological dislocation or warfare on the collective level, or serious transgression against the mores by an individual, the result can be catastrophic. The Ik, a nomadic hunting people in Kenya, were forcibly removed by a government planning agency to an evnironment where immediate adaption to a sedentary agricultural life-style was necessary to avoid physical starvation. They experienced an almost total collapse of communal institutions and attachments. They were described by Colin Turnbull (1972) as having sunk, in the space of one generation, to the level of cultural *marasmus*, being so preoccupied with individual survival that even parent-child bonds were tenuous and devoid of affection, and the elderly were ridiculed, ostracized, and left to die alone. One might say that the Ik had moved to a point beyond loneliness, a benumbed kind of depersonalization not unlike that experienced in borderline and psychotic states. Turnbull (1961) describes the Pygmy society in the Ituri Forest in the Congo Basin of Africa as a loving and intensely communal people. The most severe punishment that can be meted out for serious individual offenses such as incest is enforced isolation and social shunning. The same is true in traditional Japanese society in the sense that social ostracism is tantamount to psychological death (Kiefer, 1980).

Psychopathology

In the realm of emotional disturbance, it seems that there is a variation in etiology, quality, and capacity for endurance of loneliness. At a level where loneliness and loss are equated with feelings of nonbeing and annihilation, as in the case of schizophrenic psychosis, withdrawal from feeling and from interpersonal and reality contact may serve as protection against the full impact of experiencing the condition. Paradoxically, the internal and external shielding that is necessary to defend against loneliness also perpetuates its nonalleviation. In the case of borderline conditions, one sees extreme ambivalence about attachment and loss. Being stranded developmentally somewhere near the early part of separation individuation, the borderline person experiences overwhelming dependency needs and is at the same time gripped by feelings of rage at "bad objects." Aware of having been somehow cheated of "good-enough mothering" (Winnicott's term), he or she at the same time has neither the self-other differentiating perspective nor the inner resources to face separation anxiety. The result is a continual striving to regain a fantasied utopia, alternating with feelings of having been betrayed by others and a relative inability to sustain feelings of loneliness. Individuals with less severe character problems, but who nevertheless are dealing at the level of trying to achieve autonomy in the face of basic anxiety about separation, seem also either to fight against parent figures and social structures or cling to them. Other persons, group rules, or physical structures are seen as responsible for their feelings and for their sense of entrapment or exclusion. For them the feeling of loneliness is not so much a problem as is being responsible for the feeling and for the continuation of the lonely stance. In the case of neurotic conditions that involve compulsive or phobic covering and displacement of feelings, it appears that a variety of defensive techniques may be employed to guard against feelings of isolation and fears of "sinful" contact. These may include preoccupation with work, rigid time scheduling, selective avoidances, and voracious acquisition of objects. Higher-level neurotics seem to be painfully aware of being "on the outside looking in," whether they are observing a loving couple or a peer-sibling group. They crave love and approval and will alternately work to gain it or despair of ever achieving it.

The Current Social Context

Clark Moustakas states powerfully and succinctly some of the conditions in modern urban-dominated society that have a bearing on loneliness:

> Loneliness anxiety is a widespread condition in contemporary society. The individual no longer has an intimate sense of relatedness to the food he eats, the clothing he wears, the shelter which houses him. He no longer participates directly in the creation and production of the vital needs of his family and community. He no longer fashions with his own hands or from the desires of his own heart. Modern man does not enjoy the companionship, support and protection of his neighbors. He has been sharply cut off from primary groups and from family and kinship ties. He lives in an impersonal urban or suburban community where he meets others not as real persons but according to prescribed rules of conduct and prescribed modes of behavior. He strives to acquire the latest in comfort, convenience and fashion. He works in a mechanized society in which he is primarily a consumer, separated from any direct and personal contact with creation. Modern man, is starving for communion with his fellow man and other aspects of life and nature. (1961, p. 25)

In addition to experiencing fragmentation, depersonalization, and alienation as conveyed here, persons have a dual sense that on the one hand they are manipulated by immense forces beyond their understanding and control, and that on the other they are solely responsible for their own fate. Thomas Wolfe put the existential case darkly:

> The whole conviction of my life now rests upon the belief that loneliness, far from being a rare and curious phenomenon peculiar to myself and to a few other solitary men, is the central and inevitable fact of human existence – All this hideous doubt, despair, and dark confusion of the soul a lonely man must know, for he is united to no image save that which he creates himself, he is bolstered by no other knowledge save that which he can gather for himself with the vision of his own eyes and brain." (1941, pp. 186, 189)

It is not surprising that twentieth-century Americans, feeling lonely and responsible for their own fate and being embued with a tradition that anything is possible through technology, have become industriously involved in creating a variety of social instruments to solve their dilemma. One of these instruments has been, in recent years, the small group. We have created groups to reawaken our awareness of the nuances of human feelings and meanings. We have created groups to help us do better problem solving. We created groups to get in touch fast because by next week we may have moved. We have created groups to guarantee instant intimacy in this nonintimate world and have tried at times to pretend that we could engineer our way through or around age-old social rituals for getting acquainted and ego-mechanisms that are designed by lifelong training and perhaps by phylogenetic patterning to promote cautious interpersonal exploration and psychic integrity. But perhaps some of our short-term treatment forms are based less on valid scientific reasoning than on an unsavory conspiracy with the demands of the impersonal society – that we are training people less to make contact than we are to getting them ready to say goodbye. Let us consider the possibility that we may first *enable* people to face and understand their loneliness, then help them to find ways to deal with it. And the important point may be for group workers to understand at what level various group populations are capable of encountering loneliness and how much and what kind of assistance they will require to deal with it. A case in point is the longtime psychiatric hospital patient who has been returned to the community and suffers from psychological and social isolation. He or she may as a matter of personality structure have limited capacity for encountering the depth of that loneliness and at the same time require a lifelong support to mitigate against its effects. This means that exploration of the issue in a group might be done on a nonintensive level with opportunity for trying out getting-acquainted skills. In addition, a permanent social-support structure, such as a drop-in center, might be provided, rather than attempting to get him to be completely self-initiating in seeking out affiliations.

Loneliness and Group Development

I have proposed thus far that: (1) loneliness is universal in human life; (2) its character and identification vary across cultures and in different personalities; (3) it appears and reappears in various forms throughout the life cycle and can produce growth; (4) it occurs along with cohesive and affiliative tendencies in all human groups; and (5) group workers must exercise caution in hasty or excessive promotion of either side of this relational coin. Let us now synthesize these points with the following:

1. There is in all small groups an unfolding sequence of developmental stages, each stage haing an identifiable character and set of tasks.
2. Each stage issue is isomorphically similar to and evocative of major interpersonal themes and issues of specific life-stage issues.
3. Loneliness waxes and wanes throughout the staging process in ways that are related to and inherent in specific staging issues.
4. The loneliness issue is particularly important at the end of the second stage, and its resolution and exploration are crucial to the success of the treatment process.
5. The approach of the group worker to the issue and his or her countertransference reactions are of major importance in the process.

The points will be addressed by organizing them around a brief description of each group stage.[2]

Stage One: Preaffiliation.   The initial coming together is concerned with preliminary exploration, orientation, and establishment of trust. It is relatively nonintimate and oriented around stereotypic orientation and perception. Annihilation anxiety is present to varying degrees and mostly at an unconscious level, and projective identification is employed as both a defense and an adaption. Superficial commonality in verbal exchange and/or parallel play, approach-avoidance, arm's-length mutual exploration, and short attention span characterize the interpersonal and activity orientation.

Direct reference to loneliness at this stage of the group is rare. The major evidence that longing and disconnectedness are lurking about is to be observed in physical distancing and "other groups I've been in" stories. These tales may be of interpersonal violence or group failure, or they may contain counter-loneliness metaphors involving feeding, interpersonal fulfillment, and previous ideal group involvement. For the most part, loneliness as an *in situ* experience is denied or projected *ex situ* and dealt with metaphorically. My hunch is that members are too preoccupied with making some contact and with surviving to be able mentally to construct the profile of loneliness, much less tolerate the anxiety that would be generated by its emergence. Much as infants deal with loneliness in the early months of life by splitting good and bad objects (Klein,

1963), so the group splits in-group–out-group perceptions. At times they make out-group–out-group dichotomies, leaving the in-group neutral, unknown, and, perhaps for the time being, safe. The stereotypic mode of exchange and the sometimes strained, *as-if* emotional tone are not unlike the detached stance of the schizophrenic. Indeed, it is often schizophrenic and borderline persons who, being closest to the annihilatory underworld of the infant group, let us in most vividly on the possibilities, as they see them, of ostracism and obliteration. The schizophrenic may produce a poison gas or suffocation delusion and literally remove himself from the room or retreat into his lonely shell of psychosis. Persons with borderline conditions characteristically get into trouble in Stage I because they cannot hold back from (1) controlling group discussions; (2) making direct reference to sexual or dependency needs; or (3) telling "stories" about destruction and rejection. In the first instance, the control maneuver appears to be designed to forstall desertion and chaos, particularly if the worker is seen as not "taking care of things." The person identifies with and takes the place of the fantasied lost object. In the case of the latter two overtures, which may represent the good-bad dichotomy, the result is likely to be identical – withdrawal. But whether massive energy inputs during early group sessions are libidinal and affiliative, or aggressive and alienating, their impact is likely to be unmanageable and traumatic to the still-primitive interpersonal system and traumatic to the individual participants.[3] Again, the net effect of this energy flood may be literally to fragment the group. Or it may create a kind of intragroup isolation, an aggregate of defended and boundaried individuals, not daring to make an offer or a request and, because the group is so new and cognitively amorphous, perhaps not even knowing why. To borrow Riesman's (1950) concept, it is truly a lonely crowd.

Is the case lost? I think not. It is usually not possible for the worker to make during this nascent phase any direct clarification that could be understood or tolerated. It is possible, however, to use group structures – words, activities, physical arrangement – as a "good enough" environment to enable moderate, distance-reducing exploration and at the same time protect personal boundaries from massive encroachment. In addition, in pregroup screening interviews and in his or her beginning group statement, the worker can set the expectation for boundary respect and noncompulsive affiliation. Recalling the discusson of how much loneliness and/or intimacy a particular person can withstand, we infer that the worker, having set the basic existential stance, may vary the intensity of the message in keeping with the degree of commitment and the level of integrity of the participants' psyches.[4]

Stage Two: Power and Control.   As stereotypic momentum flags and greater competency develops, the reality of the group is encountered. Individual and collective security are sought through the establishment of group norms, rules, hierarchies, and a system (sometimes primitive) of justice and morality. Attempts at structuring succeed only partially and are assaulted not only by the permissiveness and nondirection of the worker but also because of the regressive-dependent wishes of the members. Polarized thinking and perception, scapegoating, and tendencies to leave the group appear. Utopian and paranoid fantasies, at first largely unconscious, appear, collide, and come to an impasse and the worker is de-idealized, symbolically extruded, and occasionally replaced by an idealized rescuing collective of members.

Fears of failure with respect to meeting of affective and interpersonal needs are confessed directly or through metaphor at the same time that increased group competency and interpersonal closeness emerge.

It is during the waning phases of this stage that loneliness is most likely to make its full-fledged debut. Its *mis en scène* is often preceded by a growing chorus of discontent about the competency or benignity of the worker, the adequacy of the other members, and the efficacy of the experience itself. The complaint, subtly shifting to a tone of disappointment, may be expressed with delicacy and humaneness by sell-socialized adults: "I somehow feel that we collectively are failing to meet group goals, although I know that the group worker is trying very hard. Latency youngsters put it more succinctly: "This club sucks!" Lest the reader think that this pithy phrase does not contain psychological wisdom, let us discern that the paranoid tone is subtly accompanied by a hint of yearning; the club could suck nice. Or to quote the dining hall cynic: "The food around here is poison—and such small portions."

The worker may be sorely tempted at this juncture to respond in one of two ways. The first is to the cry for nurturance, the plea for fulfillment of the utopian fantasy, a guarantee of symbiotic bliss. If the worker is not terrified by the implied enormity of the demand or the fusion that may accompany it, he or she may proceed to give increased assurance of the supportive potential of the group, the inciteful observations of the members, or in a children's group may double up on refreshments or promise a trip to Disneyland. The alternative course is to respond punitively to the dismal expectation of rejection, sadistic control, and deprivation. The worker must usually rationalize the negative counter-transference by masking critical verbal retaliation in the guise of "reality clarification" or "therapeutic confrontation." Again, on the activity treatment level, the decision to cut out snacks is construed as "helping the children to control their oral rage and regressive messing."

Perhaps this is overstating the case for effect, but the message is clear. The worker has identified with one or the other side of the message and is conspiring to defeat the first major move toward individual and collective autonomy. Better that she or he should hear first the message of despair and cynicism and mirror it, with appropriate empathic affect, back to the group. In the process, the worker must tolerate in his or her existential soul the hypothetical reality that the group could fail; the lonely prophecy could come true. He recognizes openly that the members are considering that dismal possibility, but without confirming that he either believes or disbelieves it. After a suitable period of raging and despair—artistry is required on the part of the worker to judge when the grieving is completed—the question may be posed as to whether the members can say what it was they hoped to get from the experience. It is at this crucial point that the bid for intimacy begins. It is paradoxically at this point also, as the members begin to admit their needs (the true group agenda some say) and glimpse the possibility that they may also be able to nurture one another, that loneliness may appear in its fullest flower, with poignancy and perspective.

Affect-laden revelations of personal bereavement and losses of separation, past and present, appear regularly. Some of the associations are of exclusion in the face of love and plenty. A woman describes a "flashback" of her seventh birthday party, when none of the guests showed up. A man says he suddenly feels profoundly sad, outside the group looking in. A mood of angry recrimination and resentment often may dissolve quickly into one of quiet reflection. Participants have characterized the situation "giving up," "letting go of one another." They speak of "owning" their individual feelings and "hearing other people" for the first time. A measure of the psychic and interpersonal efficacy of such an event is the dramatic sense of relief that pervades the group at the end of the session and a mood swing in the direction of optimism about the possibilities for mutual support and giving: "I thought I was going to fall apart at the start of the meeting. Now I'm real tired, but I feel great."

The transition just described appears to be based on two group dynamics. First, the capacity to bear loneliness in the presence of others is at least in part preconditioned by having experienced a safe initial entry into the group (preaffiliation state) and a subsequent "good enough" second stage (power and control), which enabled participants to negotiate out power and autonomy issues and to develop a moderate amount of personal and collective competency in the areas of problem solving and instrumental activity.[5] The second dynamic is the obverse of the structure picture. It represents the giving up of reliance on structure, which, while it supports and enables, also may serve as a barrier to full exploration of latent emotional themes and to further individuation within the group. The analogy to individual development is the separation-individuation process of early childhood, the move from the cuddling, limiting, parental lap to the freedom and scariness of walking around the room. And just as that childhood transition is seen as healthy and conducive to the development of a stable and creative adulthood, so is the transitional experiencing of interstage loneliness generic to a healthy group and to the ability of that group to help its clients.

Individuals have varying capacity for experiencing and profiting from loneliness and autonomy and display diverse reactions to this major second-stage interlude:

1. Psychotic persons are overwhelmed by the absence of protective structure and the threat of identity loss and reality dissolution. They may also become terrified by the consuming heat of impending intimacy. They may require repeated approaches to this crucial threshold.

2. Borderline persons may sidestep the developmental paradox by resorting to the good-group-bad environment split. Dube, Mitchell, and Bergman (1980) describe how this supportive mode may in time build in collective security to enable these members to risk depression and confrontation of their bereavement. Ariving at this point may require several years. It seems not to be available for short-term implementation.

3. Character-disordered persons, unable to face the separation anxiety evoked by the move from structure, most often try to regain that state by reprovoking authority conflicts. What appears on the surface to be a fight for freedom is, in effect, an escape from it. Passively oriented characters, though using seductive-compliancy as a means, seek the same result. Cuddling, whether seen as jail or playpen, is preferable to desertion and self-awareness.

4. Young children often act through the transition rather than discussing it with any consistency. Also, their natural life state is to be still attached to adults and to be sustained by the adult ego. Therefore, they should not typically be expected to experience the same degrees of separation as do adults. Any child whose integrity and safety have been assaulted to that level is already in serious jeopardy.

5. Minority persons (racial, ethnic, class, gender, sexual orientation, physical handicap) represent a very special situation as to the genesis of their sense of separation from the majority, from their own group, and from themselves. The experience can be most valuable in helping the persons to separate self-concept from the demeaning image enforced by the majority. An error frequently made by well-intentioned (and often guilty) workers is to try to confer liberation on the minority member and to deny him or her the opportunity to struggle with that aspect of himself that has internalized the aggressor's opinion. In addition, the giving up of the oppressor in one's life and mind invariably includes loneliness as at least a transitory aspect. Parenthetically, a complete view of the process may include the person deciding where to move next with regard to the majority group or community. Action on the environment, as well as internal "adjustment," can be the result of the lonely odyssey.

Stage Three: Intimacy. Having admitted and survived the fear of noncloseness, the group plunges into a familylike merging, replete with mutual admission of vulnerability and needs. Dependency bids, interpersonal jealousy, sexuality, and labile emotionality surface. Transference is high, and family associations are evident on all levels of consciousness. Group capacity to carry out cooperative activity and to meet individual needs is realtively high, but it may be disrupted at times by flare-ups of egocentrically oriented emotions and perceptions. The members identify the meaning of the group in terms of its problem-solving and need-meeting character and potential.

Issues of loneliness during the intimacy state tend to be of two types. The first is the transfer of family dramas into the group, at times abreacted without conscious connection between "here and home," and sometimes with affect-laden awareness of the recapitulation. The second type, at least partly a symbolic replay of family and other personal relational sets, is more generic to group operations. The difference between the two from an interventive standpoint is not substantial. Themes are most likely to be on the multiperson level—being left out of a love triangle or being excluded from the member (sibling) clan. There is concern about being loved and respected. Note the contrast to visions of being "wiped out" or being deserted, which were more prevalent in earlier stages. Loneliness, as well as other emotional dimensions, is more accessible to examination and collective support.

Loneliness at the point of transition between intimacy and differentiation seems to be mainly on the level of poignancy about leaving the fantasied family and moving into the reality of the here-and-now "grown-up" peer group. Some of this has to do with giving up some illusions of ideal dependency; some has to do with the fear that maturity will not be exciting. The meaning of this latter feeling may have something to do with reluctance to sublimate erotic gratification wishes into friendly altruism.

The group worker during the intimacy stage is not immune to the variety of feeling described above. In fact, the atmosphre of disclosure and vulnerability that pervades the period may make the worker more personally susceptible to longings and to upsets than was the case previously. Workers have remarked on the emergence of fantasies of being taken care of as the "littlest child" of the group, of wanting their "share" of time for talking and expressing feelings, and of being "left out" of the familylike drama. Stimulated by the heady interaction and feeling lonely in the role of nonpartaking enabler, it is not uncommon for *co-workers* to seek support from their partners. The objective counter-transference aspect of this appears to be a response on the aprt of the workers to fulfill the group's desire for a mother-father pair to complete the family fantasy. There is probably also an element of subjectivity in the urge. It is not uncommon, particularly in demanding and stimulating group residential settings, for co-workers to seek each other's constant support—to fight, to make love, even to get married—as their needs for nurturance and fears of loneliness are called forth. It is likely that the popularity of co-leadership in group work, especially among workers new to groups, is in part occasioned by anxiety over being different and alone in a crowd. In keeping with one thesis of this chapter—that loneliness can promote creativity—the worker should be aware that the lonely stance in the group has potential for increased sensitivity to group and to self and for sharpening the awareness and the understanding of one's professional brokering role.

Stage Four: Differentiation-Cohesion. This stage represents the group's move to a reality and here-and-now orientation. Relationships are no longer blurred with the past; other members are seen as distinct from self and from one another. The worker is seen as a friendly enabler in his or her own right and not as a shadow of the parent or other adult archetype. The frame of reference is now the group, which has established its own unique culture and modus operandi. Cohesion without submersion of individuality is possible and roles become flexible. The group is a safe arena for conscious replaying of interpersonal issues, for receiving objective advice, and for practicing alternative interactive styles. Contact with community and other groups is possible.

The review of life-loneliness issues continues in this stage, but it is less likely to be replicated on a transference level. Reluctance to leave the stage is conditioned partly by realization that the end is near. The group itself has become an internalized object, a source of support, and a frame of reference for humane and democratic social interaction. Members wonder whether they can get along without it.

Stage Five: Separation. When members have derived optimum benefit from the group and their association, the separation process brings on a variety of reactive feelings and behavior. These may include denial of the ending, recapitulation of early group events and characteristics, individual and collective regression, healthy and pathological flight, and review and evaluation. Upset over significant life losses is evoked by the impending termination. Transfer of skills acquired in the group into other social settings is aided by contact with the environment through trips, participation in community projects, and the like.

Gradual deinvestment in group attachments and in the operations of the group is a healthy move and appears also to be in part a means to ensure individual integrity. Acting out and regression on the part of vulnerable members are familiar to group and individual workers. What is perhaps less discussed is that for persons who have basic ego deficits, radical group termination may not be advisable. The classic concept of termination of treatment is based partly on the idea of coming to terms with loss, but it is also predicted on the assumption of a relatively intact ego and sense of object constancy. In an effective group experience, issues of loss should have been at least partially addressed as described above in the internal staging process. To the degree that continuing social support is required, a range of group programs and approaches should be considered. They are in part: group reunions; continuation of the group on a self-run basis with agency or worker consultation; referral to self-help networks and use of halfway houses or drop-in centers. The long-term presence of the community agency is important as a potential forever-transitional object.

As the session ends, the worker is left alone to experience loneliness, left by the absence of the group. He or she might entertain two fantasies as one way to evoke a test of how well separation was handled and how well he or she was prepared to help the members use the ending in the service of growth. The first scene is of the group members stopping as they prepare to leave the group room and saying in unison, "We'll never see you again and you didn't do well enough." The second and final scene is of yourself sitting alone in the room for a long time after everyone has left.

References

Blos, Peter. "The Second Individuation Process of Adolescence," *Psychoanalytic Study of the Child*, 22, 1967, 162–86.

Dube, Beatrice; Carol Mitchell; and Lynn Bergman. "Uses of the Self-Run Group in a Child Guidance Setting." *International Journal of Group Psychotherapy*, 30, no. 4, October 1980, 461–480.

Erickson, Erik H. *Identity, Youth and Crisis*. W. W. Norton, New York, 1968.

Fromm-Reichmann, Frieda. "Loneliness," *Psychiatry*, 22, 1959, 1–15.

Garland, James A., Jones, Hubert and Ralph L. Kolodny. "A Model for Stages of Group Development in Social Work Groups." In Saul Bernstein (ed.), *Explorations in Group Work*. Boston: Boston University, 1965. Republished by Charles River Press, Boston, 1976.

_____ and Ralph L. Kolodny. *Treatment of Children Through Social Group Work: A Developmental Approach*. Boston: Charles River Press, 1980.

Hartog, Joseph; Audy, J. Ralph; and Cohen, Yehudi A. eds. *The Anatomy of Loneliness*, International Universities Press, New York, 1980.

_____ "The Anlage and Ontogeny of Loneliness." In Hartog et al., pp. 13–33.

Kiefer, Christie, W. "Loneliness and Japanese Social Structure." In Hartog et al., pp. 425–50.

Klein, Melanie. *Our Adult World and Other Essays*. New York: Basic Books, 1963.

Levinson, Daniel J., et al. "The Psychosocial Development of Men in Early Adulthood and Mid-Life Transition." In D. F. Ricks et al. (eds.), *Life History Research in Psychopathology*. Minneapolis: University of Minnesota Press, 1974.

Lowy, Louis. *Social Work with the Aging*. New York: Harper & Row, 1979.

Mahler, Margaret. *The Psychological Birth of the Human Infant.* New York: Basic Books, 1976.

Moustakas, Clark. *Loneliness.* Englewood Cliffs, NJ: Prentice-Hall, 1961.

Riesman, David. *The Lonely Crowd.* New Haven: Yale University Press, 1950.

Sadler, William A., Jr., B. Thomas, and R. Johnson. "From Loneliness to Anomia." In Hartog, et al., pp. 13–33.

Sheehy, Gail. *Passages: The Predictable Crises of Adult Life.* New York: E. P. Dutton, 1961.

Turnbull, Colin. *The Forest People.* New York: Simon & Schuster, 1961.

_____ *The Mountain People.* New York: Simon & Schuster, 1972.

Wolfe, Thomas. *The Hills Beyond.* New York: Harper & Brothers, 1941.

Notes

1. I have attempted here to delineate further specific concepts of loneliness. Moustakas offers a useful and evocative discussion on the subject (1961, pp. 24–53). Also, it is necessary to forego a detailed review of some of the historical, cultural, psychological, and literary discussions of loneliness that are available. For an excellent representative collection of such material, see Joseph Hartog, J. Ralph Audy, and Yehudi A. Cohen, eds. *The Anatomy of Loneliness* (New York: International Universities Press, 1980). I have chosen to define and classify aspects of loneliness that seem most useful for relation to small-group dynamics and therapeutic intervention.

2. The group-development theory described herein was originally written by Garland, Jones, and Kolodny (1965), republished (1976), and revised and expanded by Garland and Koldony (1980).

3. For an extended discussion of the concept of early group trauma, see Garland and Koldony (1980).

4. One sociogenerational cohort that has a special investment in maintaining distance is the elderly, particularly those who have suffered catastrophic loss, such as a loved one, health, status, role, or autonomy. They often speak openly about having been deserted and bereft. They make known their intention to make no new commitments without careful assessment.

5. The distinction between problem solving and instrumental activity is somewhat artificial. It is used to allow for the differentiation between direct, verbal deliberation of issues performed in "talk" groups as compared to craft, work and, play as performed in action-oriented groups.

8

Consensus as a Form of Decision Making

Martha E. Gentry

A popular, if not faddish, word of the 1980s is *consensus*. "Can we reach consensus on this?" and "The consensus of the group was . . ." are familiar examples. Upon close examination, consensus is used to mean either a statement of agreement or a particular process used in decision making.[1] Often an inference is made that a particular process was used to reach a statement of agreement when such was not true.

This paper is about consensus as a form of decision making—a process of reaching a decision that has a long tradition as an alternative to majority rule and the use of formalized rules and parlamentary procedures. This process was developed and has been refined by the Society of Friends, or Quakers, over three hundred years. It is referred to in business-administration texts, used in the international political arena, and in constitution writing by independent nation-building countries (Hare, 1980). Consensus as a process that permeates all hierarchical levels in major Japanese corporations is attracting the interest of corporations and others interested in increasing productivity in the United States (Ouchi, 1981). Women's groups and economic cooperatives have used consensus as their major decision-making form.

This diversity of use and popularity of the term with ambiguous meaning suggest the timeliness of a review and analysis of what is known about consensus. As used here, consensus is defined as a decision participated in by all members of a group and representing the maximum area of

The author expresses appreciation to students in her Advanced Practice Theory course, Fall 1980, for reactions to a draft of this paper. This is a revision of a paper presented at the 1980 Symposium on Social Work with Groups. The paper was originally published in the Journal of Sociology and Social Welfare, 1981: 233–44.

common acceptance (English & English, 1958). Small group properties and conditions are used to analyze the literature. These include group purpose, conflict and its resolution, ownership, power or influence, size and the use of time.

Literature Review and Analysis

The Quaker Contribution

Within the Quaker experience, occasions for worship are not separated from occasions for the transaction of business. Central to this is the belief that person possesses the Light of Christ, which should serve to guide each person's life experiences as well as be available to guide a group. The process of reaching a consensus, therefore, is to seek the Spirit of God — not to seek a community of minds. This difference in purpose is essential to understand the consensus process as used by Quakers. It suggests that shared ideology in some form may be a necessary condition for successful use. Hare analyzed the Quaker experience from a Parsonian systems perspective, which is based upon an assumption of shared values.

If the Inner Light is within each person but consensus is a group process, then a natural tension should be expected. The presence of natural tension or conflict is explained by suggesting that the Spirit has not as yet been sufficiently found in all members of the group. Quakers have built in several techniques to manage conflict. Uniquely, Quakers use a period of silence in which members consider their own and others' views. During this period, self-interests that may impede seeking the Inner Light are to be set aside. A committee may be appointed to obtain more facts, and this committee may or may not report back to the larger group. The conflict-producing item may be withdrawn from consideration and perhaps introduced at a later meeting.

Within this framework, is it possible for a person to disagree with a developing group consensus? It is, but only after serious examination to determine that the different stand is based upon an objective view of facts informed by individual conscience. Pride, insensitivity, and personal ambition are to be set aside. The ability for self-reflection, self-awareness, and sensitivity to others appears to be required to some degree to all members.

Leadership of the Society in Meeting is institutionalized in a Clerk. The Clerk (1) senses the need for silence, (2) introduces the subject to be considered (though it may also be introduced by any Friend present), (3) sees that each person has the opportunity to speak, (4) delays consideration of the subject by referring it to a committee, (5) verbalizes the "sense of the meeting," and (6) records and reads the record of the sense of the meeting. This record of the sense of the meeting is called a "Minute."

Members give assent to the Minute by verbalizing "I agree" or by nodding the head. Assent does not necessarily imply uniformity of judgment but a recognition that the Minute records what the members think is right at this time—that it reflects the sense of the meeting. The extent of unity may differ according to the relative importance of the issue at hand and whether or not a decision can be postponed.

In Meeting, each member is expected to speak, is listened to, and is permitted sufficient time for full expression of viewpoints. Do some members possess more power or influence over others in the deliberations? The process of weighting individual contributions is fundamental to the Quaker method. Some Friends are held in positions of high status on the basis of reputation gained through experience and spiritual insight. Little weight is given to those who speak out of apparent self-interest. The position of high/low status in the structural hierarchy appears to be an achieved or earned position in contrast to ascribed status. Factors that influence this internal "weighting" probably are somewhat unique to Quakers and not necessarily limited to the goal-achievement behaviors noted in small-group research (Strodtbeck et al., 1957). The extent to which external group factors, however, influence internal ranking is not known.

Meeting for business in a structure that includes periods of silence and encouragement for participation by all members assumes an availability of time. Critics of the process suggest that a majority-vote decision-making process is more efficient; however, once a decision is reached by the consensus method, support for the action is assured. Compliant behavior or sabotage by the minority are well-known tactics in the majority-rule process that obstruct acting upon a decision. This may suggest that the consensus process is particularly useful when the decision outcome requires common action and support.

Limited research is available about the Quaker process. Drake (1973) was concerned that the informal socialization process traditionally used to teach Friends was not sufficient, since children are now excluded from Meeting and the adult population is highly mobile. Among other questions, he sought to identify the common elements or principles in the process that could be included in educational programs designed for Quakers. He analyzed the literature to identify principles of the process and subsequently used the Delphi technique with recognized experts in the consensus process to locate those principles most commonly accepted. Considerable agreement was obtained from these two methods.

This analysis of the Quaker decision-making process suggests that the following conditions promote successful use of consensus: (1) members are bound together by shared ideology; (2) conflict managment techniques are built into the structural arrangements of the group; (3) leadership is sensitive and responsive; (4) members understand and value the process; and (5) criteria for internal ranking of members are consistent with the goals of the group and its values.

Reaching Human Agreement

Although small-group literature historically suggested that (1) groups are more effective when all members participate, (2) minority views should be voiced, (3) the group product or decision should be developed cooperatively, and (4) the group atmosphere should be supportive, these principles have usually found expression only in the majority-rule form of decision making. There is a growing body of research, however, that focuses on consensus. This literature, primarily from the field of social psychology, identifies conditions for the consensus process to work, considers the use of power or influence, notes the relationship of conflict to the decision process, and identifies the characteristics of the consensus process as different from the majority-vote process and the effects of personal characteristic variables on outcomes.

Dodd and Christopher (1969) tried to discover some correlates of the consensus process in the variables "intent-to-agree," "discussion," and "practice." Their findings suggested three rules to use to make the consensus process work:

1. Strengthen members intent to agree
2. Provide ample time for thorough discussion among members
3. Let members practice making decisions together.

Improvement of decision making through training was studied by comparing thirty untrained and thirty trained groups (Hall and Williams, 1970). Training consisted of an instrumented T-group intervention. Their findings related to the flow of the influence process are of particular interest to an analyis of the consensus process.

Before the group sessions, when 50 percent or more of the group members subscribed to a judgment that was later incorporated in the group solution, Hall and Williams inferred that there was a majority flow of influence or a *majority power bloc*. When fewer than 50 percent subscribed to a judgment prior to the discussion, but that solution appeared later in the decision, a *minority bloc* technique was attributed to the group. If no individuals subscribed to the ultimate group decision prior to the discussion, the solution was viewed as an *emergent solution* where a free flow of influence prevailed. Those groups that received training and whose decisions were emergent also utilized the resources of their most adequate members. Untrained groups generally did not utilize the resources of their members.

Whether or not conflict was correlated with the outcome of emergent solutions was also studied. The presence of conflict was determined by measuring the extent of agreement or disagreement among members prior to group discussion. With this before-group information available, the use of emergent solutions as a response to the presence of conflict could be examined. For the groups that received training, the presence of conflict was not correlated with the use of emergent solutions. In contrast, untrained groups appeared to use emergent judgments as a response to conflict. Hall and Williams speculate that the use of the training intervention permitted a flexible and more participative power distribution in the groups.

The presence of conflict in decision making is an essential phase, however, in the work of Fisher (1970, 1974). He identifies four phases in characteristic patterns of interaction, primarily associated with the socioemotional dimension. These are Orientation, Conflict, Emergence, and Reinforcement. Decisions that emerged in the third phase were preceded by an intense period of debate and dispute over decision proposals.

Nemiroff and King (1975) compared groups instructed in the consensus process with groups not instructed in this form of decision making. Uninstructed groups used the familiar majority-rule process. Findings suggested that the two groups differed in important ways. Consistent with prediction, the instructed groups using consensus produced qualitatively better decisions, more fully utilized the average and best resources of their group members, and obtained more ideas and information from members than uninstructed groups. Groups using majority rule reached quick compromise decisions; they also used 50 percent less time than groups using the consensus process.

Effects of self-orientation, a personal-characteristic variable, have been examined in relationship to the consensus process. This variable, measured by the Bass Orientation Inventory, focuses on the extent a person describes him or herself as expecting direct rewards regardless of performance on the task or effects upon others. The researchers speculated that any of the groups, instructed or not, composed of members who measured high on self-orientation would perform less effectively than groups composed of members low on the measure. The data did not support this prediction.

An explanation was suggested by the researchers that the consensus instructions acted as a leveler on persons high on self-orientation, since no significant differences in any groups using the consensus process were noted on any performance criteria, observer reactions, or self-reports. This is in contrast to the uninstructed groups that used the majority-rule form. In these groups, significant differences on performance criteria were noted in groups composed of persons high on the self-orientation scale as compared with those low on the scale.

A straightforward examination of the manner in which groups make decisions was conducted by Hall and Watson (1970). Subjects were persons registered for management seminars. From this pool, sixteen control and sixteen experimental groups were randomly composed. The experimental groups received written instructions and guidelines on the method of group consensus in reaching a decison. Outcome variables were adequacy of decision task, utilization of member resources, and resolution of conflicts.

It was predicted that instructed groups would perform more effectively on a decision-making task than groups that had received no instructions. Instructed groups were found to produce qualitatively better decisions, to be more creative, and to achieve the synergy bonus more frequently and by greater margin than uninstructed groups. (The synergy bonus was credited to a group when the group's decisions were qualitatively superior to any of those of its individual members.)

The researchers, drawing upon knowledge about small groups, suggested explanations for the effects of the intervention that altered the usual procedures for reaching a decision. In particular, they identified the phenomenon known as the *strain toward convergence*. This strain toward convergence is often valued by group members because it is equated with group movement, efficiency, and harmony. In operation, this strain has the effect of increasing pressure upon members for closure, which serves to frustrate members who hold differing opinions. In addition, members who already have converged are less tolerant of opinion differences. Furthermore, members of uninstructed groups were observed to react to conflict and opinion differences as personal rejection.

The guidelines presented to the instructed group probably modified task and social-emotional obstacles inherent in the convergence strain and conflict-resolution attempts to the extent that different results were obtained for the instructed groups. The instructions used by Hall and Watson were developed by Hall and Williams (1970) and are the most complete and available statements of the consensus process used to reach human agreement. In shortened form, the guidelines are:

1. Avoid arguing for your own position
2. Avoid win-lose stalemates in discussions
3. Avoid changing your mind only in order to avoid conflict and to reach agreement and harmony
4. Avoid conflict-reducing techniques, such as majority vote, averaging, bargaining, coin flipping, and the like
5. View differences of opinion as both natural and helpful rather than as a hindrance in decision making
6. View initial agreement as suspect (p. 304)

Laboratory-conducted experiments obviously are not simulations of the totality of reality known in decision making. For initial isolation and study of particular variables, however, the method is advantageous. In the studies reported, consensus as a decision process comes off rather well. Findings suggest that there is flexibility in the use of power, members' resources become available, resulting decisions are qualitatively good, and self-oriented behaviors are checked by the process. In order for consensus to work, members must be committed to the process, they must have experience using it, and they must have time available for the extent of discussion necessary. The studies are less clear, however, about how conflict is expressed and managed. In addition, the tasks presented to the groups may be reasonable analogues, but they are not representative of tasks that require decisions in natural settings. However, the foundation for extending knowledge to natural settings is present and available for use in education and practice.

Examples of Use of the Consensus Process

An interesting example of the use of the consensus process is found in the League of Women Voters of the United States. The process is used to develop responses to issues selected for study. The issue itself is chosen by delegates from more than 1,300 local leagues and 50 state leagues in biennial national conventions. Following choice of the issue, materials are provided to local leagues as background for study. Questions are developed that members will need to answer to reach national consensus. The questions are as free of bias as possible and phrased to elicit members' opinions. The national study committee then assures itself that every measure of consensus reflects agreement in all sections of the country, in big cities and small towns and in large and small leagues.

In the case of the 1978 study of the federal government's urban policy options, local leagues received the questions and study materials eight months before responses were required. This provided ample time to become informed through study of the materials and additional research. In a recent speech, Ruth Hinerfeld, president of the League of Women Voters of the United States provided a description of the process.

> Such member meetings, conducted by a discussion leader who is usually assisted by a resource person and a recorder, are the central core of the League's consensus process. The interaction—questioning, debating and, most important, listening—that goes on at the meetings is what givs a League's consensus its meaning: the sense of the group. Not a collection of individual options solicited through a survey. Not a totaling of views recorded by vote. Rather, a sense of what the group, as a group, believes, a convergence of opinion which emerges in the process of discussion and debate. (Hinerfeld, 1979)

The league's use of the consensus process is based upon the conviction that it is one means to achieve the doctrine of the consent of the governed as outlined in the United States Constitution. This is their commitment and rationale for use of the consensus process. This commitment and rationale is of particular interest in the political climate of the current decade, filled with narrowly conceived special interest/issue groups.

A second example is the use of the process by a Conference of the United Nations. In 1973, the Chairman of the Committee on the Peaceful Uses of the Sea-bed and the Ocean Floor beyond the Limits of National Jurisdiction recommended that the successor body, known as the Third United Nations Conference on the Law of the Sea, adopt procedures that would provide for the use of consensus. Adlai Stevenson, former United Nations Ambassador, had earlier supported the establishment of the conference and the inclusion of this form of decision making in its rules of procedure. The conference, at its nineteenth meeting on June 27, 1974, adopted the recommendation in its rules. The rationale and the rule itself are of special interest.

> Bearing in mind that the problems of ocean space are closely interrelated and need to be considered as a whole and the desirability of adopting a Convention on the Law of the Sea which will secure the widest possible acceptance . . . , the Conference should make every effort to reach agreement on substantive matters by way of consensus and there should be no voting on such matters until all efforts at consensus have been exhausted. (Appendix, *Rules of Procedure,* p. 17)

This Convention provides for the establishment of the International Seabed Authority. The Authority establishes an assembly to develop general policies. The assembly would elect thirty-six of its members to a council, which is to be the executive organ of the Authority. Article 161 of the convention relates to voting procedures of the council. Decisions on questions of *procedure* are to be taken by a majority of members present and voting.

A three-tiered categorization of issues of *substance* was developed, to be decided by a two-thirds majority vote, a three-fourths majority vote, or by consensus (Draft Convention, 1980). This division of issues reflects relative importance and the need for common action and support.

The informal text of the Draft Convention on the Law of the Sea was completed in the Resumed Ninth Session held in Geneva, summer 1980. Completion of the convention was expected and opened for signature in 1981; however, the Reagan Administration postponed action, wishing to reexamine the issuess. Administration concerns appear to be related to perceived threats to the free enterprise system in seabed mining and the placement of the United States in an egalitarian relationship with other countries, especially those of the Third World. Unilateral action would be prohibited as a result of substantive issues reached by consensus.

Additional examples of the use of the consensus process are not so accessible in the literature. Members of womens' groups who use the process report some difficulties. It may be speculated that this can be attributed in part to their lack of common understanding of the essential features of a consensus process. They do encourage participation by all, listen to each other, allow ample time, and, generally, share a common ideology. The process is valued because of its philosophical appeal – deemphasis of use of personal and arbitrary power, respect for each member's views, and freedom from structural constraints. Critics of its use identify overemphasis on process as compared to outcome, incompatibility of task-oriented persons and interpersonally oriented group members, and periods of meetings of unbearable length. Persons associated with a variety of collectives and communal groups report similar dissatisfactions. Recent information is available about the use of the consensus process in Japanese business and industrial corporations, based upon agreement on philosophy, values, and beliefs (Ouchi, 1981).

Of the examples described, it appears that the essential feature for selection of the consensus process as contrasted to majority-rule is the necessity to develop a decision that will have the widest possible common acceptance. The nature of the decision issues, in both the example of the League of Women Voters and the Conferences on the Law of the Sea, necessitate implementation of the decision by everyone or the fact of the decision would have no meaning. Analysis of the issue to be decided may provide guidelines in practice for the choice of one decision-making process over another.

Implications for Education and Practice

The diversity of these examples and findings from research suggest that consensus as a form of decision making is available for teaching and use. To summarize, characteristics of the process and conditions for it to work are listed. This is followed by identification of areas and issues yet to be explored.

From the review and analysis of consensus, at least the following statements can be made:

1. The consensus process is time-consuming
2. The decision reached is likely to be supported and implemented
3. The process works best if members have been taught how to do it
4. Repeated use of the process improves performance
5. The process works best when members approach a decision task with an intent to agree
6. Communication skills of verbal facility and listening are important personal characterstics for members to possess
7. Shared ideology appears necessary for the process to work
8. Particular skills are needed for the person in the role position of leader
9. Members must be open to different views and information and seek all sides of an issue

10. Members must be willing to give up personal power
11. Members must be committed to participation by all
12. Members should view conflict, expressed as differences of opinion, as natural and helpful rather than a hindrance
13. Members should not seek early and quick agreement and should guard against premature strain for convergence
14. Structural arrangements—for example, use of committees for further study and deferral procedures to a later meeting—should be provided when it becomes apparent that the group is not ready to reach consensus

Knowledge development is needed in several areas. The literature is rather clear that the consensus form of decision making is preferred when the decision requires the widest possible extent of common acceptance. An area for further investigation is the identification of characteristics of tasks about which a decision is needed. This should include attention to the relative importance of the task to the group and the anticipated effects of the decision outcome. Results of this process might suggest guidelines for choosing between majority-rule or consensus. Furthermore, consideration should be given to the internal status ranking of the group to explore the extent to which a group is hindered or facilitated in reaching a consensus when high-status persons are absent. It can be speculated that implementation of a decision made without influential persons would be difficult, unless they are also supportive.

The literature does not seem to be consistent about conflict and its resolution (cf. Hall and Watson, 1970, and Fisher, 1974). Part of this can be attributed to the different ways conflict is understood—natural and helpful, or as a threat to the system. There are some who suggest that the consensus process is used in the field of business to promote harmony and group cohesion among employees under the rubric of participatory management. This use is a conflict management tool; the tasks assigned are insignificant to both management and employees, which degrades the consensus process and participatory management in its intended form. In teaching about consensus, care should be taken to explore fully the issue of conflict and the political implications of its use, since it may promote harmony/agreement when diversity/disagreement is needed.

No information was available in the research examples reviewed that addressed the issue of group size. There are reports of attempts of its use with groups of ninety persons. Size as related to time available, member characteristics, and familiarity with the process, among other variables, should be examined systematically.

In general, then, consensus as a decision-making process has been used widely. Its proponents argue that its values outweigh problems in use. Some research supports the conclusion that decisions reached by this process are qualitatively better than those achieved by other processes. This paper has suggested selected areas for further research and examination.

References

Bacon, M. H. *The Quiet Rebels: The Story of Quakers in America.* New York: Basic Books, 1969.

Brinton, H. H. *Divine-Human Society.* Wallingford, Pa.: Pendle Hill Publishers, 1938.

Comfort, W. W. *Just among Friends: The Quaker Way of Life,* 5th ed. Philadelphia: American Friends Service Committee, 1968.

Dodd, S. C., and S. C. Christopher. "How to Produce a Consensus: A Progress Report from Project Consensus." *Journal of Human Relations,* 1969, *17* (4), 618–29.

Draft Convention on the Law of the Sea (Informal Text), Third United Nations Conference on the Law of the Sea, Resumed Ninth Session, Geneva, July 28, 1980–August 29, 1980. Reproduced by Office of Law of the Sea Negotiations, Department of State, Washington, D.C., September 2, 1980.

Drake, M. C. "Quaker Consensus: Helping Learners Understand and Participate in the Quaker Way of Reaching Group Decision." Ph. D. diss., The Ohio State University, 1973.

English, H. B., and A. C. English. *A Comprehensive Dictionary of Psychological and Psychoanalytical Terms.* New York: Longmans, Green, 1958.

Fisher, B. A. "Decision Emergence: Phases in Group Decision-Making." *Speech Monographs, 37,* 1970, 53–66.

——— *Small Group Decision-Making: Communication and the Group Process.* New York: McGraw-Hill, 1974.

Hall, J., and W. H. Watson. "The Effects of a Normative Intervention on Group Decision-making Performance." *Human Relations, 23,* 1970, 299–317.

Hall, J., and M. S. Williams. "Group Dynamics Training and Improved Decision-making." *Journal of Applied Behavioral Science, 6,* (1), 1970, 39–68.

Hare, A. P. "Group Decision by Consensus: Reaching Unity in the Society of Friends." *Sociological Inquiry, 43,* (1), 1973, 75–84.

——— "Consensus Versus Majority Vote." *Small Group Behavior, 11,*(2), 1980, 131–43.

Hinnerfeld, R. J. Consensus in American Politics: A Little Help is Needed. Address, National Conference on Government, Detroit, November 12, 1979, (Published by the League of Women Voters of the U.S.).

Jones, R. M. *The Faith and Practice of the Quakers.* Richmond, Ind.: Friends United Press, n.d.

Nemiroff, P. M., and D. C. King. "Group Decision-making Performance as Influenced by Consensus and Self-Orientation." *Human Relations, 28,* (1), 1–21.

Ouchi, W. *Theory Z.* Reading, Mass.: Addison-Wesley, 1981.

Rules of Procedure, Third United Nations Conference on the Law of the Sea, adopted June 27, 1974, United Nations, New York.

Selleck, G. A. *Principles of the Quaker Business Meeting.* Richmond, Ind.: Friends United Press, n.d.

Strodtbeck, F. L.; James, R. M.; and Hawkins, C. "Social Status in Jury Deliberations." *American Sociological Review,* 22, 1957, 468–73.

"The Meeting as a Fellowship." In *Christian Faith and Practice in the Experience of the Society of Friends.* Excerpts from the London Yearly Meeting of the Religious Society of Friends. Richmond, Ind.: Friends United Press, 1973.

U.S. Delegation Briefing Materials, Law of the Sea Conference Organizational Session, December 3–14, 1973, United Nations Headquarters, New York.

Note

1. A further elaboration of differing meanings of the term *consensus* is provided in the doctoral dissertation by Drake as cited in References. He analyzed both macro- and micro-level uses of the term (pp. 18–25). Since the dissertation was accepted in 1973, confusion in usage evidently precedes the 1980s. In the political arena, an assumption of a national consensus was important to the development of the Great Society programs of the 1960s.

9

Assessment and Change of Group Conditions in Social Work Practice

Charles Garvin

The value of group experience centers on the ways that group conditions can help members attain their goals. Much of the group work literature on assessing and modifying group conditions, however, is vague and nonoperational and more ideological than practical. The purpose of this paper is to offer a useful presentation of this topic based on the current status of practice theory and knowledge from the social sciences about group processes. To accomplish this, group dimensions will be defined in a way that is conducive to assessing and changing them. Procedures will be presented for group workers and members to use to measure such group dimensions, and approaches will be suggested to maintain desirable group conditions or to change them when they are dysfunctional for member and group purposes.

One assumption made here is that knowledge of how to analyze and change group conditions often can and should be shared with group members. We do not mean that group members should be given lectures on group work and small-group theory, but rather that information pertaining to *specific* problems in the life of the group can be presented to members and used by them on their own behalf.

Group Conditions Defined

Group conditions is defined as the group circumstances that represent the social reality of the group to the worker and members. This social reality affects the behavior of the individuals in the group, their interactions with each other, as well as and the development of the group. Group conditions can be analyzed in terms of (1) group structures, (2) group processes, and (3) shared cognitions of the group's participants.

Group structure is the pattern of relationships among the members. This pattern changes from moment to moment as members interact. Structure can be studied, however, as it exists at a specified time. In addition, many patterns essential to the group's equilibrium are maintained and restored by mechanisms brought into play in the group.

There is only "one" group structure, but it is difficult to consider it without analyzing it in terms of its dimensions. These are the communications, affectional (or sociometric), power, leadership, and role dimensions.

The communications dimension consists of who speaks to whom about what and under what circumstances. The affectional dimension consists of who likes and dislikes whom in the group and consequently associates or does not associate with whom (this can be observed in the group's pattern of subgroups). The power dimension consists of who influences whom about what in the group and in what manner. The leadership dimension consists of who contributes most to the determination and accomplishment of group tasks (task leader) and who contributes the most to reducing tensions, enhancing group cohesiveness, and securing compliance with rules (social-emotional leader). The role dimension consists of who occupies formally recognized positions (such as chairperson or secretary) and who fills positions created through group interactions (such as mediator, clown, rebel, or scapegoat).

Group process consists of changes that take place in the group. Some aspects of process can be observed from moment to moment, while others are observed over longer periods of time. The latter are usually conceptualized in terms of *group development*. As is the case with structure, change in groups is a unitary phenomenon that is difficult to conceptualize without referring to one dimension or another.

In our efforts to identify the dimensions of process, we have found it useful to refer to these as "task" dimensions and "social-emotional" dimensions, thus enabling us to draw upon the array of social psychological information related to these terms. Task dimensions include that sequence of events in a group related to determining group goals (goal-determination process) and that related to choosing and carrying out the means of attaining these goals (goal-pursuit process).

Under maintenance dimensions, we have drawn upon Mills's ideas and referred to three levels: the behavioral, the emotional, and the normative (Mills, 1967). The behavioral refers to interactions directed at controlling member behavior and resolving intermember conflict. The emotional refers to changes in the feelings of attraction among members. The normative refers to the development of norms that govern the behavior of members and of the sanctions to secure compliance to these norms.

We have also identified two aspects of process that can relate either to task or social-emotional dimensions. One is "role differentiation," and this is seen in the creation of new positions in the group and the preparation and selection of members to occupy them. When the positions relate to accomplishing the tasks of the group (such as chairperson), the process fulfills task dimensions. When the positions relate to social-emotional functioning (such as the emergence of mediators among the group's members), the process fulfills social-emotional dimensions.

Another aspect of process that can relate either to task or social-emotional dimensions we call "role integration." Included here are communications among members related to defining, coordinating, and changing their roles. How this process is classified depends on the types of roles involved in the negotiation.

The third type of group condition we refer to as *shared cognitions*. This is defined as understandings of events that are held by all or most of the group members and, therefore, developed through group processes. It is a well-established fact that groups are powerful in defining reality for members. In social work groups, these cognitions may be dysfunctional to the purposes of the group, such as beliefs in the superiority of races or of one sex over the other, in the impossibility of succeeding in life through one's own efforts, or in unreal ideas about the cause of one's problems. Some cognitions are helpful to members in attaining their purposes, such as useful ideas about assessing member problems, causes of problems, and problem-solving itself.

Measurement of Group Conditions

Structural Measurement .

Since a basic tool in group work is communication among the members and between members and workers, the communications dimension of structure is often the target for change. When the concern is about the degree to which the members are talking to the worker rather than to each other, Rose (1977) suggests this be measured by a tally of member and worker communications. On the other hand, the degree to which selected members include or eliminate others from group discussion can be measured by creating a matrix that includes the names of each person as both column and row headings. Who speaks to whom can be indicated by slash marks (///). This provides easy access to information about the pattern of communications, and a sum of each column and row quickly shows who does the most talking and who is most often spoken to. This has implications for the analysis of the power structure of the group as well as the communications structure.

Often the worker and members wish to examine the content of communications as well as the frequency. Rose (1977) describes a number of measures he and his colleagues have used for this purpose. One is a measure of whether the members experience remarks made to them as either reinforcing or punishing. They do this by placing poker chips of different colors into a can, then count the chips to see how frequently each type of remark was made. Rose also developed a system for measuring other categories of content: suggestion-opinion, questions, responses to questions, self-suggestions, negative affect, positive affect, and information giving. An observer coded each remark in terms of who said it, who it was directed to, and the category.

To measure changes in the affectional dimension, workers often rely on observations of subgroups, such as who enters with, sits with, or leaves with whom, or in groups where members can choose others as teammates for tasks, who chooses whom. These observations can be charted using conventional sociometric diagrams. We have not used questionnaires given to members to measure their attitudes toward other members because of the anxiety this creates. Yalom (1975), on the other hand, reports asking members to rate others in the group on popularity, apparently without serious harm to members, and this may be an experience for which membership in a long-term therapy group prepares people.

Workers should monitor the nature of the power dimension when members are influenced by others in the group in dysfunctional ways or when some members have too little influence on the group. Such responses can be coded as (1) support or agreement; (2) disagreement; or (3) not relevant. Not all responses are coded, but only those that are made in reaction to directions, suggestions, or new ideas, that is, related to the categories just described. Some members do not contribute in this way and are likely to be low in this manifestation of power.

Leadership is an important aspect of roles present in the group. We conceive of it, following Bales (1950), as manifested in the frequency with which members fulfill task and social-emotional functions. Bales's instrument for identifying behaviors can be used by group workers. To simplify tabulation, however, we often combine the "task" behaviors into one index (that is, giving suggestions, opinions, and information) and the positive social-emotional behaviors into another index (that is, tension, release, and displays of solidarity). This type of tabulation not only demonstrates how such acts are distributed but whether they occur at all to the degree that members and workers define as desirable.

The role dimension of the group requires a more intrusive measure than the procedures described thus far. (We refer here to informal rather than formal roles.) Members can be given questionnaires (or may be interviewed) as to who, if anyone, fulfills specified informal roles chosen by the worker and the members as relevant to the group. In one group, such a list included referee, humorist, nurturer, spokesperson, and "devil's advocate." Members "vote" on whom they perceive fulfills each of these roles. When high consensus exists, it is assumed that the person does in fact fulfill the role.

Process Measurement

Now that we have described a number of ways of measuring group structures, we will do the same with regard to selected group processes. One of the most important goal-pursuit processes is group problem-solving. An instrument we developed to measure this dimension is the Group Problem-Solving Rating below (Garvin, 1981). This instrument is either rated at the end of a problem-solving discussion by an observer, the worker, all group members, or by all involved. The rating is then discussed by the worker and members in order to determine its implications for enhancing group process.

Group Problem-Solving Rating

By the end of the problem-solving discussion, the problem was:

    a. Completely resolved: All aspects of the situation were decided upon to the complete satisfaction of the members so that no further work was necessary.

    b. There has been movement toward resolution, but the group could have moved further.

    c. No change took place toward resolving the problem, yet the problem was not worsened in the process.

    d. There has been movement away from resolution during this episode in that greater verbal differences were produced and/or more "friction" occurred.

    e. The movement was completely away from the problem in that the issue was abandoned either due to frustration with it or the attraction of the group to another issue.

Another process, a social-emotional one, is the process-illumination activity described by Yalom (1975) and other group-therapy experts. We know of no specific studies of this procedure but have used the following as a first step in measurement. We have asked members in "process-oriented" groups to maintain personal journals that include their observations and reactions to "process" discussions. The workers have also maintained recordings on these events. Periodically, the workers, with the permission of the members, examine the journals to assess whether the members learned what the workers assumed they did. This is one step toward a more systematic examination of this process.

We measure the process of changes in attraction of members to each other by providing members with a short questionnaire at the end of group sessions in which we ask them how strongly they desire to return (on a seven-point scale from "not at all" to "very much"). Yalom (1975) has suggested two additional items that we have included: (1) If you could replace members of your group with other "ideal group members," how many would you exchange (exclusive of group therapists)? (2) To what degree do you feel you are included by the group in the group's activities? We included an additional item: Which members did you interact with most during this meeting?

In addition, to illuminate a number of processes, we tape-record a segment of the group's meeting in which a group problem occurs. Members are given a short questionnaire (or are engaged in group discussion) regarding the factors that they believe contribute to what occurred during the tape-recorded segment. The crucial aspect of this approach is the selection of a critical incident and the use of questions that focus members' attention on the segment.

Measurement of Shared Cognitions

Shared cognitions are difficult to observe because in many groups they are implicit in the members' comments and behaviors. Even when views are expressed, it is difficult to tell whether they reflect the views of all members or whether the silence or acquiescence of some truly reflects their opinions. Workers therefore should occasionally ask members to write down their perceptions of causes of events or their beliefs or points of view regarding them. Group discussion can be compared to these privately expressed views. With the permission of the individuals, these views can be tabulated and shared, with anonymity preserved if the members wish it.

Similarities and differences in what members say privately and in the presence of others will tell a great deal about group conditions, such as willingness of members to share opinions honestly and whether some members or even workers control the publicly expressed views of others. Some of the thoughts that are likely to fall into this category are judgments about the behavior of other group members, prejudices about social groups, and ideas about psychological phenomena.

Changes in Group Conditions

The worker can facilitate changes in group conditions by his or her impact on (1) individuals in the group, (2) several members who together constitute a subgroup, (3) the entire group, or (4) systems external to the group. The worker can use these four types of interventions to alter group structures, processes, and shared cognitions. However, there is no clearcut way to prescribe which route the worker should take among these choices, and research on the value of alternative strategies is badly needed.

Changing Structures

Individual members themselves can bring about changes in group structures, and the worker can help them to initiate this process. The communications component, for example, can be altered when the worker urges highly active participants to reduce their verbalizations or coaches low-level participants in ways of contributing their ideas to group discussions. The content of discussions can be shifted through suggestions made by the worker to individuals regarding their inputs. The sociometric dimension can also be modified when the worker helps a member to alter his or her relationship patterns in the group. If the member who changes a relationship pattern is influential, other members are likely to imitate these changes in their behaviors.

Role components of structure can also be changed when the worker helps individuals to modify their role performances. This can occur with both formal and informal roles. A leadership training approach can be taken with regard to formal roles when the group has a formal structure. Thus, the chairpersons, secretaries, and other officials of a group can be coached as to how to perform their tasks. Members who function as mediators or reduce gropu tensions in other ways can be reinforced for their constructive actions, while group "rebels" and scapegoats can be helped to find other ways of coping when their use of these roles is dysfunctional to themselves and the group.

The worker can also interact with subgroups in order to bring about changes in group structure. The sociometric structure of the entire group can be changed in this manner. The worker, for example, can help a member to interact with a subgroup other than his or hers by pointing out the advantages of interaction or through helping a subgroup to include such a member in its activities. Members can also try out in a subgroup ways of acting to enhance their leadership performance or influence on the group. The worker can alter subgroup patterns by making subgroup assignments, initiating the formation of task forces within the group or subdividing the group when an exercise is introduced.

The worker, perhaps most frequently, will seek to alter group structures through interventions with the group as a whole. One procedure is a group problem-solving process in which the problem is defined as some aspect of group structure. The worker facilitates this process as follows:

1. Help the group to identify a problem in its functioning.
2. Help the group to assess which group condition(s) serve to maintain the group problem.

3. Help the group to measure the group condition using one of the measurement approaches described earlier.
4. Help the group to identify and evaluate ways of modifying the group condition.
5. Help the group to measure the effects of the group modification approach it has chosen and implemented.
6. If the outcome is less than satisfactory, help the group to return to Number 4 and proceed again.

An example of a behavioral procedure for modifying group structure is from a group of school-age boys. The worker gave each boy a peanut each time he spoke, and this had a major effect on the communication structure of the group. (The worker also wished to have an effect on the quality of the problem-solving process, and at a later time boys were not reinforced for all comments but only those comments that were relevant to the subject under discussion.) At another session, the boys agreed that they did not express their feelings well. The "rewards" were then allocated to affective statements.

Rose (1977) reports changing a communications pattern in which some members talked too much and others too little. Low participants were reinforced by persons on their right whenever they spoke. High participants were restrained also by the persons on their right through the placement of a restraining hand on their shoulders.

Another major tool group workers use to help members alter their group's structure is program. Vinter (1974) has identified the activity dimensions that occur in any program activity, and several of these have relevance for altering group structures. The worker can help the group to choose an activity in view of these properties. One of these dimensions is *interactiveness*, which refers to the degree and type of interactions among members promoted by the activity. Thus, some activities require members to split into two teams; other activities require them to form pairs; and still others promote an ever-changing flow of associations.

Another such dimension is the *institutionalized controls governing participant activity*. As Vinter states, "Controls may be exercised by another person, sometimes a fellow participant, or impersonally (as with rules and shared norms relevant to the activity)." Different activities will have the potential of altering, at least for the moment, leadership and other roles. These are undoubtedly only a few of the program dimensions that affect group structure. We are seeking to identify others so that workers may help members select programs with greater understanding of this type of effect.

The worker can also affect the group's structure by promoting changes in the *environment* that will subsequently have an impact on the group. The worker can prompt the service agency to refer new members to the group with the anticipation that these members will have an impact on some aspect of the group's structure. In one group, for example, the only Chicana member had become a group isolate. The referral of another Chicana had an immediate positive effect on this situation. The worker can also establish conditions whereby the group interacts with systems external to the group, such as other groups as well as members' families. A group of abusive husbands held a joint meeting with their wives, and this led to some changes in subgroup patterns through the relationships that were created among the wives.

Changing Processes

Task processes can be altered through the worker interacting with individual members who have been overactive or underactive. If the overactive member has dominated the selection of group goals or means of achieving them, the worker can help that member to demand less of the group, thus allowing others to alter the course of these decisions. A simultaneous promotion of the assertiveness of members with other points of view will accelerate this change.

Social-emotional processes can be altered in an analogous manner as the worker reinforces members who are fulfilling positive social-emotional roles. Members who fulfill negative social-emotional roles by promoting dysfunctional tensions in the group will also sometimes be singled out by the worker for one-to-one work to help them cope in a different manner with stresses they may experience. This does not negate the possibility that the entire group may be involved in this process, but it recognizes that this is not possible or desirable in all groups.

Processes in the group can also be altered through the worker's intervention with subgroups. This is particularly true when the social-emotional processes in the group involve conflicts among subgroups. Workers can mediate between such subgroups, as well as help subgroups apply a problem-solving approach to identify and resolve the sources of their difficulties. Another process can occur between subgroups when a subgroup forms that opposes group purposes or activities or rebels against the worker. This of course may represent a legitimate grievance or aspiration on the part of the subgroup and should lead to negotiations among the various subgroups and the worker. The members of the subgroup, however, may seek a role and place in the group that they cannot find through acceptable behavior. Members of such a subgroup want the opportunity to influence the group and may feel that the worker hinders this.

When the worker and the members view the concerns of members of the subgroup as legitimate, they can facilitate the entry of the members of the subgroup into roles that are useful to the members, as well as to the whole group. This process inevitably modifies such components of the group's structure as communications, subgroups, and roles. When these structural revisions take place in the group, they also affect the process of goal determination and goal pursuit. Associated with this is a reduction in the tension associated with the existence of an antagonistic subgroup; thus, social-emotional processes are also modified.

Any change in subgroup patterns, and particularly changes that occur when subgroups are hostile to one another, has an effect on all other structures and processes. Some of these changes may be conducive to the group's attaining its goals, while others may not. When the worker and the group are concerned about and seek to change subgroup patterns, it is wise to monitor selected group conditions so that further problems may be identified and resolved.

As with efforts to modify group structures, the worker will frequently seek to modify group processes through interventions with the group as a whole. One such process is referred to as *process commentary*. This consists of the worker drawing the attention of the group to a sequence of events and asking the members to examine the sequence and their separate actions that created it. Through this reflective process, members learn how to take more responsibility for the group, as well as for their own effects on the group.

Another technique that we have borrowed from family therapy (Haley, 1976) is for the worker to *interrupt* a process directly and to prescribe an alternative. This is a useful approach when the group engages in a repetitive process that is dysfunctional to the group. The alternative offered may include the worker bringing another member into the sequence of interactions, asking a member to experiment with a different response, or him or her to respond in a radically different way to the set of interactions.

The worker may also use a behavioral approach, such as introducing reinforcements that have the effect of changing a group process. One example of this occurred in a problem-solving process in which several members withheld useful information. The worker asked the group to use a token procedure in which tokens were presented by the worker to members each time they made an appropriate contribution to the problem-solving discussion.

Finally, processes can be altered by programmatic interventions. The content supplied by the program often has this effect. By content we mean such things as the substantive issues introduced through a discussion or activity. New goals can be suggested in this manner, as well as new ways of attaining goals. Social-emotional issues confronting the group can also be approached through new ideas introduced in stories, role-enactments, or visual materials, such as diagrams.

The worker can also seek to modify processes through *environmental interventions*. The agency can be asked to interact with the group around agency and group purposes in order to affect goal determination and pursuit. Or the agency or community can be asked to supply resources to the group that will have an impact on the group's program. These resources may be either material or informational ones. An example of the former was an agency that secured the use of a gymnasium for a group of teenagers who needed to take a more physical approach to resolve issues of competition and aggression within the group. The latter is illustrated when the same agency provided information on forms of contraception to the group to enhance its discussion of sexual behavior.

Changing Shared Cognitions

Similar procedures to those described above have been employed to affect shared cognitions in the group. Workers can individually enable less assertive members to express their understanding of events. This may either strengthen a set of already-existing views in the group or, through introducing dissonance, lead to a change in shared cognitions. In a manner analogous to how we have worked with powerful members to alter structures and processes, we have worked with such individuals to enable them to respect the views of others in the group that differ from theirs. The resulting process has often led to a change in the views of all of the members. At times, however, the views of the most influential members can be useful to the group, and the worker will help these members to present their ideas effectively. This is appropriate when the worker "seeds" a new group with members who have developed norms and understandings conducive to the purposes of the group, and these members also have high status because of that previous experience.

The worker will seek to affect shared cognitions through intervening with subgroups when one subgroup has or develops ideas that are useful to the entire group. The worker may use the fact that one subgroup is more influential than others and will seek to develop a beneficial point of view in the influential subgroup. Alternatively, a subgroup such as that sometimes found in groups of antisocial members may be prone to develop a prosocial point of view, and the worker can make use of that fact by supporting the subgroup and reinforcing its communications to others.

The worker can intervene with the group as a whole to modify shared cognitions. A major way of doing this is through the use of program. Almost all activities introduce a set of values related to the activity. These include standards of fairness, concern for others, honesty, competitiveness, or cooperation. The worker can help the members to transfer points of view from one activity to another. For example, in some races that were held in a children's group, the younger children were allowed to begin the race several feet ahead of the older ones. This led to a discussion of the value of giving more support to some members than others until the latter "catch up." The same principle was then introduced in discussion of the meaning of affirmative action.

A set of program activities that has a strong impact on shared cognitions is value-clarification exercises. Workers can effectively use a wide range of such activities to help members to identify value positions, examine them, and reevaluate their own positions and at times change them. In addition, workers should be aware of the strong impact that statements of their own value positions may have upon the group's norms.

The way that a worker uses systems outside the group to modify shared cognitions is through promoting interactions with such systems. In one case the worker helped members develop their ethnic identity by inviting several leaders in the ethnic community to talk to the group. This cognitive input was an important factor in attaining group goals. In another situation of work with abusive husbands, the wives presented information in a joint meeting that added to the husband's understanding of family processes that led to violence.

These interactions are undertaken with the full knowledge and consent of group members and were negotiated between the members and the worker. This is still only a beginning analysis of the role of social group workers in the modification of group conditions. In conclusion, we suggest some ways to further this effort.

Conclusion

Much of the literature on group work is devoted to analyzing how worker activities affect members as individuals. As indicated here, the concept of group work has been to assist in the creation of a group that, in itself, helps members to achieve their goals. More attention must be devoted to identifying and promoting group conditions that have this desired effect. A first step in this direction is to examine group conditions in each group in more than the casual and impressionistic ways we have used in the past. This can often be accomplished through some of the measurement approaches outlined here. If workers subsequently transmit their experiences with promoting desired group conditions to others and understand how they affect member outcomes, we shall make forward strides in this aspect of practice theory.

Workers also should seek to have more research available to them on the relationships between group purposes, group conditions, and member outcomes. This research should be done in practice rather than laboratory settings so that it reflects the complexities of practice. Some studies can also be of specific groups and take the form of cases in which group factors are clearly identified. Experimental studies can also be designed that will be helpful in this respect. An example of one such study is that of

Feldman (1983) and his colleagues on group work with antisocial children. In this study, relationships were examined between such group-level variables as composition, behavioral patterns of all the members, program, and the terminal behavior of the members. Worker effects upon these variables were also studied in terms of worker experience and the practice model they employed.

We are entering an era of group work practice that will be based on a clearer specification of our concepts and our skills. This clarity, combined with worker attention to monitoring the group work process and to creating and using practice research, should introduce another golden age for those of use committed to social work practice with groups.

References

Bales, R. F. *Interaction Process Analysis: A Method for the Study of Small Groups*. Reading: Addson-Wesley, 1950.

Feldman, R. A.; Caplinger, T. E; and Wodarski, J. S. *The St. Louis Conundrum: The Effective Treatment of Antisocial Youths*. Englewood Cliffs, N.J.: Prentice-Hall, 1983.

Garvin, C. D. *Contemporary Group Work*. Englewood Cliffs, N.J.: Prentice-Hall, 1981.

Haley, H. *Problem Solving Therapy*. San Francisco: Jossey-Bass, 1976.

Mills, T. M. *The Sociology of Small Groups*. Englewood Cliffs, N.J.: Prentice-Hall, 1967.

Rose, S. *Group Therapy: A Behavioral Approach*. Englewood Cliffs, N.J.: Prentice-Hall, 1977.

Vinter, R. D. "Program Activities: An Analysis of Their Effects on Participant Behavior." In P. Glasser, R. Sarri, and R. Vinter (eds.), *Individual Change Through Small Groups*. New York: The Free Press, 1974.

Yalom, I. D. *The Theory and Practice of Group Psychotherapy*. 2d ed. New York: Basic Books, 1975.

10

The Uses and Abuses of Role-Playing

Roland Etcheverry, Max Siporin, and
Ronald W. Toseland

Role-playing is one of the most popular and frequently used technical procedures in social work practice. It is widely used in helping individuals, families, and small organized groups, as well as in helping practice with organizations, communities, and service systems. It is not only a generic set of procedures but also is part of the traditional repertoire of social work interventions. One of the first books on this subject, a forty-eight-page booklet entitled "How to Use Role Playing" (Chicago: Adult Education Association), was written by a social worker (Klein, 1956). Role-playing merits much more attention than has been given to it in the literature. It also merits much more theoretical and operational development than has been accorded to it in practice theory.

In this discussion, a conceptual framework is suggested for the use of role-playing in groups. Several purposes and benefits for its use will be identified. Also, the abuses of role-playing will be discussed, those relating to the implementation of role-playing procedures generally, and those involving the misapplication of specific techniques. To help avoid such misapplication, appropriate uses of several techniques are indicated and discussed. Our emphasis is on their behavior-change functions and objectives.

The contribution intended here relates to the presentation of a theoretical rationale for the use of role-playing in social work practice. Needed clarification also is suggested concerning structured and unstructured, primary and supplementary, types of procedures and their specific purposes. These are offered so that the techniques can be used in the formulation and implementation of more valid differential interventive programs, in which role-playing adds to helping effectiveness.

Definitions

Role-playing can be defined as the enactment of a social role, played as if "for real," in terms of "realistic behavior" in an imagined social situation (Shaw et al., 1980, p. 11). It involves an individual's spontaneous personal participation, interpersonal transactions, and experiential learning, as a member of a supportive, accepting group of people, in the playing out of a script or scene. Such enactment calls for empathic "role-taking," so as to determine both the role of another and of oneself, as well as for "role-playing" in a performance that is reciprocal to the role performances of others for a common purpose (Turner, 1956).

Role-playing, in the form of children's games (Cops and Robbers) and adult games (Charades), dramatic performances, simulations, and rehearsals of anticipated future events, has long been part of educational, socialization, problem-solving, and therapeutic processes in society. Role-playing as a purposeful helping technique for therapeutic purposes is credited to Moreno's (1946; 1952) development of psychodrama and sociodrama in the early 1930s. These techniques were adapted and further developed as role-playing procedures within group work, group therapy, and organizational development (Petzold, 1975), as well as for individual and group psychotherapy (Corsini, 1966).

Role-playing now has been formulated as a well-defined, widely accepted procedure for many helping processes. It involves a primary actor (client, protagonist), who is generally the focus and intended beneficiary of the procedure, and who may enact his or her own life role or the roles of others. Reciprocal roles are taken by the helper (leader, director, facilitator, therapist), who directs the play, by other group members (auxiliaries, auxiliary egos, alters, significant others), and also by nonparticipant observers or audience members. The role-playing process involves phases and tasks of warm-up, preparation, enactment, and closing. The content of the role-play is selected and developed so that it deals with difficulties, tasks, or dilemmas that concern and personally involve one or more members. They may deal with the loss of a spouse, rehearsing for a job interview, deciding to increase needed production, gaining skill in public speaking, or reliving a traumatic injury.

General Uses

Role-playing has two basic purposes: (1) problem-solving, in resolving a conflict, meeting a need, or completing a task, and (2) learning, in the sense of acquiring new behavior patterns through personal experience. The procedure may be used primarily for the benefit of an individual or for the benefit of the collective group. Although these problem-solving and learning purposes often overlap, there are procedural and process differences between role-playing that is primarily oriented toward problem-solving and that which is oriented to the learning and development of one or more participants. Behavior change or learning may or may not accompany problem-solving processes, particularly when related largely to environmental stresses or impediments.

Role-playing has five major uses:

1. Assessment. Role-playing often is used to demonstrate, illustrate, and to obtain objective, descriptive data. Such data may be about the characteristics, definitions, and meanings of people, situations, and problems. This information is given in concrete, vivid, personal, and emotionally meaningful terms, as in the dramatic reenactment of a child's death for which a mother blames herself. Through spontaneous performance, a person's self-disclosure is facilitated, and obstacles and resistances to change are clearly revealed. One can identify personality/ situational and antecedent/consequent variables and the nature and strength of their relationship. Behavioral deficits or excesses that make for ineffective or inadequate performance can be clearly delineated. Used for such data collection, role-playing is geared more to meeting the helper's assessment tasks, although when this information is shared with the protagonist or client, it leads to the latter's insight and understanding.

2. Stimulation. The physical activity of role-playing, the participation in action and group interaction focused on personal concerns, problems, and behavior—these stimuli provide sensory impact and arousal. Such arousal generates attention and perceptual awareness, as well as ego involvement and psychophysical excitement. It assures that important information is heard and absorbed. Group discussion is facilitated and focused. The stimulation and arousal also may result in unfreezing perceptual, cognitive, and affective structures, as well as motivational, behavioral habit patterns. A person is thus opened to behavior change.

3. Understanding. The protagonist is encouraged to gain self-awareness and insight through acting out a role in an unaccustomed way. This may result from empathic sensitivity and responses to the characteristics, feelings, and needs of reciprocal role alters. It also may result from self-observation and experiencing of one's self, identity, wants, feelings, and meanings on verbal and nonverbal levels. The taking on of different perspectives facilitates tasks of problem definition and analysis that require insightful discriminations and integrations for comprehensive knowing. The subjective meanings and distorted perceptions of social-life situations may be clarified through new and multiple views.

4. Decision Making. This involves formulating and agreeing on conclusions about facts or plans of action that are aimed to attain an objective and complete a difficult task, solve a problem, or resolve a conflict. Alternative, tentative, and experimental solutions may be explored and tested in a safe, cooperative situation through role-playing of possible or probable consequences of suggested solutions. Monitoring and evaluation are provided to assure the efficiency and effectiveness of a course of action, and to assure the generalization and persistence of the problem-solving behavior or state of affairs.

5. Behavior Change. Role-playing encourages the extinction of undesirable behavior and the acquisition, practice, and habituation of new behavior. Personal conflicts and difficulties may be worked through and the person freed for more satisfying life adaptations. Training for skills such as empathy, communication, and leadership are effectively accomplished through role-plays. New behavior may be suggested, alternatives may be explored, and skills may be practiced in a safe, trustful, accepting, expectant, and supportive group situation.

Rationale

Role-playing is a powerful technique for the realization of these purposes. Its sources are richly varied and influential. It is very productive for problem-solving and very effective in facilitating behavior change. Its operational dynamics have a creative vitality.

The powers of role-playing derive from several potent and interactive factors: sensory arousal, ego involvement, and emotional contagion; group pressures and supports for conformity, conversion, and change; and self-disclosure without devaluing consequences. Also, there is the provision of strong reinforcements for new adaptive behavior, personal identifications, and internalized cognitive representations of people and of life realities. As a role occupant, the protagonist or client is a group member and situational participant, a participant observer and actor. He or she is thus subject to the influences of strong and often new forces, of role bonds and interactive processes, and of the reference norms, expectations, perspectives, and assumptions associated with a status and role in a group.

Problem-solving of many kinds is more fruitful because the group process enables the contribution of many, often specially qualified people and resources (Shaw et al., 1978, pp. 76–86; Maier, Solem, and Maier, 1975). Frustrated, defeated, or trapped individuals are directly aided with additional resources, helped to become aware of action options, alternative goals, and path sequences. Group discussion and interthinking in simulated situations help generate creative and innovative plans and solutions, individual commitments as well as group cohesion, and consensual agreements that resolve differences and conflicts (Lonergan, 1957; Bohart, 1977). Complex tasks and group collaborative action can be simulated and rehearsed, defects ironed out, difficulties anticipated and prepared for, and group critiques provided before, during, and after a decided course of action (Blake and Mouton, 1978). All of the above makes for better decisions, with the greater likelihood that they will be successfully implemented and that they will result in effective solutions.

Role-playing procedures provide a particularly rich armamentarium for facilitating learning and changing behavior. Crucial mechanisms and dynamics for change are activated and consummated. Client awareness can promote behavior change in clarifying the irrational or dysfunctional aspects of one's cognitive schemata and basic beliefs that exercise control over one's behavior (Ellis, 1962; 1973). The dysfunctionality of one's actual behavior patterns also can be clarified. Stimulation and affective-cognitive-physiological arousal also may make for intrapsychic and interpersonal confrontation, provoke perceptual distortion or cognitive dissonance, induce tension, anxiety, and disequilibrium (Peters and Phelen, 1973), and may relax constrictions and inhibitions in regard to repressed feelings and desires. Such unfreezing is essential for modification of habitual behaviors. The stimulations, shifts, and expansions of attention and awareness are well accomplished through role-playing. In addition, insight and understanding provide new reality perceptions, the making of connections between person and situation variables, and between antecedent and consequent stimuli, or contingent rewards.

Through role-playing people can be helped to learn many abilities and skills. New patterns of problem-solving behavior, as well as of perceptions, cognitions, values, motives, attitudes, assumptive beliefs, and expectations, can be taught and learned in this way. A wide range of techniques are applicable in conjunction with role-playing procedures, particularly for training new behaviors. Among these are shaping (Fischer and Gochros, 1975, pp. 252–56), modeling and rehearsal (Sundel and Sundel, 1980), desensitization (Goldfried, 1971), and cognitive restructuring (Mahoney, 1974; Raimy, 1975). Modeling and vicarious learning, along with rehearsal and practice, are particularly effective in gaining interpersonal-relationship skills and communication skills (Gambrill, 1977, pp. 530–601; Lange and Jakubowski, 1976, pp. 69–113; Rose, 1977, pp. 86–102; Rosenthal and Bandura, 1978; Wodarski and Bagarozzi, 1979, pp. 153–61). Clients may be taught appropriate and adaptive self-talk, self-instruction, and self-control (Gambrill, 1977, pp. 438–91; Ellis, 1962; 1973; Goldfried and Merbaum, 1973; Mahoney and Arknoff, 1978; Meichenbaum, 1977; Novaco, 1978; Stuart, 1977).

Role-playing is effective in teaching problem-solving skills (Goldfried and Goldfried, 1980; Spivack, Platt, and Shure, 1976; Reid, 1978). It also has been found to be helpful in work with lower-income, welfare clients (Schopler and Galinsky, 1979), as well as in the teaching and learning of social work helping skills (Zastrow and Navarre, 1977; Shapiro et al., 1980).

The operational dynamics involved in such behavior-change processes are still incompletely understood, though some aspects have been identified. As Moreno (1952) and Blatner (1973) have suggested, the role-playing protagonist is immersed in a "surplus reality," a heightened, intensified reality, which induces experiences of emotional distance, needed objectivity and subjectivity, reduced inhibitions, enhanced freedom for choice and action, and spontaneous reflective entrance into complex subjective worlds of feelings and fantasies, of creative transformations, innovation, and synthesis. Also, there is an aspect of "act completion" (Blatner, 1973, p. 72), which strengthens the observing, controlling ego, validates emotional experience, and integrates repressed aspects of personality. Role-playing thus has many qualities of games and play and so has similar functions and dynamics.

The Abuses of Role-Playing

Such power effects of role-playing can have constructive or destructive effects. It is helpful to recognize that negative and unhelpful effects result from its misapplication and abuse. We consider here four common misuses: (1) encouraging a group member to role-play before he or she is ready or able to self-disclose or participate; (2) too little or too much direction by the group leader in casting, planning, implementing, and closing the role-play; (3) failure to protect and support the protagonist or other players; and (4) failure to use the procedures appropriately to achieve indicated objectives.

One of the most common abuses of role-playing occurs when the group leader does not thoroughly assess the readiness of the group member to engage in a role-play. The values and benefits of the experience are not clarified; the resistances, projections, and fears (as of manipulation or exploitation) are not recognized; basic trust, rapport, and cohesion with the leader and within the group are not developed; group rules concerning confidentiality, purposes, and boundaries for self-expression, criticism, and action are not clarified. To avoid these errors a specific contract needs to be negotiated with the individual group members, particularly with the protagonist. The preparation should expose them to what is involved, and they need to be given a choice to accept or refuse to participate. The leader can consciously assess readiness for involvement and for what degree of involvement and then validly engage the protagonist in a voluntary, motivated, fully participating performance.

A second common abuse of role-playing occurs when the leader gives too little or too much direction. The role-plays should not be imposed by the leader; rather, they should flow out of the purposes and desires of the protagonist and group. The leader needs to assure that the process and the tasks for each stage—warm-up, preparation, enactment, and closing—are completed at the proper time, and that transitions between stages are well made. Also, the leader has responsibility for planning, casting, and orchestrating the parts and the scripts so as to achieve the play's intended purposes and expected results. For example, in the warm-up stage, techniques to accomplish the tasks of arousing and focusing attention, fostering spontaneity and involvement, may consist of guided fantasy, games, bargaining for one's wants in "magic shop," situation tests (such as being cast adrift on a lifeboat or on a desert island), and melodrama (Blatner, 1973, pp. 40–43). Adequate time and direction need to be provided for preparation and rehearsal. Debriefing, sharing, and summarizing are techniques suitable for the closing stage.

Underdirection or overdirection may express the group leader's own personal style and needs, but direction should meet the goals, concerns, and needs of the protagonist and the group. Skilled direction should prevent or minimize impasses, delays, resistances, drifting and unfocused or overrestrictive lines of action, destructive interactions, and the imposition of undesired, unfeasible solutions upon the protagonist or the group. Provision needs to be made for continual monitoring and feedback of questions, reactions, discussions, and critique on the part of the participants to assure progression and, where needed, corrective action (Blake and Mouton, 1968).

A third form of abuse is a lack of concern for the potential for harm, or destructiveness to the well-being of one or more of the group members. Role-playing procedures are powerful in part because they ask group members to expose themselves in intimate detail, in telling how they acted, would have acted, or how they might feel like acting in a situation. Such self-disclosure might later be regretted and also might be used destructively by other group members. Casualties may be high from role-playing in therapy groups and encounter groups (Bednar and Kaul, 1978; Galinsky and Schopler, 1977; Liberman, Yalom, and Miles, 1973). In addition, role-playing often generates high levels of emotional contagion, psychophysical arousal, ego involvement, and cognitive-affective upsetness for which the client is not ready. One result may be a loss of control by the protagonist or the group. Such effects can be countered by the leader's control of the situation, and by the provision for continual feedback and monitoring. Vulnerable members should be protected from attack. A cue or gesture that action is getting out of bounds can be agreed upon to prevent abuse. In-depth self-disclosure in role-plays should be done later rather than early in the sessions. The client and other group members may need to be "brought down" from the emotional high, by group "sharing" and their reactions. Later, unanticipated, negative reactions can be avoided by providing strokes for the client, summarizing, debriefing, discussing unfinished business or future plans, and providing separation or closing rituals (Blatner, 1973, pp. 86–88).

The fourth type of misuse of role-playing concerns the inappropriate application of specific role-playing techniques. This requires a knowledge of specific techniques and their differential purpose. The leader thus can select the proper techniques and guide the process so that the role-play achieves the required tasks, solutions, and changes.

Specific Techniques

Role-plays may be structured or unstructured in type. Shaw et al. (1980, pp. 69–75) present unstructured techniques as being developmental and open-ended, allowing for spontaneous, emergent processes of problem-solving or learning. The techniques we will discuss are of this kind. Structured techniques have predetermined goals and are most commonly used in training programs. They often are designed with built-in tensions or resolutions, as in providing contradictory tasks or differences in objectives; these are used primarily to teach specific skills or attitudes. However, the degree of structure can vary so that the developmental techniques can be relatively structured when need be, and both types can be used in the same role-playing session.

In addition, role-play techniques may be primary or supplementary. Primary techniques can be used alone to accomplish particular purposes. Supplementary techniques, however, can be used only in conjunction with the primary techniques; they function to extend their impact and widen their scope, as, for example, in the use of the mirror maneuver to realize further the purposes of the modeling technique in encouraging the practice of new behavior. We present five of each type and indicate a number of variations of some of the techniques. In Table 10.1, the five categories of uses are condensed into two categories: assessment, arousal, awareness, and understanding are combined in the Awareness/Understanding column; decision making, behavior change, monitoring, and evaluation are combined in the Behavior Change column.

Primary Procedures

1. Own Role. In this procedure the client or protagonist plays himself or herself. Auxiliaries may represent persons, objects, concepts. This technique is particularly helpful for assessment purposes and the rehearsal of new behaviors. Increasing insight requires the use of such supportive procedures as soliloquy, on-the-spot interview, or doubling.

Table 10.1.   Uses of Role Play Procedures

Procedure	Awareness/Understanding	Behavior Change
A. Primary Role Play Procedures		
1. Own Role	Demonstrates and clarifies behavior/interaction patterns, concerns, and problems.	Explores-practices-rehearses new behaviors to a functional level.
	Facilitates insight into feelings, thinking, behavior of self and others.	Reduces performance anxiety associated with desired behavior.
	Identifies situational cues for own differential responses.	Prepares for obstacles and setbacks.
2. Role Reversal	Stimulates empathy for reciprocal other whose role is being enacted by protagonist.	Encourages spontaneity, participation, and unfreezing.
	Increases awareness of cognitive and affective aspects of own in-role behavior, including expectations of reciprocal other.	Facilitates shift in complementarity of expectations and behavior.
	Objectifies and clarifies situational context for own behavior.	Improves empathic skills.
3. Autodrama/Monodrama Chairing	Same as for own role and role reversal procedures.	Same as for own role and role reversal procedures.
	Identifies and clarifies own feelings at deeper levels.	Facilitates learning of adaptive "self-talk".
	Increases awareness of both substance and process aspects of own "self-talk".	Enables changes on deeper, more complex levels of feelings and meanings.
4. Modeling	Demonstration of new desired-adaptive behavior pattern.	Encourages practices, feedback, and reinforcement of desired behavior with reference to a model.
	Identifies model for mirroring, enactment, and practice.	
5. Sculpting/Choreography (Action sociogram)	Stimulates member awareness and discussion of behavior and group interactional patterns.	Enables group change in member attitudes, behaviors, and interaction patterns.

B. Supportive Role Play Procedures

1. On-the-Spot Interview	Identifies and clarifies client's thoughts and feelings while in role.	Provides practice in self-awareness and self-talk.
	Connects thinking and feeling to in-role behavior.	
2. Soliloquy	Same as on-the-spot interview procedure, in less structured terms.	Same as on-the-spot interview procedure.
3. Doubling	Same as on-the-spot interview procedure.	Same as on-the-spot interview procedure.
	Verbalizes and expresses covert thoughts, feelings, behavior for client's perception and awareness.	Gives permission and support for client's "owning" of thoughts, feelings, and behavior.
	Identifies new behaviors for acquisition.	Facilitates expression of feelings, and skills in self-expression.
		Promotes skill in use of feelings as cues for appropriate responsive behavior.
4. Mirror	Promotes realistic knowledge of consequences on own behavior upon others, and for effective task completion.	Provides practice of new behavior with reference to a model.
	Enables self-confrontation.	Enables feedback and reinforcement in learning of new behavior.
5. Sharing	Universalizes own experience as not unique.	Provides confirmation and support in reinforcement of behavioral performance and experience.
	Provides model of and experience with self-disclosure by others.	Facilitates learning of self-disclosure skills.

2. Role Reversal. Here the protagonist takes on the role of some reciprocal other; for example, the role of one's spouse. This enables the experiencing of the situation from another point of view. This technique is particularly useful for teaching empathy, especially if used with doubling or soliloquy. It also helps clarify situations and increases self-awareness. In addition, as Shaw et al. (1980, pp. 73–73) suggest, role reversal increases spontaneity, flexibility, and openness of the client and other participants. "Substitute role" (playing a symbolically substitute role) and "role distance" (playing an emotionally distant role) are variations of this technique.

3. Autodrama/Monodrama/Chairing. These three techniques are tied together in that the actor plays multiple roles (or all the parts) himself or herself. This may be done using one or more empty chairs, each representing a role, a character part, or personality aspect, with the person switching, physically or imaginatively, from one chair to another as he or she changes roles. In the occupancy of each chair, or the enacting of each part, the person initiates and maintains dialogue or interaction between the people, roles, or self-aspects, such as between a father and a son, between adult and child selves. Self-role and double-chairing are other names for this procedure. This technique is particularly powerful in activating cognitive and affective components of in-role behaviors, and thus stimulating self-awareness and insight and the learning of adaptive self-talk or internal dialogue. Cognitive restructuring, or the "disputing" of irrational beliefs or devaluing self-statements (Ellis, 1973; Beck, 1976), or learning self-control mechanisms (Meichenbaum, 1977; Mahoney and Arnkhoff, 1978), can be accomplished using this technique.

4. Modeling. This technique calls for the demonstration of new behavior to an individual by the leader or other members of the group. The model can provide immediate positive or negative feedback for the protagonist's observed practice and repeat the behavior until is is well reproduced by the client. Such activity stimulates observational, vicarious learning of behavior in terms of rewarding consequences, and it facilitates corrective feedback and reinforcement for the efficient learning of new behavior.

5. Sculpting/Choreography. This is also called action sociogram. Variations of this technique are the well-known psychodrama, or sociodrama, after Moreno (1952, 1953; Blatner, 1973, p. 46). Here the protagonist is directed to "sculpt," or position himself and key members of his family or group as if in a painting (Simon, 1972). He or she can participate with the key others in a dramatic playing out, in own or different role, of a ballet or verbal script (Papp, 1976). The psychodrama gives more emphasis to internal psychic factors; the sociodrama emphasizes social aspects. Also, the leader can provide a set of symbolic objects, such as coins, or figures, and have the protagonist use these objects symbolically to enact some problem or situation in a dynamic way. In addition to an assessment of a social situation, this technique can immerse a whole group into an intense participatory involvement, leading to self-disclosure and enactment of crucial issues and concerns. As a result, one can rapidly effect changes in the understanding, attitudes, and behavior of group members and in the group interaction patterns, for mutual reinforcement of new, adaptive behaviors and relationships. Although this procedure is widely used in family therapy, it also can be used with organized groups.

Supplementary Procedures

1. *On-the-Spot Interview.* This technique involves stopping the role-play and then interviewing one or more of the actors, asking specific, detailed questions to elicit thoughts and feelings at that point in relation to his or her in-role behavior. This increases the actor's awareness of cognitive, afffective, and behavioral aspects of role performance and identifies self-statements and self-talk that are dysfunctional and self-devaluing. It also teaches self-observation and increases self-awareness.

2. *Soliloquy.* This also involves stopping the role-play and asking the actor to disclose what she or he is thinking or feeling. However, this is done asking open-ended questions, so it is less structured than the on-the-spot interview. This may result in more dynamic data being obtained, and it also provides learning in increased self-observation and for self-talk and self-control.

3. *Doubling.* The doubling technique uses an auxiliary group member to act as the alter-ego or "inner voice" of the protagonist. In order to emphasize the identification with the actor, the double is required to speak entirely in the first person; for example, saying "I think . . . I feel." A "divided double" speaks for different parts of the actor's inner self; a "multiple double" calls for two or more auxiliaries to speak for different aspects of the protagonist's personality. In order to validate the truth of the double's statements, in offering inferences, interpretations, or alternative reactions for expression, the protagonist is required to repeat and to accept or reject them (Blatner, 1973, pp. 24–25). This technique has important functions, such as understanding the protagonist's behavior and dynamics, facilitating insight, providing support, giving permission for the protagonist "own" repressed or forbidden thoughts and feelings, and increasing emotional sensitivity and skills in self-expression. This technique is often used with own-role and chairing techniques.

4. Mirror. Here group members reenact the protagonist's behavior to demonstrate the actual performance to him or her. Other group members can verify to the actor that this replay is correct. This may be done with the use of exaggerated, amplified, or stereotyped "mirroring" of the behavior in order to emphasize particular correct or incorrect aspects. The protagonist can gain realistic self-awareness and self-insight through confronting certain aspects of self. The procedure also is useful in conjunction with modeling to teach and provide coaching, prompting, feedback, and support for the learning of new behavior. This is a way of involving participants to act as mirrors, and they also benefit by enhanced empathy, self-insight, and self-expressive skills.

5. Sharing. This is a helpful procedure to use during the role-play as well as for closing purposes (Blatner, 1973, pp. 82–86). Other members of the group share similar experiences or provide self-disclosure concerning their own feelings and reactions. This is done to provide supportive feedback to the client and mutual support for the group members, as well as mutual catharsis where this is indicated. It also facilitates the learning of self-disclosure in a supportive situation.

Conclusion

Role-playing has been presented as a very influential set of techniques. It is a basic procedure that complements the use of other techniques in group-activity programs and in group discussion within social work practice. It has generic application for social work with varied problems and clientele. We have clarified its basic purposes, offered an explanatory rationale, identified certain misuses, and suggested specific indications for the appropriate use of several techniques.

This contribution needs to be supplemented by additional research and practice to identify further specific differential indications and counterindications for the use of role-playing techniques. Further research also is indicated to clarify the dynamics that operate to make this a potent and effective procedure.

Role-playing humanizes and enlivens the helping process. It often is emotionally moving and painfully cathartic. Also, it often is a way of joyful play and fun. Used correctly, role-playing is a powerful force for helping and healing, for learning and problem-solving. It merits our greater understanding and esteem.

References

Beck, A. T. *Cognitive Therapy and the Emotional Disorders.* New York: International Universities Press, 1976.

Bednar, B., and Kaul, T. "Experimential Group Research: Current Perspectives," in S. Garfield and A. Bergin, eds., *Handbook of Psychotherapy and Behavior Change,* 2d ed. New York: Wiley, 1978, pp. 760–816.

Blake, R. R., and Mouton, J. S. *Making Experience Work.* New York: McGraw-Hill, 1978.

Blatner, H. A. *Acting-In.* New York: Springer, 1973.

Bohart, A. C. "Role Playing and Interpersonal Conflict Resolution." *Journal of Counseling Psychology,* 1977, 24, 15–24.

Corsini, R. J. *Roleplaying in Psychotherapy.* Chicago: Aldine, 1966.

Ellis, A. *Reason and Emotion in Psychotherapy.* New York: Lyle Stuart, 1962.

_____ *Humanistic Psychotherapy.* New York: Lyle Stuart, 1973.

Fischer, J. and Gochros, H. L. *Planned Behavior Change.* New York: The Free Press, 1975.

Galinsky, M., and Schopler, J. H. "Warning: Groups May Be Dangerous," *Social Work,* 1977, 22, 89–94.

Gambrill, E. *Behavior Modification.* San Francisco: Jossey-Bass, 1977.

Goldfried, M. R. "Systematic Desensitization as Training in Self-Control." *Journal of Consulting and Clinical Psychology,* 1971, 37, 228–34.

_____ and Goldfried, A. "Cognitive Change Methods." In K. Kanfer and A. Goldstein (eds.), *Helping People Change.* New York: Pergamon, 1980.

_____ and Merbaum, M. (eds.), *Behavior Change Through Self-Control.* New York: Holt, Rinehart & Winston, 1973.

Klein, A. *Role Playing.* New York: Association Press, 1956.

Lange, A. J., and P. Jakubowski. *Responsible Assertive Behavior.* Champaign, Ill.: Research Press, 1976.

Lieberman, M. I. Yalom, and Miles, M. *Encounter Groups: First Facts.* New York: Basic Books, 1973.

Lonergan, W. G. "Role Playing in an Industrial Conflict." *Group Psychotherapy,* 1957, 10, 105–10.

Mahoney, M. J. *Cognition and Behavior Modification.* Cambridge, Mass.: Ballinger, 1974.

_____ and Arknoff, D. "Cognitive and Self-Control Therapies." In S. L. Garfield and A. E. Bergin (eds.), *Handbook of Psychotherapy and Behavior Change,* 2d ed. New York: Wiley, 1978, pp. 689–722.

Maier, N. R. F.; Solem, A. R.; and Maier, A. A. *The Role-Play Technique.* San Diego: University Associates, 1975.

Meichenbaum, D. *Cognitive-Behavior Modification.* New York: Plenum, 1977.

Moreno, J. L. *Psychodrama,* vol. 1. New York: Beacon House, 1946.

_____ *Who Shall Survive?* New York: Beacon House, 1952.

Novaco, R. W. "Anger and Coping with Stress." In J. P. Foreyt and D. P. Rathjen (eds.), *Cognitive Behavior Therapy.* New York: Plenum, 1978, pp. 135–74.

Papp, P. "Family Choreography." In P. J. Guerin (ed.), *Family Therapy.* New York: Gardner, 1976, pp. 465–79.

G. A. Peters, and Gardner, S. "Role Playing Techniques in Industrial Situations." *Group Psychotherapy,* 1959, 12, 148–55.

Petzold, H. "Psychodrama and Role-Playing in Group Work." In K. D. Benne et al. (eds.), *The Laboratory Method of Changing and Learning.* Palo Alto: Science and Behavior Books, 1975, pp. 365–92.

Raimy, V. *Misunderstandings of the Self.* San Francisco: Jossey-Bass, 1975.

Reid, W. J. *The Task-Centered System.* New York: Columbia University Press, 1978.

Rose, S. R. *Group Therapy: A Behavioral Approach.* Englewood Cliffs, N.J.: Prentice-Hall, 1977.

Rosenthal, T., and Bandura, A. "Psychological Modeling: Theory and Practice." In S. L. Garfield and A. E. Bergin (eds.), *Handbook of Psychotherapy and Behavior Change.* 2d ed., New York: Wiley, 1978, pp. 621–58.

Schopler, J. H., and Galinsky, M. J. "Role Playing: Insights and Answers for Welfare Clients," *Public Welfare,* 1979, *37* (1), 23–32.

Shaw, M. E., et al. *Role Playing.* San Diego: University Associates, 1980.

Shapiro, C. H., et al. "Performance Based Evaluation: A Diagnostic Tool for Educators." *Social Service Review,* 1980, *54*, 262–72.

Simon, R. "Sculpting the Family." *Family Process,* 1972, *2*, 49–57.

Spivack, G.; Platt, J. J.; and Shure, M. B. *The Problem-Solving Approach to Adjustment.* San Francisco: Jossey-Bass, 1976.

Stuart, R. B. (ed.), *Behavioral Self-Management.* New York: Brunner/Mazel, 1977.

Sundel, S. S., and Sundel, M. *Be Assertive.* Beverly Hills: Sage, 1980.

Turner, R. H. "Role-Taking, Role-Standpoint, and Reference-Group Behavior." *American Journal of Sociology,* 1956, *61*, 316–28.

Wodarski, John, and Bagarozzi, Dennis. *Behavioral Social Work.* New York: Human Sciences Press, 1979.

Zastrow, L., and Navarre, R. "The Nominal Group: A New Tool for Making Social Work Education Relevant." *Journal of Education for Social Work,* 1977, *13*, 112–18.

Part IV

Innovations in Practice

Part IV, "Innovations in Practice," presents four chapters that deal with practice techniques and worker behaviors in interventions with clientele whose problems are especially amenable to group treatment. Included in this section are discussions of recent developments in techniques that are applicable to groups and how these can be incorporated into practice.

Chapter 9, "Uses of Groups with Relatives of Dependent Older Adults," deals with a subject that has received little attention. This group approach uses a reality orientation and an educational/functional focus that are of direct relevance to the tasks of daily management of group members responsible for the care of older relatives. The chapter points out the necessity for the leader of such a group to be an expert in both group work and gerontology, as well as being subjectively comfortable with the process of aging, familial demands of the aged, and general family dynamics. The chapter is a record of an actual group run by the authors; it describes in detail the situational characteristics of the members and the patterns that emerge in the various stages of group development, including several common themes; actions taken with the older person, feelings, relationships, and knowledge of the aging process.

Chapter 10, "Treating Postdivorce Adjustment in Latency-Age Children: A Focused Group Paradigm," describes a model consisting of (1) a parent-child assessment system; (2) concurrent parent and child group sessions that deal with traumas of postdivorce children in the latency stage that include a structured set of exercises and group games. The methodology takes into account criteria for group composition, pregroup preparation of members, and clearly delineated group-outcome goals. Measures of outcome are based on subjective reports of participants of specific behavioral changes, such as reduction in undesirable behaviors and the development of coping skills to deal with their changed reality.

Chapter 11, "Social Group Work and Alcoholics Anonymous," is a comparative study of the major themes of the AA self-help programs and social group world. It focuses on the problems and issues confronted by social workers in work with alcoholics. Some of the problems are seen to reside in the philosophical differences between the two modes of help, a reality that must be confronted if the trend to integrate social work into AA counseling programs is to be effective. The chapter suggests that social group work can play a complementary role, as opposed to a competitive one vis-à-vis AA groups and can serve persons who are unlikely to avail themselves of AA facilities. Characteristics of such populations are described and stategies of intervention suggested.

"A Group Work Framework for Teaching Assertive Skills to the General Public" describes an educational model for teaching assertive behaviors through an education program. The program consists of a five-week structured behavioral course, providing participants with both didactic and experiential information. The paper gives a step-by-step description of content and exercises related to the acquisition of desirable assertive actions and demonstrates the logical progression of learning through home assignments and peer feedback, role playing, and practice sessions. The authors emphasize the supportive and nonthreatening nature of such an educational model vis-à-vis a therapy group, and they support this position with empirical data related to desired behavior change by class participants.

11

Uses of Groups with Relatives of Dependent Older Adults

Margaret E. Hartford and
Rebecca Parsons McCoy

Rationale for the Group

The decision to offer time-limited, closed-membership groups of people who had an aging dependent relative came as the result of many kinds of requests by people who were seeking assistance in dealing with an older relative. Frequently, the request for assistance or understanding was not for the older relative who was becoming increasingly dependent or deteriorating, but for the concerned or care-taking relative—daughter, son, niece or nephew, brother or sister, spouse or friend. The need was not only for emotional support but also for gaining greater understanding of the processes of aging, for help in planning and direction for future action, for locating resources, for understanding roles and relationships, and for acquiring behavior appropriate in the particular situations. While each request was unique, there were common or similar themes in each family. Previous life patterns of family relationships, socioeconomic status, and the current physical and psychological condition of the dependent relative made each situation unique, but there were enough similarities in the feelings and experiences of the concerned relatives that a group modality appeared to be useful. All potential participants seemed to need the kinds of assistance a group could offer.

While word-of-mouth reports would suggest that many groups of this sort are offered in mental health, social work, and other counseling services, an extensive literature search did not produce much written evi-

This is an expanded version of a paper delivered at the Conference on Social Work with Groups, Arlington, Texas, 1980. It first appeared in Social Work with Groups, 5(2), Summer 1982: 77–90.

dence about relative groups. There were a few articles about groups of adults whose older relative was in a nursing home or long-term care facility. There were reports of groups of primary caretakers for excessively frail and dependent older adults with diagnosed mental disorders. But lacking any clear formulation of group approaches through perceived experiences, it was decided to establish our own approach based on our understanding of the nature of the problems and group processes, and the orientation of the available leadership; an experienced practitioner and group work educator/gerontologist, and student trainees in gerontology/ social work and gerontology/psychology in their last semester of professional education (Margaret E. Hartford, Ph.D., Rebecca Parsons McCoy, M.S.G./M.S.W., and Sam Popkin, M.A., a trainee in Clinical Aging and Psychology).

Pregroup Planning

In pregroup planning, account was taken of the influence of the context, which was the Adult Counseling Center of the Andrus Gerontology Center on the campus of the University of Southern California. The potential participants were people who had called the center requesting help about an older relative, or who were currently receiving individual counseling at the center.

An eclectic group approach was used, drawing from various theoretical orientations as it seemed appropriate for the needs of the participants. Less of an encounter approach or of long-term psychotherapy were used, and more of a supportive, current-functioning, reality orientation, dealing with crises as they occurred, with some didactic educational approach to understanding the normal and pathological changes in aging, and with an emphasis on helping participants cope with and master their current situations.

The focus of the group was to assess and bring to current awareness through the group processes the needs of the individual participants relevant to the pressures they felt about their relatives, to assess and begin to work on some ways of coping with the tensions, feelings, and responsibilities of the concerned, and/or care taking relatives about their older relatives; and to develop an understanding of the aging processes, their own and their relatives'; to deal with role changes and other areas of stress. Attention was given to an examination of current and life-long patterns of relationships between older and younger family members to see how these tended to impede or help cope with their current situations. On the basis of their current situations, assessments were made as to anticipated and inevitable changes in the condition of the older person and planning for future courses of action.

From the standpoint of the group, the objective was to establish an atmosphere that would permit and support expression of ambivalent or even resentful feelings about current conditions, responses, and relationships, and to offer empathetic responses. The focus was also to support planning and direction for current and future dealing with self and older relative. The development of the group was for support, belonging, mutual aid (without advice giving), and strength, which the participant could carry outside of the group, plus practical help in carrying the family support role. To the extent appropriate, group discussion included helping participants to gain some insight to their own feelings and behavior and that of their relatives. From a research standpoint, the purpose of the group was to determine major themes of concern about aging relatives, care taking, and intergenerational relationships.

Worker Choice

With these goals for the group, certain criteria began to emerge for worker choice and assignment. It should be noted that while the original groups were developed there was also some analysis as to qualities that would be important for the best working relationship with the particular participant population. The worker as a well-educated and experienced professional in social work needed a good theoretical and working knowledge of the normal aging processes and pathology in aging, including the bodily changes, the emotional and psychological impact of aging on the older person and on relatives, spouses, and friends, the symptomatic behaviors of organic brain syndrome, of genuine senility, and reversable pseudo-senility caused by illness, crises, depression, drugs, social isolation, or other factors; and the physical symptoms, effect of depression on memory, circulatory, respiratory, digestive, and gastrointestinal and urinary systems, the bodily and psychological effects of particular drugs—in general, basic social gerontological knowledge. The worker also should have worked through or at least worked on his or her own family relationships and feelings about aging to be able to identify with or empathize with both the position and the responses of the caretaking person and needs of the older person. In an attitudinal sense this means that the potential worker would have confronted personal attitudes about aging and growing old, and the older population in society, and about middle age, since most of the caretaking relatives were middle-aged. He or she should have understanding about parent-child relationships, especially as these change throughout life transitions, and understanding of authority, about role functioning and familial responsibility, not to over- or under-emphasize either. In this area the worker needed to understand also the effect of unresolved family conflicts from adolescence and young adulthood on the establishment of helpful family relationships in the later years, when roles and responsibilities shift. Workers also needed a working knowledge of community resources for services for the elderly or access to information and referral services. Workers, of course, needed a good working knowledge and skill in group process in order to facilitate the organization of a group from an aggregate of people who had in common their concern about an older relative, so that the group could become the instrument for learning, helping, supporting, problem-solving, and growth of the participants. In other words, the worker needed group counseling skills as well as group facilitating skills, and some teaching skills. The worker's teaching skill was necessary for helping participants learn to use the group for their growth, and also for helping participants learn about aging, to bring cognitive content about aging and the diseases of aging. The counseling skills were necessary for helping participants grow in self-awareness and learning to work better on the relationships with their dependent relatives and to manage appropriate roles and responsibilities in their families, but also to help participants see the need for their own independent lives as so not to be smothered in their caretaking responsibilities.

In some groups we learned that the worker needed to have worked on his or her own attitudes about death and dying as well as feelings and knowledge from a psychological and sociocultural perspective. This was important to assist participants whose relatives were dying or had died. The worker needs knowledge and sense of comfort in grief work, of the various sociocultural ways of dealing with death, as well as the impact of a dying relative on the caretaker and subsequently on the group. The worker needed to understand the behavior of separation and termination of guilt in wishing for the death of an ill relative and subsequent feelings of loss when the relative dies.

Time and Size

In the pregroup phase, decisions were made to offer an eight-session one and a half hour closed-membership group. Size was to range from six to ten, depending on availability of participants at the hour set, 1:30–3:30 on a weekday. Initially, the time was set because of availability of staff and space and because the area is safer for travel during daylight. It was determined later that a time after work might be more feasible in the future if a safe location for evening attendance could be located, because the time as set eliminated some working people with older parents, and others had to take off from work or other activities to attend the group. The eight sessions were set with anticipation of the amount of time necessary for the group to go through the phases of group development and the content that would need to be covered. The time-limited approach also gave an opening for escape for those people who were uneasy about the group approach but could accept a limited number of sessions. Size was determined on the basis of the time/size ratio of participants in relation to the depth of problems and problem focus for each participant (Hartford, 1971).

Composition

Intake for the group was done through individual interviews by the co-therapists, who were graduate students in gerontology and social work. Potential participants came from referral from caseloads of individual counselors in the Adult Counselling Center, or from intake of people who called inquiring about help in managing their relatives.

Initially, there was thought of composing a group along a single dimension, such as relatives of a person with diagnosed Alzheimer's disease, organic brain syndrome, or severe depression. There was also consideration of including only relatives who were the primary caretakers, or only persons whose adult relative was institutionalized. But during the intake it became apparent that there were some common and unique factors in each of these categories, and that a mixed group might prove more beneficial for the participants, since they could share with each other some of their different experiences.

Group Development

With these criteria one group of six was composed, including the following: two cousins, Faye and Alice, whose mothers were sisters. Alice had given up a job and an apartment in another city to move in with her mother, who had become increasingly dependent, confused, and unable to maintain herself alone. This daughter had found another part-time job. She was seeking some psychological diagnosis or greater depth in understanding of her mother's problems, some help in anticipating the problems ahead, and also some psychological support for herself in the responsibilities she had taken on. The other cousin, Faye, who was herself undertaking some graduate study, was concerned because her mother, who though still able to maintain herself in senior housing, had developed a serious chronic illness, diabetes, and was not taking her medication regularly. Also her mother was becoming increasingly withdrawn and had dropped some of her volunteer and senior-center activities. Faye sought assurance that there was some pill or some other medication that would return her mother to a former mental state of independence. She wanted more cognitive knowledge of aging, denied what she and her mother were experiencing, and had some difficulty recognizing her mother's symptoms of depression and deterioration. At the same time, she was experiencing some guilt about her feelings and the rejection of responsibility for her mother, which she turned onto her cousin by suggesting that Alice was being a martyr by moving in with her mother and caring for her. The presence of these two in the group set up a subgroup conflict that the whole group worked on to some degree.

A third participant, George, was a retired man in his seventies whose wife had had a very rapid onset of senile dementia, probably diagnosed as Alzheimer's, and whom he had had to place under constant institutional care. He had cared for her as long as he could. However, she had been unable to continue at home because she had become dangerous to herself, to him, and to others. He was in individual counseling, dealing with understanding her problem and handling his loneliness, guilt, and anger. His use of the group was to gain better understanding of her illness, to have a place to talk out his concerns, and to gain support. He also contributed to the understanding of others with some insights regarding the feeling of having to take the responsibility for a relative who is deteriorating, making decisions, and taking action where the ill person can no longer participate responsibly. This contribution was useful to those facing the same future. He also offered empathy and understanding to the others.

A fourth group member, Celia, was an affluent, successfully married society matron, who lived in elegance at the beach with her successful and wealthy husband, teenage children, and father-in-law. The father-in-law was a wealthy business man who had suffered a heart attack and tended to be sedentary but independent, but was somewhat angry and frustrated at his limitations. He had his own suite in the beach house but generally took his meals with the family. The presenting problem for Celia was her mother, who still lived in the family house, of considerable size, in one of the older sections of the city, with a housekeeper and a driver. In her slight deterioration and confusion and excessively demanding style, she was no longer able to keep service personnel very long; consequently, according to Celia, she was suffering from being robbed of money and jewelry and exploited by housekeepers who tended to be transient. She was also constantly demanding of her daughter by telephone, sometimes in the middle of the night. She still maintained her affiliations with downtown clubs, the alumni association of her college, and community activities in which she had previously served on the board. Celia would frequently take her mother to the beach house for overnight or weekends, but she would immediately want to go home. On arrival at home she would want to go back. Celia had attempted to get her mother to move to a condominium, or to one of the elite retirement hotels not far from her present home. This action would mean selling the family home, now of course of considerable value. None of these proposals was acceptable to her mother. Celia, who stated that she was in individual psychiatric therapy, wanted to participate in the group to gain help in how to manage her mother better. She also had a younger sister, Debby, who was in business in one of the resort beach towns and who, Celia said, was not assuming any responsibility for her mother. Celia brought Debby to the group sessions twice without any preparation of the worker or other members. Celia said she brought Debby for the group and the worker "to tell her how to understand mother, and to make her take more responsibility." Debby sat quietly in these sessions, except for reinforcing her sisters' description of their mother's demanding behavior.

A fifth member of the group, Elizabeth, was the wife of a business-man and mother of two college-aged children, whose mother-in-law was her concern. The mother-in-law had lived in her own house until she had a stroke. When she recovered, she moved in with the family because the physician thought she should not live alone. While the home was of ade-quate size, the young people in and out of the house annoyed her. Also, she did not maintain her personal hygiene, resisted bathing and chang-ing clothes, had some problems with bladder control, and seemed lonely and isolated. Elizabeth decided her mother-in-law should be moved into a retirement home. After exploring several such places, a home was cho-sen and the mother-in-law was moved. It was apparent that the older woman was in no way involved in the decisions about moving. At first she was angry, and the daughter-in-law felt guilty. This was the point at which Elizabeth joined the group. Her concern was that her mother-in-law would become more ill or dependent and could no longer be main-tained in the particular setting, which did not have hospital or nursing health care. Her solution for her mother-in-law was to find her a senior center and keep her busy. Her denial of the actual needs of her mother-in-law or of anticipating the future were problems to be worked out, plus her own problem of guilt and rejection. She needed a place to talk out these factors. She also had a horror of her own old age and her husband's pend-ing retirement, which emerged subtly in the group.

A sixth participant, Helen, was a retired professional person who was working as a volunteer and part-time paid worker in a senior nutri-tion program. Her mother was of concern to her. She too wanted a quick solution for her mother's deterioration and increased dependency. By the time she arrived at the group she had made a decision to provide day care for her mother. Since some of the discussion in the group during the first session she attended was relevant to understanding some of the normal changes of aging in the very old, her response was, "I know all of this, I am a gerontologist, I work in a nutrition program and we have had this content in training." Yet her responses or descriptions of her behavior re-garding her mother indicated that her understanding did not apply to herself and her mother, and she apparently did not want it to. She dropped out of the group, sending a message that she was too busy to at-tend further meetings. She did not respond to worker's efforts to offer her either individual or group counseling. Apparently the approach of the group came too close to her experience and she was not ready to handle her feelings. The group stabilized at five members.

Beginnings

The worker attempted to create an atmosphere of support and reinforce-ment that encouraged the participants to share their concerns and to sup-port each other. Participants introduced themselves by first names only and stated the problems that had brought them to the group. They defined their concerns variously: with relatives, with themselves, or with relationships between themselves and their relatives. Some took an intellectual approach of only seeking more knowledge about aging, or wanting to understand senility, or to learn about the availability of resources. As an approach to the beginning phase of the group, the workers encouraged the participants to listen to and support each other, to ask questions of each other for further information, and to draw associations from one experience to another. Workers discouraged advice giving and rather attempted to lead the group into a problem-solving approach, of listening, analyzing, sharing, and caring. From the beginning session, members were inducted into the group process by doing it rather than making the group process explicit. The workers did some instruction by presenting information on understanding the aging processes, on senility and reversible confusion and memory loss, on the nature of the brain diseases such as Alzheimer's and its control and medication. Although the material was carefully presented with consultation of medical personnel of the center, some of the participants found the material threatening, especially when they had hoped that a pill had been invented that "would make mother like she was twenty years ago." The workers used the group to help participants to work through some of these feelings and reactions. One of the members, whose wife had been institutionalized after several years of his attempts to care for her after she developed Alzheimer's disease, was particularly helpful in the follow-up discussion of the presentation.

Progression

Each session was concluded with a summary of content covered during the session and problems worked on by each of the members, and a review of the progress, including ways members had supported each other and challenged each other. The group as a whole indicated what it would like to talk about or work on the next session, and individuals stated particular concerns that they had and would work on with their relatives between sesssions. At each new session one of the workers gave a brief review of the previous session and agenda items set for the current session. The agenda was not always followed, but it did provide continuity from one session to the other. The session usually began with some particular pressing experience a member reported that had occurred during the previous week.

Process

Alliances formed among most members. They showed interest in each other regarding how various approaches had worked out during the week. They encouraged each other to express frustrations. They gave evidence of gaining greater insight, both of themselves and of their relatives, in the way they responded. Several recognized that they were being overprotective and not engaging their older relatives in decisions affecting them. Two of the participants who seemed to be deadlocked in battles for power with their relatives began to show signs of relaxing, not correcting their relatives for accuracy when a person was confused, not blaming the relative for willful negative and controlling behavior. Participants reported that they found themselves in more cooperative and comfortable relationships.

After approximately three-fourths of the sessions one of the cousins, Faye, reported that she was dropping out of the group for two reasons. First, her mother had resumed taking her medication, with the assistance of a public health nurse, and had attended the senior center nutrition program again. Faye commented that she guessed that by changing the way she responded to her mother as she had learned in the group, she and her mother were not arguing so much about the medication. Faye said she was enrolled in a class that met at the same time as the group and could not miss any more sessions. It should be noted also that this withdrawal from the group also followed the session in which one of the workers had discussed some of the physical decrements of aging as it affected the brain behavior and social behavior. He had also been definitive in stating that so far there has been no discovery of a pill that would reverse the aging process. Faye had been notably disappointed that there was no miracle drug. Her cousin, Alice, did not return the week after, but called to say her car had given out. She also indicated that she had located a job that would prevent her from coming to the last session. The last session was attended by three participants, two of whom indicated that they would like to join another group if it was offered. The third indicated that she would like to become a senior volunteer at the center, and while she wanted to continue contact she did not need any help like the other group members.

Common Themes

Several common themes were identified from the initial groups; those having to do with actions taken with relatives, those related to feelings, those dealing with relationships, and those related to knowledge.

One of the major actions that relatives are concerned about is the relocation of a person who becomes too frail or dependent to remain in the original residence alone, or too deteriorated to remain in the community. The issue is around helping the relative to move. In many cases this was the precipitating event that brought the family to the center. An important aspect of this theme is to help the caretaker to understand how difficult relocation can be for the older person. Another aspect is involving the older person in the decision every step of the way. The choice to move the older person into the family home, where there are in-laws and may be children of assorted ages, may have greater implications and carry more responsibility than anticipated. If the relatives are considering moving the older person, it is important for families to see that the older relative needs to maintain some sense of control and participation in the decision and the act of moving in order to maintain some sense of self-esteem, as well as avoiding disorientation that may follow a major move for anyone. Relatives need to anticipate the changes in relationships, pressures, use of family resources, both physical and emotional, and the allocation of space that result from the addition of another adult to a household. Roles and responsibilities are also affected. If the choice is to move to an institution, the family also needs to be aware of some of the effects of institutional living after maintaining an independent family household, and to anticipate the changes. Some of the rights and responsibilities of the older person and the families in selecting and monitoring an institutional arrangement also surfaced in the consideration of this theme. The issue was discussed in several sessions and apears to be a common theme of concern to many families.

A second theme, involving action, was the engagement of other relatives or secondary care givers. Some of the group members felt "bombarded" by "helpful" suggestions from other relatives, while others felt resentful that others did not help more. Group members frequently found it necessary to learn how to use their relatives or friends more appropriately in care giving and to relieve themselves of the total responsibility.

A third action-related theme was the recognition that there were appropriate times and circumstances for making decisions and taking responsible action when an older relative can no longer manage or at least decide alone. Family members need help in learning that while they make every effort to place the mastery and management in the hands of the old relative, there are times when the older persons may feel deserted, or cannot manage responsibilities, and will become overly anxious if support is not given. The group gives the opportunity to role-play the feelings around these actions and to gain some empathy for the feelings of the older relative.

A fourth theme, related to dealing with feelings, that emerged almost constantly was that of impatience and frustration, especially when a relative is mentally impaired. Not only did the participants need a chance to express their frustration but they frequently needed to accept the fact that it was appropriate and important to plan for some respite care so that they could get some emotional relief. They needed to combine dealing with their feelings with a plan of action that provided a means of sometimes getting away from their caregiving responsibilities.

A fifth theme and closely related to the above was a feeling of entrapment in a difficult situation with an increasingly dependent or disoriented older person. Participants with this feeling sought the group as a safe place, and a permissive place to express their anger without fear of criticism or increasing guilt. In this sense the group was used for catharsis, accepted with empathy and understanding.

Expressions or feelings of guilt was a universal theme, regardless of the amount or quality of care given by the person. Members were helped to view their situations and limitations realistically and objectively and to gain some insight and relief from their guilt by understanding why they felt that way. The group process was used to help people work through their relationships with their relatives with the support of the group in order to work on their feelings of guilt.

A seventh theme that occurred was the importance of communications and sharing between the members of two generations in the family. When needs change and dependence increases, many older people cannot ask for the help that they need because of their belief in independence, their dread of being a bother to someone, or their fear of being taken over and stripped of their autonomy if they ask for any assistance. Many of the families in the group apparently had a very indirect way of communicating with their relatives, and through the group experience they learned to be more direct and to encourage their relatives to be more expressive in their thoughts, opinions, and needs.

Closely related to the communication theme was the theme of interpersonal conflict that resulted from mutual misperception and response between the relatives of two generations. The group helped the family members to see the roles that they played in perpetuating certain of these conflicts by the way that they responded to each other and to the older relatives. The group helped members to see that while some behavior results from life-long patterns, other results from pressure in the current situation, and not necessarily the results of old age. Some of the group members discovered that when they responded differently to their older relatives, and with some understanding of some of the feelings, fears and concerns of the older relatives, this behavior elicited different responses from the relatives. In several instances this behavioral approach taken in the group improved family relationships.

In the realm of knowledge, a major theme was that of understanding the physical and psychological changes of aging and what is at stake for the older person. This included understanding the emotional response of bodily changes and feelings of loss and status, of friends, of control over self, and coping with these feelings. Basic knowledge of aging and refuting stereotypes and misinformation was a theme that ran through every session.

A final theme closely related to the above was the knowledge of reversible and irreversible losses in brain functioning, in dementias and evidence of what is popularly called senility. Some members associated slow responses and minor memory loss to mental impairment, while others were sure that severe dementia could be reversed with a pill. Each group sought cognitive content in this area. These were the major content areas that occurred in the groups, not stimulated by the workers but introduced by the members.

Conclusion

There appears to be an increasing need for relatives who have a care-taking role with older adults to have some assistance with handling their feelings, their realistic planning, their understanding of aging and support for their day-to-day responsibilities and frustrations. They need help in learning how to take on appropriate roles and care in working through their problems in the caretaking role. People who share these stresses in common, guided by an educated professional who has expertise in group leadership and in gerontology, can be helped to manage their responsibilities more adequately.

The experiences reported here would suggest the participants in groups created for the purpose of helping them work with older relatives evidenced some change in their behavior, their beliefs and attitudes, and grew in their understanding of aging, of their relatives and themselves.

A second conclusion is that workers with such groups need to be skilled in group leadership, in understanding of human behavior from a development standpoint, and a psychodynamic view of the family and individual, and must be particularly knowledgeable about aging processes as well as attitudes and stereotypes about aging.

With skilled leadership, groups can be a most useful and helpful means of providing caretakers of their older relatives to be able to function adequately and appropriately, hopefully to improve the quality of life for older adults and their families.

References

Hartford, Margaret, E. *Groups in Social Work*. New York: Columbia University Press, 1971.
_____ "Use of Groups in Mental Health of the Elderly." In J. Birren and Sloane, *Handbook of Mental Health in Aging*. Englewood Cliffs, N.J.: Prentice-Hall, 1980.

12

Treating Postdivorce Adustment in Latency-Age Children: A Focused Group Paradigm

Emily Tiktin Schoenfelder
and Catherine Cobb

The divorce experience for a child is universally fraught with confusion, loss, and insecurity. Regardless of the circumstances that precede marital disruption, children are unprepared to cope with the drastic readjustments that follow. A child's inherent security is grounded in the family context and is largely predicated upon his or her unconditional belief in the permanence of the parental marriage. Divorce can rupture this stability and create fragmentation in a previously ordered world.

Divorce frequently constitutes a developmental crisis in the lives of children of all ages, a phenomenon amply supported in the literature (Benedek and Benedek, 1979; Derdyn, 1980; Hetherington, Cox, and Cox, 1979; Wallerstein and Kelly, 1980). Uniformly, children experience a pervasive sadness at the loss of the family unit and one parent's departure from the home. The intensity of these losses has been shown to temporarily impede the emotional, psychological, and social growth of children (Anthony, 1974; Kelly and Wallerstein, 1976; McDermott, 1970; Wallerstein and Kelly, 1976; Westman, Cline et al., 1970).

Many children of divorce were formerly well adjusted. The problems they develop during and after divorce are in reaction to uncontrollable stresses that leave them feeling helpless and greatly reorder the structure of their lives. The traumatic impact of divorce often causes acute adjustment problems and can leave these children more vulnerable to future psychiatric difficulties (Anthony, 1974; Derdyn, 1980; McDermott, 1970; Wallerstein and Kelly, 1979).

145

How children react is determined by a complex set of variables related to each child's level of cognitive function and subjective perception of reality, his or her parent's ability to cope, and the degree of postdivorce turmoil to which the child is exposed (Wallerstein and Kelly, 1979). However, some clearly discernible syndromes have been identified (Wallerstein and Kelly, 1980) that show remarkably age-consistent patterns. Particularly during the latency period (7 to 12 years), children exhibit many uniform emotional and behavioral reactions. The reactional symptoms characteristic of this age, in conjunction with specific developmental tasks undertaken during latency, make latency-age children especially vulnerable to the impact of divorce.

Latency is the most significant age period for formative growth and personality development. Critical ego and identity development occur; cognitive, moral, and social structuring begins; and the equilibrium of inner- and outer-family relationships is challenged. Latency-age children depend heavily on both parents for nurturing, protection, and control, as well as for the consolidation of age-appropriate identification. The stress of divorce interferes with the normal developmental process by absorbing the child's mental and emotional energy, thus inhibiting his or her ability to work and play effectively (Hess and Camara, 1979; Wallerstein and Kelly, 1980). As the child struggles to sort through conflicts, reorder perceptions, and mourn the intense loss, his or her ability to concentrate is diminished and social interaction with peers declines.

During the postdivorce period latency-age children often experience depression, manifested by clinical symptoms, including loss of appetite, sleep disturbance, and joyless play (Derdyn, 1980; McDermott, 1970). Withdrawal from siblings and peers, increased somaticism, and outward aggression may accompany the internal depression that is characteristic of the grieving process (Anthony, 1974; Hozman and Froiland, 1976). Behaviorally, children may react to all the change with such regressions as increased clinging behavior and neediness, tantrums, and bedwetting. Nightmares, newly appearing discipline problems (such as demands for attention) and decreased school performance are also characteristic of latency-age postdivorce adjustment (Fulton, 1979; Gardner, 1977; Kelly and Wallerstein, 1976; Kurdek and Siesky, 1979; Wallerstein and Kelly, 1976).

Despite the abundance of literature discussing the effects and implications of divorce on children, there is a paucity of material describing interventions with such children. Wallerstein and Kelly (1977) advocate inclusion of the children within a family-counseling model. Gardner (1976) has written extensively about individual psychotherapy with children of divorce, and Hozman and Froiland (1976) present a model of individual treatment based on the Kubler-Ross (1969) concept of "loss." Only two sources present group work with children of divorce (Cantor, 1977;

Wilkinson and Bleck, 1977), both of which were conducted in informal school settings. While each of these approaches addresses a crucial component of postdivorce adjustment, an integrative element is lacking.

The authors' model incorporates several elements of the above-mentioned strategies. It is designed for children experiencing acute reactional syndromes and offers preventive intervention for less distressed children. Two specific components contribute to the uniqueness of the model. First, the child's participation in a therapeutically developed peer group is thought to be the optimal mode of treatment. The group provides a supportive milieu where the children can increase their inter- and intrapersonal awareness. A progressive series of innovative games and exercises has been devised and constitutes the "focused group paradigm," which is the foundation of the treatment program.

Second, the authors contend that latency-age children are strongly influenced by their parents and that parents are, in fact, instrumental in impacting the child's adjustment or failure to adjust following divorce. Thus, intervention with the primary parent (the parent that provides the greatest amount of custodial care), in conjunction with child-centered treatment, is viewed as an essential combination. The parents of participating children form a group of their own, which is offered as an adjunct to the child-directed treatment.

Introduction of the group-treatment model into practice began through Divorce Lifeline, a nonprofit counseling agency in Seattle. Divorce Lifeline was established in 1968 to provide professional group counseling for adults undergoing separation and divorce. In 1979 Divorce Lifeline incorporated a program for children, using the authors' model.

The Treatment Model

Intake/Assessment Procedure

Preceding the formation of the group, the therapist conducts an intake/assessment interview with each prospective parent-child dyad. The parent is asked to complete a questionnaire detailing current custody and visitation practices and providing subjective input as to the child's functioning at school and at home. The parent fills out a checklist of specific behavioral or emotional problems demonstrated by the child, such as depressive symptoms, acting-out behaviors, and regressions. Simultaneously, the child is asked to do a family drawing, depicting each family member "doing something." The act of drawing eases the child's anxiety about the interview and provides important projective information as to the child's view of present family relationships, his or her significance in the family structure, and feelings about self.

The interview involves both parent and child and focuses highly, if not exclusively, on the child's perceptions. Of greatest importance are the child's beliefs about the causes of the divorce, preseparation memories of the family unit, and changes that have taken place. The therapist describes the nature and structure of the group, explains confidentiality, and asks the parent to give permission for the child to discuss openly all family issues.

Although the intake procedure is primarily a psycho-social assessment for the therapist, a corollary function is to screen out a child who might be unsuited for group therapy. Contradictions for inclusion are: (1) history of excessive interpersonal conflict that would interfere with group interaction; (2) severe behavior problems that if manifested in the group would significantly disrupt the group process and impede the therapy of the other children; and (3) emotional or personality difficulties of a long-standing nature (unrelated to the divorce) that would warrant individual psychotherapy.

Parent Group: Goals

The purpose of the parent group is twofold: (1) to provide a vehicle whereby the therapist can give feedback to the parents that will guide them in facilitating adjustment for their children; and (2) to promote peer support where parents can share their experiences and exchange suggestions. Although these were the planned goals, during the pilot session it became evident that the group was meeting an additional need.

During discussion of their personal divorce situations, many parents indicated they had sustained animosity for their spouses that endured long after the divorce. The children in these cases were often, intentionally or not, caught in the middle. This phenomenon has frequently been reported to be characteristic of postdivorce spousal relationships (Benedek and Benedek, 1977; Bernstein and Robey, 1962; Cline and Westman, 1971; Derdyn, 1980). Although the parent group was not designed to provide therapy for parents, the group setting is an excellent arena for exposing prolonged hostility and the harmful effects it can have on the children. The group offers a place for parents to ventilate residual anger and receive support in resolving these conflicts without involving their children.

Because of the lingering bitterness expressed by many parents for their former spouses, only one spouse from each family is included in the parent group. In most cases, the parent with primary custody is the preferred parent for group involvement. This does not discount the important influence both parents have on the child. The parent spending the most time with the child, however, has a greater opportunity to effect and maintain behavioral changes on a consistent basis. In addition, the postdivorce adjustment of this parent seems to be more directly related to the child's overall recovery. All nonparticipating parents are given the option of individual appointments with the therapist.

Parent Group: Structure

The parent group meets three times for one and a half hours each session. The first parent session is held following completion of all intake interviews and prior to the first children's group. The second session follows the fourth children's group (midway), and the final parent group is after the last children's session.

It is imperative at the outset that the therapist clarify his or her role. The therapist's commitment is clearly defined as assisting the child in postdivorce adjustment. In no way must the therapist be drawn into advocacy for one parent over the other, since this would be inconsistent with child-focused teatment.

The three parent sessions are minimally structured, allowing parents to guide the course of the group according to their specific needs. The first session follows the pattern of newly forming groups, where the emphasis is on introductions and establishing common themes. In the middle session the therapist provides feedback about the children's work in the group, while parental exchange and support develop. The therapist also presents the children's concerns about parental behaviors that cause them discomfort and may be interfering with the child's adjustment. The final session continues to promote group-sharing and problem-solving, with time allotted for the therapist to summarize observations and for parents to evaluate the program. Emphasis in the sessions is on interaction among the parents. The therapist provides some direct information relayed from the children's groups but primarily uses his or her knowledge of group process to facilitate group movement.

Children's Group: Goals

The eight sessions that comprise the children's treatment represent a time-limited, brief intervention directed toward three identified goals: (1) to broaden the child's understanding of divorce by dispelling common misconceptions and offering accurate information; (2) to provide an arena for teaching the recognition and healthy expression of feelings; and (3) to present an interactional peer setting where normalization of the divorce experience can occur.

A "game" format is used to focus each group session. The games, developed by the authors, serve as vehicles to structure the therapeutic milieu. The games also keep the children attentive and provide an indirect method for them to disclose anxiety-producing thoughts and feelings. Edible reinforcers (primarily nonsugar items such as raisins and peanuts) are used to help the children remain task-oriented while simultaneously rewarding their appropriate participation.

Children's Group: Process

The beginning children's sessions are designed to promote trust and provide a forum for mutual sharing. Early establishment of group structure is essential to guide and shape the boundless energy of latency-age children. Through a tightly focused structure, the children are provided with constructive rather than chaotic group learning and interaction. As the children begin to discover similarities and differences in their family situations, group cohesion and commitment develop quickly.

The first session opens with a brief review of the group's purpose and the setting of basic group norms. The therapist then directs the children in an introduction exchange. Each child responds to prepared questions that are designed to elicit "neutral information" (such as age, favorite activity), as well as "divorce-related" material (such as how long parents have been divorced). This is an ice-breaker that provides an immediate base of comparisons and contrasts.

The remainder of the first session uses an exercise to help the group identify divorce-specific issues. The therapist has the children take turns writing two lists on the blackboard indicating things that are "different" and things that are "the same" since the parents' divorce. A reward (a raisin or peanut) is given to all the children each time a new item is added to one of the lists. Writing on the board and sharing a common goal help the children relax and promote group interaction. The lists show the children that many families undergo similar changes after divorce, that some things do not change, and that improvements can occur (such as "less fighting at home").

In the next session the children identify and explore feelings. It is important to establish early a common language for the children and the therapist to use as a basis for communication throughout the remaining sessions. To facilitate this process a "balloon-feeling" game was devised. The game begins with the children identifying feelings and listing them on the board. Each child then uses a felt marker to draw a face on a balloon, depicting one of the feelings as it relates to the divorce in their family. The children take turns sharing their balloons with the group. All the children describe how they experienced the feeling and how they behaved in connection with it. Different ideas for handling the feelings are exchanged. To conclude the exercise, several balloons (which again represent feelings) are crowded into a paper bag (representing a person) to demonstrate what happens when too many unexpressed emotions build up inside; a person becomes overloaded. If the feelings are talked about, then the bad feelings do not build up and there is more room for other feelings.

As the sessions progress, the therapist and the group help the children break down and analyze their divorce-related experiences. The children are guided to explore and talk about their individual situations. Emphasis is on identifying problem areas and generating problem-solving ideas within the group. This is accomplished by using role play and puppetry. The therapist provides the scenarios, which are based on problem areas that have already surfaced in the group. The children act out the scenes, discuss optional ways to handle the situations, then reenact the scenes employing alternate problem-solving ideas. Variations include the use of puppets, substitution of vignettes composed by the children, and enactment via pantomime.

The following sessions continue with more direct problem-solving. The therapist teaches the children new ways to cope with stressful situations in their families. Communication skills are introduced and practiced as the children are helped to recognize what aspects of their situations they can change and how to make the changes. For example, many children are distressed when parents continue to fight openly in front of them. The therapist helps the children understand that the argument is the parents' problem to handle, not theirs, and discusses options the children have when this happens, (such as telling the parents how it upsets them and asking them politely to go elsewhere, or leaving the situation themselves to get involved in a pleasurable activity out of earshot).

The authors employ a board game patterned after Richard Gardner's "Talking, Feeling, Doing Game" (1974) to provide a structure for this process. The game is played by each child rolling the dice and moving a marker on the board. The child selects a card corresponding to the colored space he or she lands on. The cards consist of questions developed by the therapist to elicit feelings, attitudes, and the practice of healthy adjustment skills. The game is a format only; there is no competition or winner. Each child is rewarded for his or her independent answers. The children are encouraged to discuss in detail any issues that arise. Playing the game generates high enthusiasm and maximum group interaction, and it is an excellent forum for teaching the children ways to effect favorable changes in unsatisfying situations.

The later group sessions are designed to help the children summarize and consolidate their group experience. Discussion and activities focus on helping the children accept those aspects of the divorce situation that they cannot change and work on the areas that they can change. The children also receive assistance in determining positive outcomes in what they most often perceive as negative situations. A technique used to address these concepts is a "good/bad" drawing exercise, where the therapist provides a statement for each child that reflects an area of particular concern for that child. The statement instructs the child to draw both a positive and a negative aspect of the given situation. For example, "Draw on half the paper something that would be good about your mother getting married again, and on the other half draw something that would be bad about it." After the drawings are completed, they are shared and discussed with the group. As the children continue to talk about their feelings and concerns, they not only recieve the therapeutic benefits of ventilation but also become aware of their increased abilities to communicate and negotiate change within their lives. The children also learn how to perceive things in new and different ways.

The final session integrates the essential concepts covered throughout the groups and addresses termination issues. The review process occurs in a game where the children select colored circles off a board, each containing a question or statement that pertains to material discussed in the sessions. The children take turns and are rewarded for their responses. The review has two benefits: (1) the children have the opportunity to consolidate their learning and demonstrate newly acquired skills; and (2) the therapist uses the exercise to determine how well the children have assimilated the major concepts and their abilities to implement the new learning.

How the children feel about the group's ending is extremely important, and appropriate termination time must be provided. The termination process allows each child to express feelings that often reflect how he or she is handling the "marriage termination." Therefore, constructive group closure may contribute to a successful resolution of some of the divorce-related issues. The children are encouraged to acknowledge ambivalent feelings about the group's ending and are asked to discuss the positive and negative aspects of their group experience. Finally, each child is asked to identify the most important thing he or she gained from participation in the sessions.

Conclusion

To date, seven group programs have been completed, involving a total of forty-one children. Reports from parents and children, coupled with therapist observations from within the groups, strongly support the presented group model as having a positive impact upon the participating children's postdivorce adjustment. Although researchers frequently question the reliability of self-report evaluations, the authors as practitioners believe that subjective reports warrant significant consideration when assessing the therapeutic value of a treatment program such as this. Even though much of the reported data are not statistically quantifiable, the fact that the parents and children found the experience to be personally beneficial is of paramount importance in exploratory work.

On written evaluation forms and through verbal feedback, many parents have reported specific behavioral changes in their children over the course of treatment. Most predominant were reports of marked reductions in such regressive reactions as tantrums, bedwetting, and excessive clinging. Conversely, significant improvements were noted in school performance and resumption of play activity with peers. It is reasonable to assume that reported reductions in depressive symptoms and apparent increases in self-esteem could be attributed in part to various components of the treatment model. Through greater awareness of divorce issues, the children are likely to experience less guilt and feel less responsible for their parents' separation. This may decrease their need to "cure" the problem and might consequently relieve some of the anxiety associated with these concerns. In addition, as parents increase their understanding of the child's feelings through participation in the parent groups, they are able to provide a better structure for managing the behavior problems.

It is important to note that several chidren displayed an increase in depressive symptoms after the group began. The delayed onset of depression may occur as a result of two things: (1) open group discussion may cut through previously maintained denial defenses, allowing the child to then feel his or her pain more acutely; or (2) situational changes that continue during postdivorce months may create new conflicts and losses for the child. For those children whose depressive symptoms surface late, termination at the end of the brief intervention model may be premature. In these situations, the children should be referred for additional therapy.

An important index of the program's value has been the parent's response. Without exception, parents report that their children have benefited from the group experience. Along with behavioral changes, parents report the most pervasive impact to be the improved communication between themselves and their children. Parents have attributed the improved communication to their child's heightened awareness of divorce issues, greater comfort with the subject of divorce, and new willingness to inquire about things he or she did not understand.

The children's own feelings about their treatment experience are also extremely important. The children's reactions to the group have been overwhelmingly positive. Attendance has been consistently high, and the children have shown sustained enthusiasm throughout the sessions. Comments from the children indicate that they have derived benefits from the experience that are consistent with the identified treatment goals. Many children have expressed great relief in discovering that other children have similar feelings about divorce, thus making them feel more "normal" and accepted. The children also have reported that learning new problem-solving methods has helped reduce their frustrations and feelings of powerlessness. Many children indicated they would like to participate in a continuation group if it were offered.

The therapists have observed several overt behavior changes within the group sessions. Several children showed a notable decline in disruptive, attention-getting behaviors as the groups progressed. Part of this might be attributed to their decreased anxiety about participation in the group. It also suggests that the children can become more comfortable with divorce-related issues, and that focused discussion of these issues seems to have a desensitizing effect. This, combined with the catharsis of mutual sharing, appears to help the children alleviate feelings of shame and self-doubt. Feeling better about themselves, the children have less need to act out in group-disrupting ways.

Regarding the parent sessions, most parents responded favorably to their group experience. They have expressed relief in realizing that their children's adjustment reactions represent common responses to postdivorce distress rather than faulty parenting. Parents have reported that the groups helped them understand their child's needs better, particularly the importance of providing an open atmosphere for the child to ask questions about on-going changes. Through increased discussion with their children, parents have been surprised to discover the misconceptions that the children had about the divorce. This knowledge has enabled parents to clarify inaccurate information, which subsequently eases the child's confusion and anxiety. The only recommendation from parents regarding their group has been to increase the number of parent sessions in the program.

In addition, several significant changes in parental attitudes have been observed by the therapists as the parent sessions progressed. Two changes have been most evident. First, many parents have become more accepting of the range of feelings expressed by their children, particularly anger. By understanding the child's anger, parents are able to be more tolerant of outbursts, thereby allowing them to help their child handle the feelings more constructively. Second, several parents have recognized that their own negative feelings toward their former spouse do not necessarily reflect the child's feelings about that parent. Accepting this has enabled some parents to stop using the child as a "pawn" for continued spousal conflict. These reports from parents have confirmed the importance of combining the parent group with child-focused treatment.

Although the data to validate this treatment model are not quantitative and is therefore primarily subjective, based on available subjective reports, the authors believe that the group program has had therapeutic results for both parents and children. It is recognized that in many respects this program is a pioneering effort that provides groundwork for future study where objective program evaluation can be incorporated. Given the increasing number of children who are victims of the rising divorce rate, there is a continuing need for practitioners to respond with innovative programs for helping these children. The ideas presented here represent such a plan and invite further attention from the social work profession.

References

Anthony, E. J. "Children at Risk from Divorce: A Review." In E. J. Anthony and C. Koupernik (eds.). *The Child in His Family: Children at Psychiatric Risk*, vol. 3. New York: John Wiley & Sons, 1974.

Benedek, R. S., and Benedek, E. P. "Postdivorce Visitation: A Child's Right." *Journal of the American Academy of Child Psychiatry*, 1977, 16, 256–71.

_____ "Children of Divorce: Can We Meet Their Needs?" *Journal of Social Issues*, 1979, 35, (4), 155–69.

Bernstein, N. R., and Robey, J. S. "The Detection and Management of Pediatric Difficulties Created by Divorce." *Pediatrics*, 1962, 45, 956.

Cantor, D. W. "School-Based Groups for Children of Divorce." *Journal of Divorce*, 1977, 1 (2), 183–87.

Cline, D. W., and Westman, J. C. "The Impact of Divorce on the Family." *Child Psychiatry and Human Development*, 1971, 2, 78–83.

Derdyn, A. P. "Divorce and Children: Clinical Interventions." *Psychiatric Annals*, 1980, 10 (4), 22;047.

Fulton, J. A. "Parental Reports of Children's Post-divorce Adjustment. *Journal of Social Issues*, 1979, 35, (4), 126–39.

Gardner, R. A. *Psychotherapy with Children of Divorce*. New York: Jason Aronson, 1976.

_____ *The Parents Book about Divorce*. New York: Bantam Books, 1977.

Hess, R. D., and Camara, K. A. "Post-divorce Family relationships as Mediating Factors in the Consequences of Divorce for Children."; *Journal of Social Issues*, 1979, 35, (4), 79–96.

Hetherington, E. M.; Cox, M.; and Cox, R. "Play and Social Interaction in Children Following Divorce." *Journal of Social Issues*, 1979, 35 (4), 26–49.

Hozman, T. L., and Froiland, D. J. "Families in Divorce: A Proposed Model for Counseling the Children." *Family Coordinator*, 1976, 25 (3), 271–75.

Kelly, J. B., and Wallerstein, J. S. "The Effects of Parental Divorce: Experiences of the Child in Early Latency." *American Journal of Orthopsychiatry*, 1976, 46 (1), 20–32.

Kubler-Ross, E. *On Death and Dying*. New York: MacMillan, 1969.

Kurdek, L. A., and Siesky, A. E. "An Interview Study of Parents' Perceptions of their Children's Reactions and Adjustments to Divorce." *Journal of Divorce*, 1979, 3 (1), 5–17.

McDermott, J. F. "Divorce and Its Psychiatric Sequalae in Children." *Archives of General Psychiatry*, 1970, 23, 421–27.

Wallerstein, J. S., and Kelly, J. B. "The Effects of Parental Divorce: Experiences of the Child in Later Latency." *American Journal of Orthopsychiatry*, 1976, 46 (2), 256–69.

———— "Divorce Counseling: A Community Service for Families in the Midst of Divorce." *American Journal of Orthopsychiatry*, 1977, *47*, 4–22.

———— "Children and Divorce: A Review." *Social Work*, 1979, *24* (6), 468–75.

———— *Surviving the Breakup*. New York: Basic Books, 1980.

Westman, J. C.; Cline, D. W.; Swift, W. J.; and Kramer, D. A. "Role of Child Psychiatry in Divorce." *Archives of General Psychiatry*, 1970, *23*, 416–20.

Wilkinson, G. S., and Bleck, R. T. "Children's Divorce Groups." *Elementary School Guidance and Counseling*, 1977, *11* (3), 205–12.

13

Social Group Work and Alcoholics Anonymous

F. J. Peirce

Marty and her husband, Ronnie, were married while he was serving in Vietnam. He is from a working-class family in an area called "Little Dixie," and she is from a well-to-do farm family in the Mekong Delta. In both cultures women are subordinated to the men in the family and typically devote their lives to caring for their husbands and children. Ronnie was discharged from the army for various medical reasons complicated by heavy use of drugs and alcohol. They have lived in a college town for several years, with both of them working and going to school intermittently. They have a nine-year-old son, Harrison. Ronnie drinks heavily, has been in and out of AA and alcohol-counseling programs, and sees himself as an alcoholic.

Marty has been to Alanon but found it too religious and serious. She wants to help Ronnie and has come to accept that he must do it for himself. She joined a group for spouses of alcoholics at the alcohol-treatment center in her community. The group was led by a social worker with a background in group work in mental health and similar programs. In the first meeting Marty talked of her pain and fear. Ronnie was beating her and told her that she could not leave him or she would lose her citizenship and be deported. Sex with him was a brutal rapelike activity, and Marty was growing increasingly anxious about the effect of this on Harrison.

As soon as Marty paused in her tale, the other five women in the group—there were no men in the group at that time—expressed deep concern, care, support, and outrage. Information, especially regarding her legal status, was offered. Two members offered bed and board for the times when Ronnie became violent. One reached out and held her as she described her situation. As this occurred, Marty began to appear more calm and even cheerful. Others spoke of similar experiences. The group leader used these experiences to open up first a discussion of the feelings of Marty and the others and then an exploration of the options available to Marty. This discussion continued through three sessions. Marty decided to leave Ronnie, go on welfare, find an apartment, and go back to school. The leader and group members helped her list, organize, and find these resources. Marty left the third session a cheerful, organized, goal-direct person.

Marty came to the fourth session late. She looked tired and appeared to have been crying. Everyone was concerned and asked her if she had moved. She had not. She had told Ronnie of her plans. He stormed out in a rage. He returned later much calmer and with their pastor and an alcohol counselor. They convinced Marty that Ronnie would begin drinking and require hospitalization again if she left him. She could not resist this and agreed to stay if Ronnie would not abuse her. He did not, but he continued to threaten her. She became depressed and angry with herself.

In the eighth session of the same group, Delta, a woman in her mid-fifties with much experience in Alanon, began the session by asking, "How does this group differ from our 'regular' Alanon or AA groups? I know it is different, it adds something, but what is different? Is one better than the other, should I be in both or just one? My husband says that I spend more time in meetings than I do with him. I try to explain, but it is hard, and he doesn't listen anyway." The worker reflected the question to the group and listened to a rather sophisticated, sensitive discussion of the issue Delta had raised. Among others, the group reached the following conclusions:

1. In both groups "you have to do it yourself, have to take care of yourself, 'cure' yourself; no one can do it for you."
2. In both groups "you can't be responsible for someone else's illness, behavior, or life."
3. The AA-Alanon groups are "more like a religion, a way of life with helpful rules, directions, guidelines. You have to believe if it's going to work. You have to give it up to God. It provides answers."
4. In the treatment group no answers are provided by the leader. He and the others help, but "the idea is that the best answer is the one you work out for yourself. It may not be the one everybody else thinks is best, but it will probably work best for you."
5. "Sometimes it feels like the Alanon members who have been around a while know what is going to happen before you do, or when it happens, they tell you all about it. They know what it's like, they have been there, but sometimes it's like a script and they know the end before you do."
6. "Sometimes it feels like he (the social worker) doesn't know what it is like to be an alcoholic or to live with one. It's not as easy as talking with someone who is an alcoholic or lives with one. But he really learns from us. He wants to know about me, about each of us. That sure helps me figure out what's happening to me."

The same social worker also served on the Board of Directors of an alcohol-treatment program. Board meetings usually were routine and brief. On one occasion alcohol research was being discussed. The social worker mentioned the Rand Report (Armor et al., 1976). Most other members, including all from AA, firmly and vigorously attacked the Rand studies. The social worker tried to suggest that the findings were simply suggestive and merited further study. It was pointed out that this would be the "wrong" kind of research. It was also clear that no one else had seen the report.

The excerpts above highlight some of the key issues in social work practice focused on alcoholism. This paper is a discussion of some of the major themes of the AA self-help perspective and of social work methodology with groups. Some of the apparent similarities and differences of the two approaches will be identified, followed by a discussion of issues and problems for social workers in their work in this field.

A number of assumptions undergird this paper:

1. AA and its related activities provide more effective help to alcoholics and their families than other approaches or programs. Whatever its true success rate, it is more effective than any other large-scale program.
2. There are identifiable populations of people with alcohol-related problems who are simply not helped by or amenable to help by AA programs.
3. Social workers and other mental-health professionals cannot and must not try to duplicate AA programs.
4. Social work services with groups, as well as with individuals and families, can effectively supplement and complement AA programs. The obverse is also true; social workers must continue to use AA as a vital community resource.
5. Social workers must continue to develop alternative services for those who cannot or will not participate in AA programs.

There are large areas of agreement and similarity in the AA perspective and that of social group workers. These include:

1. Both value the dignity and integrity of the individual.
2. Both believe that individuals can change.
3. Both believe that recognition of the problem is a prerequisite to change.
4. Both rely heavily on the use of the group as a supportive, challenging, and clarifying means of change for individuals.

Some major differences or issues include:

1. Social workers tend to be pessimistic about the likelihood of most alcoholics changing, even though they believe that all have the capacity to do so.
2. Many social workers believe that there are acceptable alternatives to abstinence as one of the major treatment goals for alcoholics.

3. AA promotes a set of values perceived by many social workers and other professionals as directive and dogmatic (Gartner and Reissman, 1977, pp. 25–26).
4. AA is perceived by many social workers as tending toward "blaming the victim (Gartner and Riessman, 1977, p. 26).
5. Social workers – group workers – see the group as a means to an end. The AA group is perceived as an end in itself. Social workers believe that membership in the group is transitory and that long-term or permanent membership in a helping group is a form of inappropriate dependence.
6. The AA perspective and that of most alcohol counselors relies heavily, if not exclusively, on the use of identification of the recovering alcoholic with the recovered alcoholic. Social workers capitalize on this process and also recognize the significant force in other treatment dynamics.

These and other differences result in very real problems. It is clear that social workers must take the initiative to begin the process of working out these differences. There is little evidence that AA and alcohol-counseling programs aggressively recruit social workers to staff programs. On the contrary, there appears to be real distrust of social workers and other professionals. Gartner and Riessman (1977) note:

> Implicit in the self-help thrust is a profound critique of professionalism. Traditional professional models . . . are seen as outmoded for modern needs, and the traditional relationship between professionals and consumers is not only inconsistent with the participatory ethos emerging out of the 1960s but also seems to be correlated with inefficient and ineffective service delivery, in large measure, because of the unwillingness and inability of professional organizations overly intellectualized orientation, excessive credentialism and limited reach in regard to various populations. (p. 12)

Clearly, recovered alcoholics as a group are not convinced that traditional mental-health and social-service programs are as effective as AA or the alcohol-counseling programs that identify with AA. The professional approach to the work appears to be overstructured, impersonal, and uninformed. King, Bissell, and O'Brien (1979) suggest that this results from the lack of formal education focused on alcoholism; the psychoanalytical approach of social workers, which leads to seeing alcohol abuse as a symptom; the expectation of social workers that the patient will be able to discuss the problem if asked the right questions; the possibility that some aspects of environmental manipulation can be counterproductive, and that social workers are easily drawn into the alcoholic's power struggle with the bottle.

It is not clear that all of these are valid or realistic issues. For example, fewer social workers are so easily tarred with the psychoanalytic brush. However, it is clear that these perceptions are real and must be confronted. There must be more formal and informal educational and training opportunities for students and practitioners motivated to work with and understand alcoholics. Greater emphasis should be given to the specific dynamics of alcohol and other forms of chemical dependency. Further, attention must be devoted to two major issues: dependence on the group and the controversy regarding abstinence.

Most literature focused on the use of the group as a form of professional treatment emphasizes the use of the group as a means to an end or a vehicle of change (Garvin, 1981; Konopka, 1983; Northen, 1969; Yalom, 1975). The helping group tends to be seen as one with specific goals and tasks and a limited existence. The group may take on many of the characteristics of a primary group, but the group is not an end in itself, and these qualities are seen as features that facilitate change. Some group features are also recognized as a potential danger in group work since the member can easily develop a debilitating, change-resistant dependence on the group that transmogrifies the basic purpose of the group. A major focus of professional group work is to use the group experience to help members find healthy and satisfying primary-group relationships outside the treatment group. Thus, a major operational objective of professional group work is to minimize dependence to the point that the treatment group is no longer needed by the individual.

The AA group, on the other hand, is built on the premise that recovery depends on continued group participation. For many, this participation may be peripheral and less meaningful. It appears, though, that for most, recovery requires significant dependence on the group. Even among social workers who are not psychoanalytical, this is often seen as substituting one obsession for another. Professionals tend to forget, however, that the new obsession is socially desirable and productive. Those who worry unduly about this dependence also tend to forget that for most life is a series of compromising, coping, and crutching that can lead to existential wholeness and even joy. Instead of "I'm OK, you're OK," one can claim the reality that "I'm not OK and you're not OK, but that's OK" (Kapp, 1980). Social group workers can then focus on the provision of short-term goal-focused groups that supplement and compliment the AA experience. Social workers need not compete; they can help.

The supplemental focus of social work services merits some discussion. There are apparently significant numbers of persons dependent on alcohol who cannot make effective use of AA or traditional alcohol-counseling programs. One large group is the unattached men and women who live on the fringe of society, on skid rows and in similar areas. This population is alienated from society and makes little use of either self-help or more traditional mental-health services. The most appropriate professional priority for this population is to focus first on basic survival needs. Programs focused on personal change appear to have little relevance for this population until and unless these needs are met.

Another population appropriate for social group work services are those who reject some of the norms and values of AA and other alcohol-counseling programs. These are individuals who cannot accept that "there is a power greater than any of us" and who cannot "give it up to God." They are often also those for whom abstinence is not an appropriate goal. Social workers and other mental-health professionals must help develop and staff effective programs for this group.

Abstinence is a major issue for many social workers practicing with alcoholics. King, Bissell, and O'Brien (1979) handle this by accepting that abstinence from alcohol is necessary to recovery. If the circular logic of AA is adapted—that an alcholic is one who can never drink again—this is acceptable. However, this would appear to classify unnecessarily many as alcoholics and also suggest that "problem drinkers" who do not return to controlled social drinking were never alcoholics in the first place. It would lead to the possibility of many "problem drinkers" receiving less attention because they are not seen as alcoholics. Also of importance in terms of intellectual honesty are the reports of the Rand Institute regarding treatment of alcoholism (Armor et al., 1976). These are a collection and a collation of outcome studies done throughout the country. As with collections of this sort, the usual set of methodological problems is present. The studies suggest and certainly do not prove that some alcoholics can return to controlled social drinking. As noted in the introduction, these studies have generated much controversy and heated argument. The minimal position of social workers in the face of the evidence, however, would be that further research is needed. Blumberg (1977) suggests that AA will continue to confront this issue and that,

> What may occur is a challenge to the total abstinence (ultraist) component of AA ideology by those who argue that it is possible to resume social drinking. . . . Can AA encompass the moderate as well as the ultraist position . . . without setting loose too many schismatic tendencies? (p. 2128)

Social workers should participate responsibly in this debate, should it occur, by respecting the values of AA while seeking improved and expanded services through change in programs. Other issues of significance to this discussion include transparence, the use of interpretation, and the leader's responsibility for group members.

Social work practitioners can probably best be described as ambivalent regarding the issue of social-worker openness and honesty. Traditionally, they have avoided transparency because of well-founded fears of the contaminating effects this has on transference and counter-transference relationships. It is probable that this position was held firmly because of professional insecurity, including the desire to be as much like "real" psychotherapists as possible. This has changed dramatically. In some respects the current period can be described as an era of "be yourself" and "anything goes as long as it is genuine." Still, there is recognition of the continuing problems with unqualified openness. Yalom (1975) notes that transference and counter-transference are still of important concern, even if not in the traditional analytical context. He further suggests that freedom and spontaneity in extreme form can result in a leadership role that is as narrow and restricted as the traditional blank screen and can also result in the provision of no leadership at all. Despite these concerns, practice is and should be more open and transparent than the traditional models. This does not include, however, the kind of openness that is common in many of the newer forms of group work. Social workers are disciplined professionals who use transparency as an additional dynamic in the helping process, but not as an end in itself or as an objective with intrinsic virtue and value.

While AA can be described as "primarily suppressive and inspirational" (Gartner and Riessman, 1977, pp. 25–26), a major force of its work is the development of frank and sometimes brutal openness in all participants. The professional stance, on the other hand, can and often is seen as aloof, holding distance, and even being cold. Two equally unfortunate responses are common in the face of these attitudes. Social workers may open up and "let it all hang out," or become even more "properly" professional, explaining in great and dull detail the most picayune and arcane details of the transference and counter-transference phenomena. Neither is helpful. Professionals must avoid defensiveness and be as open and transparent as is appropriate. They should be open about this balance. They can, for example, tell group members that openness and full disclosure by the social worker are not routinely helpful and that this will be emphasized when it appears that it will be helpful.

In another paper, the author (Peirce, 1980) has noted that a major objective and skill in social work practice is the identification and clarification of social reality and of its meaning and significance to participants. This takes place in the "here and now" context of the group. This focus strongly emphasizes the use of the current experience in group interpersonal processes as a means of recognizing, understanding, and dealing with social reality. Yalom (1975, pp. 105–68) refers to this as "activation and process illumination of the here and now" and suggests that this is done by thinking in the "here and now," relating the "here and now" to the group's task, moving the focus from the outside to the inside and encouraging responses from members of the group.

The here-and-now focus can be difficult for those who have experienced various AA programs. AA members do concentrate on living "one day at a time"; however, a major focus of AA meetings is discussion of one's past history and drinking and the effect of this on one's life and on others. The confessional quality of these meetings leads to an emphasis on history, which serves as a useful suppressive and directive dynamic. Discussions of current processes and feelings may be seen as avoidance and denial of the fact of alcoholism. Social workers will try to refocus such discussions on the reality of current group experience and use this process as a means of exploring new behavioral modes and coping processes. It must be remembered that this process is a tool and not an ultimate objective. The ultimate goal is to help members improve their lives outside the group.

Because process illumination emphasizes cognition and intellectual analysis, it may be perceived as incongruent with the spiritual features of AA. Social workers can accept that these spiritual features in the AA value system help clients add insight and greater self-acceptance. This is not easy, and is it not appropriate for many. It can be done and should be one of the major complementary features of social work service.

A major feature of AA is the twelfth step: the provision of help and the assumption of caring responsibility for other alcoholics. This includes both those who assume leadership roles and those who do not. AA members get personally involved in each other's lives. The practice of social group workers tends to run counter to this in one and possibly two ways. First, professional distance is maintained. The professional lives separate from group members and believes that it is therapeutically sound to do so. This distance does make it harder to understand clients and often convinces them that the professional has less insight into their situation. They may also see this behavior as less caring and concerned than that experienced in their other group experiences. Social workers also do not routinely encourage extragroup relationships among group members. This is seen as contaminating the helping process and adding dynamics that confound growth and change. As with other issues noted here, this position is professionally appropriate. This does not negate the value and utility of relationships within AA groups. Rather, the professional view must be seen as complementary and supplemental.

The purpose of this paper has been to explore the relationship of professional group social work with Alcoholics Anonymous, Alanon, Alateen, and similar self-help and alcohol-counseling programs. The major premise is that each perspective is of great value to persons suffering from the ravages of alcohol dependency and its associated problems. Social workers can work harmoniously with AA and related programs. This can be done with integrity so as to supplement and complement existing programs.

References

Armor, D. J., et al. *Alcoholism and Treatment.* Santa Monica: The Corporation, 1976.

Blumberg, L. "The Ideology of a Therapeutic Social Movement: Alcoholics Anonymous." *Journal of Studies on Alcohol, 38,* no. 3 (1977): 2128.

Garner, A., and F. Riessman. *Self-Help in the Human Services.* San Francisco: Josey-Bass, 1977.

Garvin, C. D. *Contemporary Group Work.* Englewood Cliffs: Prentice-Hall, 1981.

Kapp, S. Correpsondence, 1980.

King, B. L., et al. "Alcoholics Anonymous, Alcoholism Counseling and Social Work Treatment." *Health and Social Work, 4,* no. 4 (1979).

Konopka, G. *Social Group Work: A Helping Process.* Englewood Cliffs: Prentice-Hall, 1983.

Northen, H. *Social Work with Groups.* New York: Columbia University Press, 1969.

Peirce, F. J. "The Methodological Components of Social Work with Groups." Unpublished, 1980.

Yalom, I. D. *The Theory and Practice of Group Psychotherapy.* New York: Basic Books, 1975.

14

A Group Work Framework for Teaching Assertive Skills to the General Public

Sandra Stone Sundel and Martin Sundel

The availability of psychological knowledge through the mass media and the growth of the self-help movement, among other factors, have created a market for short-term classes that focus on self-improvement topics. Community-sponsored courses on topics such as assertiveness training, personal growth, overcoming shyness, stress management, coping with divorce, child management, weight control, and smoking clinics proliferate in communities around the country. In this consumer-oriented environment, individuals are increasingly self-diagnosing their deficits and seeking out courses that address their concerns and interests. These developments have provided opportunities to apply short-term behavioral group concepts (Sundel and Sundel, 1985a and 1985b) in programs sponsored by university continuing-education departments, mental-health clinics, social-service agencies, and women's groups.

Assertiveness-training groups have proven to be of particular interest to the public (Alberti and Emmons, 1974; Jakubowski and Lange, 1978; Sundel and Sundel, 1980). We have conducted assertiveness-training groups for such diverse clientele as women law students, women's political-caucus groups, realtors, health and human-service professionals, and administrative staff in federal and state agencies.

The focus of this paper is on assertiveness-training courses offered to the general public by the first author through a university-based continuing-education program. A description of this program will be presented, including objectives and activities for each session. The results of seven classes are discussed. Participants signed up for a five-week, ten-hour course described in the continuing-education brochure and paid forty-eight dollars. The course has attracted both men and women,

166

including college students, senior citizens, blue-collar workers, artists, business executives, middle managers, and clerical workers. Problems presented include interpersonal difficulties with family, friends, work associates and superiors, and self-assessed "low self-esteem." The typical size of these groups has been twelve members, although the range has been from ten to twenty-four. A description of the operation of these groups will be presented according to an assessment, planning, intervention, and evaluation format (Sundel and Sundel, 1980; 1982; 1985a).

The average person who signs up for this course is not interested in psychotherapy, but wants a stigma-free setting in which to solve a particular problem. The class setting is appealing because individual assistance is largely unavailable outside of therapy, and participants are attracted by the educational rather than the intense emotional experience encountered in individual or group psychotherapy.

The mental-health professional who is the leader uses group concepts such as cohesiveness to facilitate individual goal achievement. Too much emphasis on building relationships among group members, however, will divert the group from concentrating on assessing and modifying the problematic behaviors that brought them to the class.

Orientation and Assessment

All individuals who sign up for the course are accepted as group members. They usually present a specific problem area to work on. At the first meeting, the leader explains the purpose of the group and its operating procedures. Group members are told that all discussions within the group are confidential. Individuals are expected to participate in group activities and exercises. In addition to working on their own problems, they will participate in role-plays and discussions aimed at solving other members' problems. After class size is determined, the chairs are arranged into a horseshoe or circle so that the members and leader face one another.

To optimize the time available for problem-solving, the leader attempts to establish conditions conducive to participants discussing their difficulties in acting assertively. The leader assumes an active role in directing group activities during the first and second meetings. The leader models behaviors that are unfamiliar or difficult for individuals to perform. These behaviors include praising each other for discussing their problems in the group, for asking each other relevant questions, and for giving each other constructive comments and feedback.

The leader's role during the assessment phase is to (1) help each member identify an assertiveness problem to work on in the group, and (2) teach group members how to specify target behaviors and their controlling conditions (antecedents and consequences). The members are taught a behavioral-assessment format for analyzing their problems: Situation (antecedents), Target Action (response), and Results (positive and/or negative consequences).

Assessment procedures and activities for sessions one and two are described below.

Session 1

I. Introductions: The leader introduces herself first, thereby presenting a model for each group member to provide a similar introduction. Introductions are brief and include name, job status, and personal goals for the course. Typical areas of concern expressed by group members have included self-confidence in dealing with people, getting a job, disciplining children, and relationships with family members.

II. Goals: The leader then states the goals for the five two-hour sessions. "After this class, you should be able to (1) express yourself assertively in your target situation, (2) assert yourself with less anxiety, (3) increase the range of assertive responses you can make in your target situation, (4) evaluate your assertiveness in new situations, and (5) develop your own assertiveness program to deal with new situations."

III. Definition of terms: Assertiveness, underassertiveness, and overassertiveness are defined (Sundel and Sundel; 1980), with specific examples given by the leader and group members. The leader points out the relationship between behavior and its consequences. Underassertive behavior has certain negative consequences for the individual. Acting assertively may also produce negative consequences, however, when it results in a shift in reinforcement for someone else. The leader also points out the necessity of using one's own behavior as the focus of change, rather than attempt to change the behaviors of others.

IV. Obstacles to asserting oneself are addressed, giving specific examples: (1) lack of awareness of an assertive option, (2) anxiety, (3) belief that assertive expression of one's right is unimportant, (4) verbal deficit, and (5) behavioral deficit.

V. Discrimination exercise: The discrimination test from Lange and Jakubowski (1976, pp. 41–53) has been adapted and is used to help each group member correctly identify and discriminate assertive, underassertive, and overassertive responses.

This exercise gives the leader the opportunity to highlight assertive statements and phrases ("I would prefer . . ."; "I wouldn't feel comfortable . . ."; "I'd like to talk about changing this situation.") and to contrast these with underassertive ("I hope you don't mind." "Well, uh, I guess it's OK") and overassertive phrases ("You've got your nerve." "Are you crazy?"). It also allows the leader to correct misconceptions about the definitions of terms. Some observations made during this exercise include:

1. Many people have difficulty correctly identifying inappropriate responses in situations that make them personally uncomfortable. For example, an individual who has trouble ending phone conversations with friends is more likely to identify an underassertive response to that situation as assertive than someone who does not have difficulty ending phone conversations.
2. Group members sometimes recognize their own situations as similar to those in the exercise but are not satisfied with the responses given. The leader can then initiate a discussion of other assertive responses to those situations.
3. Group members are given the opportunity to discuss differences of opinion and standards of behavior that can help them to formulate their own assertive-response style.
4. Individuals frequently can identify assertive responses but state that they would not be comfortable performing them. The leader and group members point out the negative consequences for continuing to perform the nonassertive responses and help these individuals identify assertive behaviors they can perform.

VI. Homework assignment: Members are asked to keep a record of situations they want to handle differently; that is, in which they are either over- or underassertive when they want to be assertive. In addition, they were instructed to keep a list of assertive, underassertive, and overassertive behaviors they observed in others.

Session 2

I. Assessment: The STAR system for analyzing target behavior was developed to teach participants how to assess their target behaviors.

$S \rightarrow TA \rightarrow R$

S = Situation

TA = Target Action (the target, or problematic, behavior)

R = Results or consequences, which can be positive (R^+ or R^-) or negative (R^- or R^+).

This assessment method was introduced to the group as a way of identifying target behaviors and their controlling conditions. Group members were asked to give examples of situations from their homework assignments to be analyzed using this method. The leader points out the negative results of acting nonassertively in each situation. Positive results are also discussed. Negative results include missed opportunities for reinforcement, "feeling bad or incompetent," and somatic complaints. Positive results include avoidance of confrontation or conflict and sympathy from others.

Each individual was asked to select one problem for assessment. Most individuals selected interpersonal problems related to family members or work associates.

II. Behavioral reenactment (Sundel and Lawrence, 1974): This role-play assessment technique was used to help identify target actions that are the focus for change. The leader and group members observe reenactments of situations that involve nonassertive behaviors and point out problematic responses and their antecedents and consequences. Behavioral-change goals are formulated based on the assessment.

III. Developing assertive responses: Based on the information obtained in the behavioral reenactment, role-plays are arranged in which other group members demonstrate assertive responses to the same situation for the participant with the problem. He or she then attempts to perform the assertive responses observed in the role-plays. If group members are unable to demonstrate assertive responses, the group leader acts as a model, demonstrating appropriate behaviors.

When group members are reluctant to divulge personal target situations, several general examples are suggested by the leader as a way of eliciting responses from participants: (1) discussing an unsatisfactory performance evaluation with a superior; (2) saying no to unreasonable requests from family members or work associates; and (3) dealing with an elderly parent who is worried about you and phones several times a day. Participants provide the details that make these situations personally relevant.

IV. Homework assignment: Members are instructed to continue recording difficult situations and to use the STAR system to analyze their target situations. They are also instructed to write goals for change, specifying behaviors to increase and behaviors to decrease.

Planning and Intervention. The major tasks of the group leader during the third and fourth sessions are to help each member: (1) specify desired assertive responses, and (2) evaluate the benefits and risks of acting assertively. The group leader sets up role-plays, coaches individuals during the role-plays, and models assertive responses. The leader also demonstrates for group members how to model and coach each other and give feedback. Feedback is designed to reinforce assertive behaviors the individual has performed and provide suggestions for improving future role-play performances.

Group members are encouraged to become actively involved in planning and implementing each other's assertiveness-training programs by serving as: (1) assertive models, (2) actors role-playing the parts of significant others, such as co-workers or family members, (3) reinforcers, (4) feedback givers, and (5) evaluators. Participants are also involved in formulating behavioral assignments, or "homework," which includes specifying behaviors to be performed between meetings. Initially, the leader assumes major responsibility for giving behavioral assignments. As the members increase their problem-solving skills, however, they take a more active role in structuring their own assignments, as well as those of others. In order to make it more likely that they can perform their assignments, members rehearse the assertive responses in the group, getting feedback and suggestions for improvement.

Behavioral rehearsal is an essential component of an assertiveness-training program. Some group members are able to specify their desired assertive responses with minimal difficulty, and they can then proceed to rehearse these behaviors. Other members have more generalized problems of assertiveness, requiring a variety of behavioral rehearsals to give them opportunities to practice a range of assertive responses to many different situations.

Session 3

I. Discussion of homework assignment: Participants discuss their behavioral-change toals related to a target situation. They provide feedback to each other regarding the appropriateness of the goals and make suggestions for improvement. Group members who continue to have difficulty choosing a target situation are helped to zero in on problematic behaviors and their controlling conditions. Most individuals have completed the STAR assessment of their target situations. They should be encouraged to use these situations in the behavioral-rehearsal exercise described below.

II. Risks and benefits: The leader discusses the importance of weighing the risks and benefits of acting assertively (Sundel and Sundel, 1980). Examples are given of situations in which individuals have decided to refrain from behaving assertively because the risks outweighed the benefits. The leader helps group members evaluate risks and benefits in a realistic manner.

III. Behavioral-rehearsal exercise (adapted from Lange and Jakubowski, 1976, pp. 108–10): The class is divided into small groups of four or five individuals. These small groups position themselves around the room and stand in a circle to facilitate realistic role-plays. Members are told to re-create the conditions of their target situations as realistically as possible within the confines of the small group. One person is selected to describe a target situation. This individual rehearses an assertive response in that situation, using one or two other group members to play the parts of significant others. The group members provide feedback, first by commenting on what they liked about the person's performance, and then making suggestions for improvement. The scene is repeated, with the individual attempting to implement the group's suggestions. Feedback is again provided by the group after two or three verbal exchanges, and the person rehearses the same scene once more. Then the next person presents a situation, and the procedure continues until all members of the group have role-played their target situations.

For individuals who have selected inappropriate target situations or who have difficulty keeping up with the rest of the class, the leader can suggest several situations for them to use in the exercise: (1) asking a friend for a favor, (2) canceling travel reservations, (3) returning an item you don't want to a store.

IV. Homework assignment: Participants are instructed to try out assertive behaviors they have learned and to report the results.

Session 4

I. Discussion of homework assignment: Participants discuss the results of their attempts to act assertively in their natural environments.

II. Behavioral-rehearsal exercise: Using the exercise described in Session 3, participants continue to work on developing assertive responses to difficult situations.

III. Homework assignment: Participants are instructed to try out assertive behaviors they have learned and to report the results.

Evaluation. During the fifth and final session, the primary task of the group leader is to help each member evaluate goal progress and improvement in assertive skills. Group members use records of their behavioral assignments in evaluating their progress. Members also help each other evaluate changes in assertive performances they have observed in role-plays and interactions in the group. The leader identifies other resources that are available in the community for further work in assertiveness, as well as for other problems that were not addressed in the group.

Evaluation occurs on an ongoing basis in these groups because members comment on each other's performances in class from week to week. Members role-play different situations each week, giving the group many opportunities to provide evaluative feedback.

Session 5

I. The leader, together with the group, summarizes the concepts and techniques covered in the previous sessions.

II. Assertive phrases to remember: The following phrases have been found to be helpful to individuals trying to asssert themselves in various situations:

It is my policy . . .
I prefer . . .

This is unacceptable . . .
In the future, I would appreciate . . .
It has been my experience . . .
I feel strongly about this . . .
I understand what you're saying, but . . .
I would like . . .
I feel . . .

These phrases communicate "I" messages, rather than focusing on another person's behavior. Class members have reported that these phrases were helpful to them when asserting themselves in difficult situations.

III. Generalization: The leader presents each group member with a situation that requires an assertive response. They are each given one chance to respond assertively to the situation. Some examples include:

1. Would you loan me $150?
2. No, your order is not ready.
3. I don't believe you have a justifiable cause to question my evaluation of your performance.
4. Can I borrow your car?
5. Will you look after my pets while I'm on vacation?
6. What do you think I should do?

This exercise gives each class member the opportunity to demonstrate assertive responses to new situations. The exercise provides an additional evaluation tool by which the individual, leader, and other group members can evaluate the assertive performance of participants.

Course Evaluation

During a two-year period a total of 110 individuals in seven classes completed the course. Of this number 95 (86 per cent) were female and 15 (14 per cent) were male. The age range of participants was 10 to 56.

At the end of the course, participants were asked to complete a four-question evaluation form:

1. To what extent is your assertiveness problem solved?

    A. Completely or mostly solved   -   52.7%(58)
    B. Moderately solved   -   42.7%(47)
    C. Very little or not at all solved -   4.5%(5)

2. Were your expectations for the class met?

    Yes   -   77.3%(85)
    Somewhat   -   18.2%(20)
    No   -   4.5%(5)

3. Would you recommend this class to a friend?

Yes   -   95.5%(105)
No   -   4.5%(5)

4. What is the most important thing you have gotten out of this class? Typical answers to this question included the following comments:

"Awareness of my rights to express my opinions."
"How to say no without feeling guilty."
"Feeling better about myself when assertive; not worrying about people liking me."
"Dealing with others saying no to me."
"Think before speaking."
"More confident."

These findings indicate that most of the participants found the course to be helpful in solving their assertive problems and would recommend it to a friend. Comments offered by participants were consistent with their ratings.

Although significant improvements in assertiveness among participants were observed over the course, the maintenance of these changes and the extent to which they generalized to the individual's environment are unknown. An improvement in the course design would include a behavioral pretest and posttest, as well as a follow-up evaluation regarding maintenance of each individual's assertive performance. Although desirable from an evaluation standpoint, it would be impractical to carry out given the time and resource limitations.

Conclusion

Assertiveness continues to be a popular topic, and courses offered to the general public can help individuals improve interpersonal skills. Research on assertiveness in the general population has reported assertiveness to be inversely related to anxiety and depression (Sundel and Lobb, 1982). The course described here provides an inexpensive, socially acceptable way for individuals to improve communication skills without entering psychotherapy. The course also provides an opportunity to influence significant numbers of individuals who identify themselves as having certain interpersonal difficulties.

References

Alberti, R. E., and Emmons, M. L. *Your Perfect Right.* San Luis Obispo, Ca.: Impact Publishers, 1974.

Jakubowski, P., and Lange, A. J. *The Assertive Option: Your Rights and Responsibilities*. Champaign, Ill: Research Press, 1978.

Lange, A. J., and Jakubowski, P. *Responsible Assertive Behavior*. Champaign, Ill: Research Press, 1976.

Lawrence H., and Sundel, M. "Behavior Modification in Adult Groups." *Social Work*, 1972, *17* (2), 34–43.

Sundel, M., and Lawrence H. "Time-Limited Behavioral Group Treatment with Adults" *Michigan Mental Health Research Bulletin*, 1970, *4*, 37–40.

_____ "Behavioral Group Treatment with Adults in a Family Service Agency." In P. Glasser, R. Sarri, and R. Vinter (eds.), *Individual Change Through Small Groups*. New York: The Free Press, 1974.

_____ "A Systematic Approach to Treatment Planning in Time-Limited Behavioral Groups." *Journal of Behavior Therpay and Experimental Psychiatry*, 1977, *8*, 395–99.

Sundel, M., and Lobb, M. "Reinforcement Contingencies and Role Relationships in Assertiveness Within a General Population." *Psychological Reports*, 1982, *51*, 1007–15.

Sundel, M., and Sundel, S. *Behavioral Modification in the Human Services: A Systematic Introduction to Concepts and Applications*. 2d ed. Englewood Cliffs, N.J.: Prentice-Hall, 1982.

_____ "Behavior Modification in Groups: A Time-Limited Model for Assessment, Planning, Intervention, and Evaluation." In D. Upper and S. M. Ross, eds., *Handbook of Behavioral Group Therapy*. New York: Plenum Press, 1985, pp. 3–24.

_____ "Behavior Modification with Time-Limited Groups." In M. Sundel, P. Glasser, R. Sarri, and R. Vinter (eds.), *Individual Change Through Small Groups*, Second edition. New York: The Free Press, 1985b.

Sundel, S., and Sundel, M. *Be Assertive: A Practical Guide for Human Service Workers*. Beverly Hills, Calif.: Sage Publications, 1980.

Part V

The Minority Focus in Work with Groups

Part V includes four chapters that deal with methodologies and techniques specifically applicable to work with minority groups. Chapter 15, "Group Work in a Desegrated School," describes an experimental school-desegration program in Buffalo, New York. Ten to twelve member groups of fourth and fifth graders composed of equal numbers of black and white children were formed. This chapter uses a sociological perspective to analyze various phases of group development. Standardized tests are used to assess behavioral changes in group participants. The report provides a graphic description of both leader and group behaviors and critically evaluates the strengths and weaknesses of the program. The effects of group intervention on facilitating integration are discussed within each systematic step of group development. The focus is on selected variables crucial to a successful desegration plan in a black neighborhood where white suburban children were transported through busing.

Chapter 16, "Reaching Out to Alienated, Chronically Ill, Black, Elderly Minority Groups at Inner-City Primary Health-Care Centers," describes two group approaches in work with poverty-level, socially isolated, black, seriously ill, elderly clients. The techniques used are based on "activity-centered" and "problem-solving" interventions. Black elderly clients are characterized as alienated, powerless, self-neglected, and underutilizers of health care. The group approaches are designed to combat these alleged problems. Attention is given to group development, group processes, and worker functions. Member selection criteria are delineated, as well as a number of practical considerations that are crucial for the optimal achievement of the groups' primary purpose;that is, an improved relationship between the alienated, chronically ill, black elderly and primary health care.

177

Chapter 17, "A Model to Evaluate Group Work Practice with Ethnic Minorities," applies 2×2 matrix of group goals and group process to the analysis of intervention efficacy. The sample used in the study is a group of Native American female divorcees. The methodology emphasizes cultural variables and accordingly modifies both process and goals traditionally associated with therapeutic groups. The chapter stresses the need for concreteness as a relevant process and outcome-goal for working with such clients. Data are collected both from client ratings of group sessions and analysis of verbal contact transcribed from audiotapes. An eclectic treatment approach is used involving optimal member involvement. Based on tabulated results of the Practice Outcome Inventory, measurable outcome gains are reported. Actual descriptive examples of group sessions illustrate how this model may be generalized to work with other ethnic minorities.

Chapter 18, "Group Work with the Chicano Youth in the School Settings: The Multimodel Perspective," makes use of specific aspects of the three most prevalent models of group work practice as delineated by Papell and Rothman. The first part of the chapter explores sources of prejudice toward Chicano youth, particularly in the school system. Group work practice is seen as a way to deal with both the environmental systems that carry out what has been referred to as institutional racism as well as the individual effects of such systems on the members of the group. Thus, it is an attempt to combine the social-goals model with the remedial-rehabilitation model. This can be particularly effective with Mexican-American youth. The final section of the chapter demonstrates the theoretical discussion with an example of work with a Chicano teen-age boys' group, illustrating the integrated model throughout the discussion of worker roles and intervention strategies.

15

Group Work in a Desegregated School

Louis A. Colca

Currently, nearly every major metropolitan area is experiencing the impact created by the historic Supreme Court decision declaring segregation unconstitutional. Despite the fact that the court ruling has created a multitude of problems surrounding implementation for many school districts, desegregation of schools is in fact taking place. The population that has been most vulnerable to the desegregation order are the students who are involved on a daily basis. They are being exposed to new experiences under less than ideal circumstances.

A review of the literature on school desegregation indicates that the mixing of black and white children does not necessarily reduce racial prejudices or increase positive interaction. Conversely, a considerable number of studies indicate that increased interaction may in fact increase racial stereotypes and tensions (Pettigrew, 1971).

The purpose of this paper is to relate the experiences of one program that was implemented on an experimental basis at a desegregated school in Buffalo, New York. The paper will report on the experience of using a small-group-process approach to facilitate integration. The focus is on the various factors and issues that are significant, how the problems were resolved, and what we have learned from the experimental program.

The Setting

Buffalo, like most metropolitan cities, has a history of feeble attempts at token desegration. However, as a result of an NAACP suit in 1976, the Buffalo Board of Education was put under a federal court order to develop and implement a comprehensive desegregaton plan for city schools. As a result, a voluntary citywide Magnet School Program was initiated in 1977. It involved an open enrollment and bussing service to eight elementary and high schools offering a variety of specialized alternative-

179

educational programs. Students were accepted on the basis of achieving a 50/50 black/white ratio in these schools.

The group project to be discussed in this paper was implemented in one of these magnet schools. The school had been an all-black, lower-income neighborhood school. White students are bussed to the school, and it presently has a 60/40 black/white ratio. The prekindergarten through third grades are substantially more racially balanced than grades four through eight.

Since there are no data available on the students' racial attitudes or behavior before desegregation, we cannot make any empirically based statements about the effect of desegregation on the students at this school. However, based on personal experience as a parent of children in the school and from personally working in the school, we can give a subjectively formulated profile of the racial situation existing in the school after desegregation. Most of our observations were substantiated by the pretest results of our study and feedback from the teachers.

The smoothness of the desegregation process has been impressive, with few overt signs of racial tension. The principal and teachers do not tolerate negative racial remarks or even references to a pupil's race. All the equality cliches are frequently voiced by the school staff. Any discussion of race is immediately squelched, except when it is part of the curriculum of multiculturalism.

However, a clear distinction between the "bus kids" (white) and the "neighborhood kids" (black) has always been apparent. Racial cleavage is notable whenever students interact informally, and it seems progressively more pronounced in each higher grade level. The cafeteria seating pattern is a strong indicator of the degree of racial cleavage at the school. The higher the grade level, the less often black and white students are seen sitting next to each other or interacting on an informal basis. The students seemed to have developed a certain sophistication in realizing what is acceptable and not acceptable to say within earshot of adults. It was common to hear children quoting the equality cliches, denying prejudices and asserting the unimportance of a person's skin color. Yet the behavioral evidences of racial cleavages and mistrust were very evident on the buses, in the cafeteria, or in other situations where adults were not controlling the situation. It is also apparent that cross-racial friendships rarely continue outside of school hours and are usually not encouraged by parents. At parent meetings the subtle hostility and mutual distrust became apparent and began to emerge between black and white parents.

Program Design

The program was developed and implemented by the author and a faculty member from the Social Work Program at the State University

College of New York at Buffalo. It was initiated as an experimental project used in conjunction with the field-studies program for undergraduate social work students. The program was not funded and resources were extremely scarce.

One fourth-grade and one fifth-grade class were chosen as the target population, since the desegregation literature indicates that racial tension and social cleavage tend to become more pronounced at this age (St. John, 1975, pp. 68–71). One class of each grade was randomly selected as the experimental group and one as the control group. Two undergraduate social work students were trained in the skills of group dynamics and were selected to co-lead four small (ten to twelve students) racially balanced groups.

The groups met for sixteen weeks, one hour per week, during school hours. A three-phase program was developed to provide a nonthreatening forum in which students could explore and communicate their positive and negative feelings regarding various racial issues. The first phase included establishing a group purpose and giving students a sense of themselves as a part of the larger historical process of desegregation. Several nonthreatening exercises were used to develop a trusting atmosphere. Films and filmstrips were also used to stimulate discussion of racial differences, similarities, and sources of conflict. The films enabled students to identify and discuss issues without exposing too much personal material too quickly.

Phase II employed exercises that gave students an opportunity to explore their feelings and concerns regarding attending a desegregated school. All of the exercises contained an element of fun so that students would be more likely to become involved. A typical exercise was "Hot Seat," which they enjoyed and which was productive in facilitating discussion of their feelings about racial issues. Students were able to support and confront one another to obtain a better understanding and appreciation of each other.

In Phase III role-play incidents were developed whereby students would have the opportunity to experience different racial situations. The videotaping of the dramas enabled members to explore and discuss some important concerns and issues. The use of role-play situations removed many of the barriers that students normally have regarding talking about sensitive issues and taboo subjects.

Group Dynamics and Group Work Skill

Applying basic principles of small-group processes and group work skills is just as crucial and relevant in working with groups of children as it is with the most sophisticated adults. The next section outlines how basic group work principles were applied to planning and implementing children's groups. It also highlights the special factors that were unique to working with children.

Group Size

The group dynamics and group work literature is rich with documentation on how the number of group members and the group composition need to be determined by the purpose of the group and the nature of the interaction desired. Klein states:

> The smaller the group the more it demands involvement and the greater the potential for intimacy. The smaller the group the greater are pressures, the easier is the access to the worker and also the greater is the flexibility in modifying goals.

> Larger groups allow greater anonymity and hence a person can hide, withdraw or get lost in the group. The larger the group is, the less members know each other and the less the worker can know them. (Klein, 1972, p. 65)

Our stated purpose for the group was to increase communication and improve interracial relations. Based on this, we divided the students into racially balanced groups of ten to twelve students. We expected this size to be ideal in maximizing the potential for member participation. The groups wold be small enough to allow for intimacy and a high degree of interaction, while at the same time they would be large enough to allow some degree of anonymity and thus avoid a highly threatening situation.

The group size proved to be ideal in some respects and problematic in others. The groups were small enough that participants felt free to express themselves openly, but they were secure and anonymous enough to withhold when they wanted to without undue pressure. There was also a sufficiently large number to provide diversity and a lively sharing of ideas.

A disadvantage occurred when all twelve members were present; control sometimes became an issue. This was especially true with the fourth-graders, who tended to have a shorter attention span and were more likely to engage in disruptive behavior than the fifth-graders. At the other extreme, several students had a high absentee record and never became fully assimilated into the group. At a few group sessions several members were absent or were unable to attend because they were involved in a special school activity, leaving the group smaller than ideal. However, overall we feel that the decision on size was sound, but more planning needed to be done to deal with the absenteeism, conflicting school activities, and the issues of control.

Space

The effect of the physical environment of the meeting place cannot be understated. Klein states:

Space is a variable to be considered and used. If the room is too small it causes jostling and tempers become aroused. Crowding produces anxiety when closeness is an issue; it enforces body contact which can exacerbate fear and anger; it can cause withdrawal and also acting out. If the room is too large it encourages running, social distance fragmentation, and wool-gathering. If the room contains interesting equipment such as laboratory apparatus, sewing machines, typewriters, and similar distractions, these seduce the members to touch and play with these objects. (Klein, 1972, p. 65)

Unfortunately, we were not in a position to select an ideal meeting place. As in most school settings, the space available to us was limited and not well suited for running discussion groups. The room usually assigned to us was much too large, had too few chairs, and was adjacent to the noisy cafeteria. Since the room was used by other personnel for various activities, it was sometimes unavailable or being used as a storeroom for equipment or materials, which were inevitable distractions for curious group members.

Two group work skills became crucial in overcoming these obstacles. One involved developing a positive working relationship with those on whom we were dependent for acquiring space. In our situation it was the assistant principal and the maintenance man. Because of the group leaders' abilities to elicit their interest and understanding of our needs, many obstacles were either alleviated or lessened as they arose. Continual reinforcement and renewal of group purpose also became an important skill in overcoming these obstacles. It was clear that at the beginning, when the leaders were relatively weak in clarifying purpose, the problems around space seemed insurmountable. As this skill became stronger, the problems with the available room could be confronted and resolved. For example, in the tenth week, when we entered the meeting room, we found it half-filled with several thousand dollars' worth of candy from a school candy sale. We began the meeting by discussing the purpose of that week's meeting and raised the potential problems of the candy. Not one of the children in any of the four gruops touched any of the boxes of candy, which could have easily jeopardized the group session and our relationship with the school.

Group Structure

In planning the group activities and exercises we did not distinguish between the four groups. We came to realize, however, that the fourth-grade students needed greater structure, a faster pace, and more concrete exercises. Several skills were important at this point. Tuning into the students' immediate needs and interests without losing the purpose of the group was one successful technique. Another crucial skill was being flexible and spontaneous enough to change gears midway in a session. It was often necessary either to change the rules of an exercise or change the activity altogether when it was not productive. At other times, the group leaders chose to allow the group to go off on an unplanned tangent when it was deemed appropriate and of value to the group purpose.

Co-Leaders

The original plan was for the two undergraduate social work students to co-lead the groups. In retrospect, this was an unrealistic expectation despite their preparatory training in both group work and in co-leadership. One major obstacle was their opposing natural styles of group leadership. One tended to be authoritarian, the other democratic. Although they were able to compromise in working out the weekly planning, it was difficult for them to work together spontaneously in the group meetings. Being students and thus still insecure about their professional identity and strengths and weaknesses, they were reluctant to cut in or change direction or make suggestions that were not already agreed upon. The unhealthy rivalry and differences in style were easily perceived and played on by the children. An enormous amount of energy was expended by the supervisor and social work students to improve the communication between the student workers and help them to co-lead the groups more effectively.

It was decided after several sessions that the two supervisors would each co-lead two groups with the students. This had the advantages of on-the-spot modeling and provided a structure for feedback. On the other hand, the students were self-conscious and reluctant to assert their own leadership on par with their supervisor. These disadvantages required a great deal of pre- and postsession communication between the supervisors and the student leaders. Although the student/student and the supervisor/student co-leadership models present some unique problems, many of these potential obstacles to effective co-leadership are also present with experienced group leaders and need to be constantly addressed.

Beginning Phase

The major role of the group leader during the beginning phase of any group is to help clarify the group purpose, group goals, and the expected role of the leaders and group members (Schwartz, 1971). In retrospect, we realize that the two undergraduate social work students who co-led the beginning sessions were not adequately prepared for this phase. They were initially hesitant to be direct about the purpose. For example, they avoided any reference to students being of different races. Instead, they tended to talk in generalities, which left the group purpose vague. In setting down role expectations, they described only what they were not ("We're not teachers") and what they did not expect ("You don't need to behave like you do in the classroom"). This left the students confused and opened the door for a lot of testing behavior in the first two sessions.

The student group leaders were made more aware and given additional training in this area. Then they were able to clarify the purpose and the role expectations and developed a contract with the group members. At this point, there was a drastic turnabout and the sessions became focused and goal-directed.

We found that the fifth-grade groups were better able to maintain their sense of purpose and were self-motivated to pursue it throughout the life of the group. Because the younger age group had a shorter attention span and needed more work to stimulate them, the group purpose became obscured more often. One important skill in dealing with this issue was attempting to be more creative in developing exercises that would hold their interests longer. A second strategy was to involve them more in the planning of group sessions. The third was to make a "demand for work."

Demand for Work

Shulman recognizes that part of the client or group, "representing their strength, will move towards understanding and growth. The other part of the client or group, representing the resistance, will pull back from what is perceived as a difficult process" (Shulman, 1979, pp. 65–71). This process of pulling back surfaced periodically. It sometimes manifested itself in disruptive behavior that distracted the group from its work. The "entertain me" syndrome was also a means of expressing it. After viewing a ten-minute film they might ask to see it again rather than discuss the implications of the film. At these times the group leaders needed to employ the demand for work skills of holding to focus, challenging the illusion of work, and checking for underlying ambivalence (Shulman, 1979, pp. 65–71).

The use of these skills was sometimes effective and sometimes not. When they were not successful, it could usually be traced to a failure to tune into the group's need for a change of pace. In working with children it is especially helpful to have a large repertoire of activities to draw from.

Group Competition

One rather surprising development in the group was the intergroup competitiveness and jealouses. For example, one group would boast to another that they were doing better exercises. One group began to feel that the group leaders favored the other group. The leaders slowly became aware of this through subtle remarks made by students. It reached a critical point when there was an angry outburst by one student, after one of the leaders announced that he would be out of town and would miss the following week's session with that group. The leaders were able to use this incident to help the students verbalize their feelings and competitive resentment. When appropriate opportunities arose, the group leaders were prepared to process this issue with the other groups. The group competition we observed was a predictable occurrence, which the group leaders should have expected and been prepared for. As a "good bond" or "we feeling" develops and they begin to see themselves as a group, it is also natural that they will begin comparing themselves with other groups. The leaders need to be tuned into the side-effects of group cohesiveness so that they can effectively address the confronting issues.

Outcomes

The evaluation component and our observations both indicated that the program was successful in several areas. The evaluation component, which consisted of the Semantic Differential (Osgood, Suci, and Tannenbaum, 1957), a Modified Social Distance Scale (Moreland, 1976, pp. 21–25), and the Ohio Social Acceptance Scale (Raths and Schweichart, 1946, pp. 85–90), used a pretest/posttest experimental design. Each of the measures indicated a significant positive change in at least one area for the experimental groups. The Semantic Differential shows that the control groups demonstrated slightly more negative stereotypic thinking, while the experimental group was significantly less negative toward members of the other race. On the Modified Bogardis Social Distance Scale, the control group showed a slight tendency toward greater distance, while the experimental group showed significantly less social distance. The results from the Ohio Social Acceptance were mixed. White students in the experimental groups became more accepting of black students of the same sex. The change did not take place across sexual gender or for black students toward white students.

Unfortunately, the outcomes of the Cafeteria Seating Pattern (Schofield and Sagar, 1976) did not corroborate the outcomes of the attitudinal tests. The major disappointment was that the program did not have any effect on the racial cleavage in the Cafeteria Seating Patterns. Differences occurred across grade level rather than between the experimental and control groups. The fifth-grade classes by the end of the school year were less likely to sit next to a classmate of a different race, whereas the fourth-graders showed no significant differences between the pretests and posttests. This would indicate that the project's impact was not strong enough to affect the age-related tendency toward racial cleavage, which begins at the fifth grade.

The observations of the group leaders and the school personnel indicated that the program had made some inroads in improving the racial climate in the school. The most impressive area has been in the area of verbal communication. The majority of children in all four groups became more honest in expressing their own feelings and more comfortable in confronting one another on racial issues. This was especially true of the two fifth-grade groups. The children looked forward to the group, and on several occasions it became a meeting ground where they were able to discuss racial issues that occurred on their bus or in their class. An excellent example occurre done week when one of the more popular black children in the group had been ostracized by the rest of the children in the class because he wanted the part of a white person in a class play. This issue surfaced in the group and following a group discussion increased understanding, and a lessening of the tension was observed.

A second example was when one of the black children had invited a white child to a family affair. The white child had agreed to attend but did not show up. The group explored the feelings of the white youth being the only white person at a party and the feelings of his friend who was disappointed by his friend's absence. These two excerpts are examples of the kinds of interchanges that occurred and appear to increase students' awareness and understanding of each other and some of the obstacles hindering the positive interaction between blacks and whites.

Considering how resistant and afraid the group members were at the beginning of the program even to refer to race, this opening up of communications was indeed a giant step toward alleviating some racial tension at school.

Other indicators of the effectiveness of the project has been the change in attitude toward the program from the principal, teachers, and aides. As progress with the children was made, the school staff began to demonstrate their active support for the program by making sacrifices to provide us with more adequate space, equipment, and supplies. The teachers and aides demonstrated their acceptance of the project by their willingness to meet with group leaders and exchange information critical to both the group and the classroom situation. Conversely, these meetings were extremely important in enlisting the support of the school staff in developing a team atmosphere. Another measure of acceptance of the project was that one of the teachers proceeded to refer favorably to the group as "Sociology 101."

Program Modification

The consensus among those involved in the project was that the program was successful in increasing students' awareness of racial issues and in reinforcing the positive views that emanated from the desegration experience in the two classrooms. However, some important learning experiences took place for the author, and some definite modifications would be needed if similar programs were conducted with this target group in the future.

1. The author was unrealistic regarding the time that would be necessary to develop, implement, and supervise a new program. The utilization of students who are inexperienced as group leaders is an excellent learning experience for the students, but it requires the supervisor to commit a great deal of time to support, supervise, and model the group work skills needed for them to be successful. This is an important factor that must be taken into consideration before embarking on an experimental project without funding or support.
2. The mismatching of the co-leaders adversely affected the initial progress of the students in developing their group work skills. The author was too concerned with having racially balanced group leaders and neglected personality and leadership styles, which were far more important.
3. More structured contact with parents and school officials needs to take place to develop complementary programs that would build on the gains of the groups. One example is engaging parents, teachers, and students in the development of recreational, political, educational, and/or community development projects that might emerge as common interest areas. This would also give program ownership to the teachers and parents and improve the possibility of the program's continuation. Unfortunately, our meetings with teachers and aides were often rushed. They would have been more fruitful if we had put in additional time and energy. Our contacts with parents were rare.
4. A referral network needs to be developed for students who demonstrate the need for specialized individual attention to be linked to the appropriate services. During our work with the groups, some children were identified as needing specialized services, but since the group program was not a part of the school system there were obstacles to referring them for needed services. More attention by program staff in being recognized by school personnel as an integral part of a child's educational experience is an important factor that needs to be built into the program.

Conclusion

Schools are complex institutions that mirror many of the problems we face as a society. Prejudice, discrimination, racial cleavage, and racial tensions are a few examples of the societal problems that are also occur in the schools. Schools and school social workers need to be active and innovative in addressing these issues. The inclusion of groups in an elementary school represents a potentially effective interventive strategy. It is critical for the social worker to be knowledgeable in group dynamics and skilled in the group work process and systems interventions.

References

Klein, Alan. *Effective Group Work: an Introduction to Principle and Method.* New York: Associated Press, 1972, pp. 65, 178–79.

Moreland, J. Kenneth. "Racial Attitudes and Racial Balance in Public Schools." National Institute of Education Grant # NIE–G–76–0040, Randolph-Macon Women's College, Lynchburg, Virginia. October 1976, pp. 21–25.

Osgood, Charles; Suci, George; and Tannenbaum, Percy H. *The Measurement of Meaning.* Urbana: University of Illinois Press, 1957.

Pettigrew, Thomas. *Racially Separate or Together?* New York: McGraw-Hill, 1971.

Raths, Louis, E., and Schweichart, L. F. "Social Acceptance Within Inter-Racial School Groups." *Educational Research Bulletin,* 1946, *25,* 85–90.

Shoefield, Janet W., and Sagar, Andrew. "Inter-Racial Interaction in a New Magnet Desegrated School." Paper presented at 84th Annual Convention of American Psychological Association. Washington, D.C., September, 1976.

Schwartz, William. "Groups in Social Work Practice." In William Schwartz and Serapio Zalba, *The Practice of Group Work.* New York: Columbia University Press, 1971, p. 15.

Shulman, Lawrence. *The Skills of Helping: Individuals and Groups.* Itasca, Ill.: F.E. Peacock Publishers, 1979, pp. 65–71.

St. John, Nancy. *School Desegration Outcomes for Children.* New York: John Wiley and Sons, 1975, pp. 68–71.

16

Reaching Out to Alienated, Chronically Ill, Black Elderly Through Groups at Inner-City Primary Health-Care Centers

Hisasi Hirayama and Hugh Vaughn

Being "old" in this fast-changing, youth-oriented society is by no means easy, but the degree of difficulty seems to increase if the aged person is poor, ill, or a member of a racial minority. McCaslin and Calver (1975) once described the fate of racial-minority elderly as being in "double-jeopardy"; being old in this society is one "jeopardy" and being a minority in life is another. They proposed that ethnic consideration should be included in the design and delivery of health services to the elderly at two different levels: (1) preferential considerations of minority elderly in response to their double-jeopardy situation; and (2) the need for differential considerations of the various ethnic groups being served.

The poor and ill black elderly require special help in dealing with both the managing tasks of health-care problems and the particular struggle in day-to-day functioning. They also need, just as any other older person, enriched opportunities for socialization and the expression of feelings and thoughts because the emotional overlay of life problems can further deter their effective coping and adaptation. Yet, health and social services available to these black elderly are still limited. The opportunity for receiving adequate services is limited because existing programs are usually not geared to their special needs, particularly those programs for the chronically ill black elderly who reside in inner-city areas.

This paper describes our efforts and experience in developing a group program responsive to the needs of the chronically ill black elderly at an inner-city primary health-care center in Memphis, Tennessee. This program has been a part of the five-year training grant awarded to the

190

University of Tennessee School of Social Work by the National Institute of Mental Health in order to train social work students to work on mental-health problems of the chronically ill elderly at primary health-care centers.

The Setting

The Cawthon Primary Health Center is one of six primary health centers operated by the Memphis–Shelby County Health Department in Memphis. Situated in a predominantly black community, the center provides a variety of health and medical services to a large number of black elderly who suffer from a variety of chronic health problems, including diabetes, heart disease, hypertension, and strokes.

The primary health center, being a public health agency, with its historical roots in preventive care, places heavy emphasis on prevention of illnesses, health maintenance, and the promotion of health. A staff of nurse-practitioners, rather than physicians, assumes major treatment and educational responsibilities, while the physicians provide consultation and support to nonmedical staff. The majority of the elderly patients known to the center not only have chronic illnesses but also are experiencing severe social and economic deprivations.

The following case excerpt perhaps illustrates a typical health and life problem of chronically ill elderly patients who were referred to the social worker by a nurse-practitioner:

This case involves two elderly sisters, Ms. X and Ms. Y. Ms X is sixty-seven years old, blind, senile, and severely diabetic. She looks much older than her chronological age. Ms. Y is sixty-three years old and solely responsible for Ms. X's care. The nurse felt that Ms. X was not receiving the care that her condition requires, which includes daily bathing, daily urine testing, and daily insulin injections. The nurse-practitioner's particular concern was Ms. X's cleanliness. Ms. Y was involuntarily referred to "discuss it with the social worker." Ms. Y recognizes her sister's medical needs, but her sister presents her with much resistance in this area. Ms. X has been blind for only a few years and has not adjusted to it. The blindness occurred after she became senile (the result of a stroke); therefore, her capacity for adjustment may be limited, but she refuses to make even limited adjustments such as using a cane. She is uncooperative about bathing and frequently refuses to allow her sister to take a urine sample. However, she does allow the daily injection.

The problem is further complicated by the fact that Ms. Y is in very poor health herself. She has a heart condition, advanced diabetes, and arthritis. She seems mentally alert but depressed. She is angry with her sister and ashamed of her, specifically when she becomes irrational in public. She is also highly resentful of the confinement that her sister's condition imposes upon her. She has had exclusive responsibility for her sister's care for seven years, with no relief. She recognizes that she must have periodic relief from this responsibility in order to maintain her present state of physical and mental health. The clients are from a lower-class, rural black family of fourteen children. Six siblings are living, but only one brother lives in the Memphis area. All of their siblings are older and have serious health problems.

The clients in the case require a wide range of services, from rehabilitative and psychiatric services for Ms. X to homemaker and home health services and ego-supportive casework and/or group work for both Ms. X and Ms. Y. Some relief from the care of Ms. X is essential for Ms. Y in order to maintain her present state of physical and mental health. However, in reality, not all these needed services are readily available for the clients. Speaking about mental-health services alone, despite the greater needs, all the evidence shows the chronically ill black elderly receive little service from the existing mental-health centers. A plethora of reasons have been given as to why the black elderly have been underserved by the existing mental-health facilities. For example, Shader and Tracy (1973) argue that: (1) few black elderly seek and are referred for aid to mental-health centers because they often seek help through somatic channels in medical clinics; (2) the black elderly have a basic negative attitude toward mental-health clinics and hospitals because of fear, lack of information, and social stigma; (3) the black elderly in general define mental illness differently than white elderly, so such illnesses as senile dementia are more readily accepted as part of aging rather than as a pathological condition.

The root of alienation, powerlessness, and underutilization of health services by the black elderly in the South lies in the experience of racial discrimination and oppression that they have been subjected to and endured with throughout their lives. Unlike more assertive and socially conscious younger generations of blacks, most elderly blacks known to the primary health center have never learned to assert their rights. Their distinctive behavior appears to be that of compliance, passivity, and submissiveness in facing the professional personnel at the center or at other organizations.

One student recorded his encounter with a sixty-six-year-old man:

> In the beginning stages of work together, the client assumed a passive, compliant attitude. A recurring statement was, "I always do what the Man says." By the term "Man," he was referring to those persons whom he perceived to be in a position of authority. These persons were usually Caucasians. In this case he was referring to the physician and myself. The type of response seems to occur more frequently in older clients who have suffered various forms of oppression because of their race. He had learned at an early age that more aggressive techniques for manipulating his environment, such as competition, did not work well for those of his race. The client's sense of powerlessness had a basis in reality.

One inevitable consequence of the oppression is that the black elderly have learned experientially that they must not depend too greatly on social- and health-service agencies to meet their needs. They have fear that their concerns would not be heard and, if heard, not responded to appropriately. Thus, many black elderly have developed an inherent distrust in health and welfare systems, and they have learned to expect to live with minimal organizational support.

The health-care professionals by and large are white, with middle-class value orientations. They have been socialized into a certain life-style that is significantly different from that of the life-style of the poor and undereducated chronically ill black elderly. They have developed the professional attitudes with certain established methods and procedures of treating patients.

Communication becomes a barrier to the relationship between the elderly and professionals, not to mention other external factors as travel to or waiting at the center, which further deter effective utilization of health services by the elderly. Thus, in short, alienation, powerlessness, self-neglect, although mostly unintentional, and underutilization of health services are some of the most significant social and behavioral characteristics of this population.

Effective management of any chronic illness requires that an elderly person have good self-help and self-care knowledge and skills. Any major long-term health problems such as hypertension and diabetes requires constant self-monitoring. It also requires help from sympathetic and understanding health-care professionals who emphasize health maintenance and health education rather than treatment of acute illnesses. Reaching out to elderly patients poses a major challenge to social workers who assume responsibilities of providing health-social services to this "at high risk" population in the primary health center.

In the spring of 1979 and 1980, we developed two group approaches at the primary health center as a means of reaching out to the alienated black elderly, and those groups were carried out by first-year social-work graduate students. One such approach was an "activity-centered" group, which focused on the development of social relational skills of the participants related to their abilities to deal with people, bureaucratic organizations, and linking themselves with community resources. Another was a "problem-solving" group, which focused on the tasks of increasing participants' knowledge and skill for problem-solving of health care and for effective coping in their daily functioning. In both approaches the organizing theme was aiding the elderly to establish or restore control over their lives and/or to gain power over their powerlessness as much as they were capable of achieving. Both approaches were designed to be a group experience that would rely heavily on activity as a vehicle of communication to emphasize mutual aid, problem-solving, and encourage the sharing of feelings and thoughts concerning common tasks.

The focus in this paper is on the design for formation of such group programs. However they were planned, started out, and carried out, the critical issue in each stage of group development in view of group formation, interaction, and functions of the group worker, as well as issues in the relationship between black elderly and white group worker, will be examined. It is hoped that it will provide a method of working with this specific population, with a model of group work that can be more widely used at primary health centers, as well as at other health-care facilities.

Group Formation

William Schwartz (1971) offers a model that would bring together the need of the elderly to use the health-care system and the need of the health-care system to serve the elderly. His conception has been referred to as a "reciprocal model." This particular model appears to fit well with our effort to strengthen a "symbiotic" relationship between the chronically ill black elderly and the primary health center. Schwartz defines the nature of the client group as "a collection of people who need each other in order to work on certain common tasks, in an agency that is hospitable to those tasks," and he further states that "this simple definition carries within it all the necessary ingredients for a strategy of practice" (p. 10).

Forming a group of the chronically ill elderly requires special considerations. Such questions as what would be the goals, who should be included, how should it be carried out, where should it take place, and why use a group approach rather than individual work must be carefully considered.

Although the field instructor and student social workers spearheaded the planning of groups, from the onset other health professionals at the center were also asked to become involved in the planning process so that the group program would not become a social-work monopoly. Involving other professionals in the planning process not only assured their full support and cooperation with the program but also prevented potentially damaging professional jealousy and turf-guarding around the development of new programs. In fact, it opened the door for nurse-practitioners to participate in groups as invited resource persons in some of the group sessions.

For the "activity-centered" group, criteria for membership was that any one who was over sixty and who was having difficulty coping with life stresses relating to their health condition would be eligible. In particular, the elderly who were considered to be at high risk, such as the people who had limited mobility because of physical handicap, solitary living, social isolation, or experiencing stress under special circumstances (such as Ms. Y in the case illustration) were heavily recruited. On the other hand, the membership criteria set for the "problem-solving" diabetic patient group were more narrow and restrictive. The requirement was that a person must be at least sixty years of age and diabetic and have a problem of self-care for a diabetic condition.

The recruitment was done using several different channels, asking the professional staff to refer potential members, reviewing social workers' caseloads, and reviewing the center's patient records. One unexpected and useful source of referrals came from the center's receptionist, who happened to be a longtime resident in the neighborhood and knew practically every elderly patient in the center.

Besides recruiting prospective members for groups, the worker had to undertake many other tasks in the planning stage. We learned early that the availability of transportation plays the most crucial role in the participation of the elderly in any program. Simply, we thought that we could not expect reluctant elderly to participate in groups by asking them to arrange their own transportation to the center. A combination of such factors as the lack of transportation and their general reluctance to ask for assistance often discourage the black elderly from obtaining even emergency medical services. With the cooperation of the local Easter Seal Society, a door-to-door pickup service had been arranged for the prospective members.

There were many special considerations in preparing the elderly for group membership. The initial fear of the unknown that grips everyone at the beginning of a new experience was magnified for these alienated elderly. The worker contacted the prospective members either by telephone or in writing at first and then made a visit to their homes in an effort to persuade the reluctant patients to participate in groups.

Interviewing the elderly in their familiar environment where they had some control over the situation was very important. At the homes, in plain language, the worker tried to explain the goals and the nature of groups to each prospective member by emphasizing the commonalities of group members and the opportunity for sharing feelings, thoughts, and social activities. Although most elderly responded favorably to the idea, some were openly suspicious and so fearful that they declined to participate. The elderly who were physically disabled did express their particular concerns about physical arrangements, and wondered whether they could participate fully and safely in the program. They all needed strong encouragement and assurance from the worker.

Once the members were selected, the worker made at least two or three telephone calls prior to the first meeting, while a few people required a second home visit by the worker. The worker also rode in the van with the elderly on the first day of the meeting, which helped to reduce anxiety and tension.

The Activity-Centered Group

We thought that doing or sharing of activities should serve as the central medium to stimulate interactions among group members, since we judged this approach as the most suitable to this less verbally oriented group of the elderly. We deliberately avoided dividing a group into the categories of "doing" and "talking." We wanted to provide an opportunity for the alienated and powerless black elderly to come together in a group and to make meaningful human contacts with the worker and with one another while they engaged in activities as the medium of interaction. Thus, the activity-centered group was organized with a variety of planned activities, such as games, arts and crafts, films, and trips.

This group was formed with ten members with ages ranging from sixty-seven to seventy-eight, with eight women and two men. Three of the members had partial paralysis as the result of earlier strokes and their mobility was greatly limited. Their speech also was greatly affected by strokes. The other members had a variety of illnesses, such as arthritis, diabetes, heart disease, and/or hypertension. Some suffered from periodic mild to moderate depression. All were on some kind of medication. Five members lived alone in either substandard apartments or equally inadequate "shot-gun" houses in one of the poorest neighborhoods in Memphis. They relied on Social Security and food stamps as sources of income. The other half of the members lived with their adult children or sibling. This group met once a week for six weeks. Sessions were held for two and half hours at the center. Lunch was prepared by the worker at each meeting.

At the opening of the first meeting, the worker explained the purpose of group in clear and simple language; the commonalities of being old and chronically ill, doing, talking, and helping each other through group experience were emphasized. The worker then introduced a game, "Getting Acquainted with Each Other." The game was played for the purpose of helping members to get to know each other and of learning the names of the members. The initial use of the game opened many new avenues for reaching this group of elderly, and it certainly helped to ease initial anxiety and tension in the group.

Prior to the meetings, all program ideas and materials were prepared by the worker. The worker presented the plans to the group for approval, modification, and solicitation of new ideas, but the response from the members was minimal; they suggested no new ideas. However, for these essentially less verbally inclined members, engaging in and sharing activities together made the meetings more meaningful. For example, the sheer joy of accomplishing a simple drawing, "Draw someone you love most," was expressed by a seventy-eight-year-old illiterate woman who had enormous difficulty in the use of hands because of paralysis. She drew a barely recognizable human figure whom she called her grandchild who lived in California, and she expressed her hope that someday he would come to visit her.

As the group proceeded toward greater trust and intimacy and became freer in the expression of thoughts and feelings through engaging in activities together, the worker also encouraged more meaningful discussions. The discussions moved into some depth. Themes central to their lives, such as the meaning of old age, being poor, and ill health, were touched upon in the discussions. Those themes usually came out as a form of exchanging life stories with each other with considerable reflection on their past experiences. For example, one woman talked about her experience of having two strokes in the past that left the left side of her body paralyzed. She also reported without emotion that she never went to see a doctor after the stroke. Since the incident of not seeking medical service after strokes is not infrequent among the black elderly, no one but the worker reacted to her story with any dismay. When the worker pressed her as to why she did not go to the hospital, the woman's reply was that she did not have transportation. The worker took this opportunity to discuss how serious the transportation problem had been with the elderly. They talked about various degrees of difficulties with transportation, then the discussion was further extended to other reasons for not seeking medical assistance, such as their profound dislike of the hospital they must use for the secondary-care facility. They cited such factors as long waiting periods (six to eight hours) and the rude and unkindly treatment they had frequently received from some of the clerical staff. They said that there was nothing anyone could do to change the system; however, they hoped to get some help from the worker or the staff at the primary center the next time they needed to go to the city hospital.

A central function of shared activity was to provide members with the opportunity for contact with one another. The participation in the group gave these elderly members new goals and new experiences and something they could look forward to engaging in each week. Furthermore, playing games and sharing activities not only facilitated the interaction with each other but also opened the door for the acquisition of new information. For example, in the course of group interaction, some members expressed interest in learning more about the care of chronic illness, such as the proper diet for diabetes and hypertension. This interest prompted them to invite a nurse-practitioner and nutritionist to speak about the subject. The invited speakers brought a film and film clips to explain about diet, and viewing of the films helped the group members to grasp some of the more complex ideas about dietary management. The function of such an activity was described by Shulman (1971) as "data-gathering." The notion was that as group members worked on their common tasks they might need access to data that were not immediately available within the group itself and must be sought from outside. Another example was a trip the group made to the county mayor's office. The members were flabbergasted that the mayor and also a representative from the Department of Aging received them graciously and took time to explain various county programs for the elderly and also listened to their complaints. There was no doubt that most of the information was new to these people. Furthermore, prior to the visit to the mayor's office, the members spent some time talking about subjects they would present to the mayor. The group did engage in the function that Shulman called "rehearsal"—a chance to rehearse roles prior to actually confronting a situation. This type of exercise was greatly needed by the members who had difficulty presenting their ideas and wishes clearly to others. Incidentally, the group chose to discuss transportation problems with the mayor; however, they also wanted to express their appreciation and gratification about how well they were treated at the primary health center.

A trip to the zoo provided the best opportunity for socialization. It turned out to be one of the highlights of all activities, since it involved an enjoyable picnic lunch as well as seeing the animals, which stimulated the members' curiosity.

The Problem-Solving Group

Unlike the activity-centered group, which had broader objectives, the problem-solving group had a sharper focus—that of helping the group members to develop better management skills for diabetes through group interactions. The ultimate goals were problem alleviation and related task accomplishment for each group member. Although group members had common problems, each also presented unique problems.

The problem-solving group was formed with eight diabetic elderly, ages ranging from sixty-two to seventy-four, who were having difficulty managing their diabetic conditions. They were included in the group primarily because the physicians and nurse-practitioners expressed their concerns that "something has to be done to help them to improve the level of care they receive." Six of the participants lived with their relatives; only two lived alone. They all required daily insulin, but appropriate dietary management was the key issue for all of the participants. Not only must they avoid sugar, but they must also avoid excessive use of fat and salt, since most of them also had other illnesses such as hypertension and heart disease. This group met at the center six times once a week for two hours each.

Initially, the worker presented the purpose of the group as "learning more about diabetes and its care" and downplayed the participants' poor management records. Just as in the activity-centered group, the worker relied heavily on activities as a medium of communication and interaction, but the activities were geared toward helping the group members to develop more accurate knowledge and better skills in dietary management. For example, nurse-practitioners and nutritionists were invited to participate in the group as resource people. They brought films, raw food, and other teaching materials to demonstrate techniques for problem-solving. However, the learning was essentially a two-way street. Not only did the elderly learn some new information and problem-solving skills, but the professionals learned something about the effect of their past and present work with the elderly. The professionals learned how little knowledge the elderly had about diabetes and dietary management, despite repeated teaching that the professionals had done with them individually in the past. As the members felt free to express their feelings and thoughts in the meetings, much unexpected information was divulged. One example was that several members thought that insulin worked more or less as an antidote. They thought that whenever they ate a piece of cake, they should take a double dose of insulin afterward.

Unfortunately, there were more dropouts in this group than the activity-centered group. Bad weather, which forced cancelation of two meetings, and transportation problems contributed to the dropout of a few members. Nevertheless, this type of group appeared to be useful for educating the elderly and the professionals.

Termination

The termination of the group meant a separation, a loss of relationships that had developed over a period of time. It was a painful moment for many group members. We also thought that perhaps separation was harder and more painful to the elderly than to younger people because in one respect, old age itself signifies a loss of many relationships. The fact is that old age is full of losses with few gains, loss of jobs by retirement, loss of physical stamina, loss of social roles, loss of spouses and friends, and, finally, loss of one's own life.

It appeared that the termination was particularly hard for those elderly who lived alone in isolation because their degree of dependence on the worker and other members of the group had increased. The worker needed to be sensitive in handling the termination. As she anticipated difficulty of termination for the members, the worker talked about the ending of the group long before the final meeting. Nevertheless, in the final meeting, sadness and tension were visibly heightened, and perhaps this was the only occasion that a strong emotional current was felt in the group. For example, in the ending of the activity-centered group, the worker talked about what the group had meant to her by emphasizing many positive experiences she had with the group. Then, one by one, each member expressed his or her feelings. Finally, one man stood up and said how much he and other members appreciated what the worker had done and concluded his statement by saying the worker (white) was now considered one of them, which meant she was accepted as a member of his race. The worker thanked the man and the group and talked about how closely she felt toward them. At last, the worker and the members exchanged home telephone numbers for future contacts and the meeting was adjourned.

Functions of the Worker

In both the activity-centered group and the problem-solving group, the worker's central function was to mediate the engagement between client need and agency service. The intent was to strengthen what Schwartz (1971) called the "symbiotic" relationship between the alienated, chronically ill black elderly and the primary health center. The worker acted as mediator to activate both clients and services. She reached out to the alienated black elderly and brought them to the center, and, at the same time, she mobilized resources in the center and in the community to meet the needs of the elderly more responsively. Such examples were that the worker in both groups acted as a catalytic agent between the elderly and the clinic personnel, since both needed improved communication. Another example was the visit the activity-centered group made to the county mayor's office. Both the elderly and the mayor came to understand each other more, and the mayor learned more about the needs and problems of the elderly. Of course, in the group the worker consciously acted as a mediator to activate and stimulate human interactions, mutual aid, and problem-solving among the members.

We learned that the work with the chronically ill elderly demands far more active worker participation in many areas of the client's life both in and out of the group situation. Because of poverty, illnesses, and social disadvantages, these elderly were more prone to have problems in life than their well-to-do counterparts or younger generations. Continued participation in the group alone requires a good deal of effort on the part of the elderly. Thus, the worker must give close attention to meeting the individual needs in and out of the group in order to help the client to fulfill the "contract"—to attend the group regularly and to maintain a cohesive group. For example, on the day of a meeting, a group member called the worker to tell her that she could not attend the meeting unless she got her Social Security check from the mailman. She was afraid that the check might be stolen if it was left in the mailbox. The worker offered to look for the mailman with the client until she got the check.

In working with the elderly, the worker must be aware of a risk of creating excessive dependency of the client on the worker. We observed that some elderly, particularly those who live alone in isolation, tend to develop a stronger dependency on the worker once they saw that the worker was caring and willing to help. The worker must keep in mind that creating excessive dependency not only defeats the whole purpose of the group but also is more damaging to the elderly in the long term. One way to prevent this is for the worker to keep her attention on the tasks that the clients are to perform and help them to perform those tasks well rather than doing for them. In work with the elderly, an attitude of "the worker knows best" is risky because it increases their dependence in a group in which independence is a primary goal (Twente, 1970).

Although we are not certain, our limited experience tells us that handling the dependency needs of the elderly might be a more difficult problem for a white worker than a black worker, particularly for social workers in a southern city. The black elderly, because of their historical experience, view whites as being more powerful and as having access to more resources. The historical race relationship based on the pattern of the white domination and black submission is well entrenched in the minds of the black elderly. Thus, both the white worker and black clients could easily fall into this old pattern of the dominant "giver" and the submissive "receiver."

For example, the activity-centered group was carried out by a mature, middle-aged white female who was resourceful, caring, and deeply committed to the black elderly. In the beginning, the elderly approached her with caution and apprehension. They were polite, submissive, and appreciative. The difficulty was that, despite the worker's effort to transfer the power to the group members and help them to become more independent in decision making, her efforts were only partially successful. The balance of power and decision making appeared more heavily weighted toward the worker's side than toward the group members'. Throughout the group the members remained generally submissive, appreciative, and well satisfied. We are not at all certain at this point whether this pattern was the result of the unique characteristics of the elderly of this socioeconomic group or the result of unique transactions between the white worker and the black elderly. In any event, these intricate transactions must be studied further.

Conclusion

Based on our conviction that the poor and ill black elderly require special help in dealing with managing tasks of health care and day-to-day functioning, we have developed and experimented with two group approaches at the primary health Center—the activity-centered group and the problem-solving group. We are able to affirm our beliefs that groups are one of the most useful tools for reaching out to the alienated black elderly who are isolated and have a problem with the use of the available health-care services.

Brody (1973) estimated that today nearly 81 percent of the people over sixty-five have at least one chronic illness. Among them, approximately half are somewhat disabled because of chronic illness. Approximately 16 percent of the elderly are estimated to have some kind of mental impairment. Thus, the most pressing health problems of the elderly are not the treatment of acute illnesses, but the management of chronic illnesses. Furthermore, life-styles, environment, and associated behavior patterns of the elderly are known to affect their illness, disability, and health-care utilization. Many chronically ill black elderly have problems coping with the stress of their health condition. Helping the elderly cope with chronic illnesses poses a new challenge to social workers who are responsible for enhancing the social functioning of the client and must assume a vital role in a health-care facility such as a primary health center.

The student workers who participated in groups reacted favorably. The experience provided an exciting and creative opportunity for them to work with the elderly. The program had a lasting impact on the entire program in the primary health center through the worker's collaboration with other health professionals and the participation of the key professionals in the groups. However, the use of groups requires further refinement and development. The search for new social-work group approaches must be continued at primary health centers because they offer invaluable opportunities for social work to experiment with efforts to discover more effective and efficient ways to deliver services to the elderly.

References

Brody, S. J. "Comprehensive Health Care for the Elderly: An Analysis." *Gerontologist, 1973,* 13.

McCaslin, R., and Calvert, W. "Some Indicators in Black and White: Some Ethnic Considerations in Delivery of Service to the Elderly." *Journal of Gerontology,* 1975, 30, (1).

Shader, R., and Tracy, M. "On Being Black, Old, and Emotionally Troubled: How Little is Known." *Psychiatric Opinion,* 1973, 10, (6).

Shulman, L. "Program in Group Work: Another Look." In W. Schwartz and S. Zalba (eds.), *The Practice of Group Work.* New York: Columbia University Press, 1971, p. 227.

Schwartz, W., and Zalba, S. *The Practice of Group Work.* New York: Columbia University Press, 1971.

Twente, Esther. *Never Too Old.* San Francisco: Jossey-Bass, 1970, p. 14.

17

A Model to Evaluate Group Work Practice with Ethnic Minorities

Man Keung Ho

This chapter introduces a model for evaluating group work practice with ethnic minorities. Experience derived from using this model in work with a group of Native Americans is presented to illustrate the model's applicability and value.

The need for ethnic-minority content in social-work education has been recognized for a number of years, and serious efforts have been made to incorporate the study of ethnic and minority-group life into the social-work curriculum (Crompton, 1976). Yet no attention has been directed to evaluating whether this minority content is relevant and successfully transformed into practice to meet the existing needs of minority clients. Group life and group experience are integral components of most ethnic-minority societies, and social workers should capitalize on the value of the group concept in their work with ethnic minorities (Lewis, 1980). The introduction of this conceptual model aims to provide group workers with a means to evaluate their practice with different ethnic-minority clients. In addition to facilitating evaluations, the model itself can serve as a group-treatment technique.

Model Conceptualization

This evaluative model of group work practice consists of two important elements of effective practice: relevant goal and relevant process. Present group work practices are often heavily biased toward knowledge obtained in formed or "unnatural" small groups, as well as toward the Anglo-European middle-class culture, including class values and language factors (Jones, 1979). However, in actual practice situations, many ethnic minorities do not value the "I-Thou" focus. They believe in restraint of strong feelings, may not place a high priority on insight, may not make a clear distinction between physical and mental health, may seek immediate answers or solutions to problems, and often do not speak fluent standard English (Queen and Habenstein, 1969). Thus, an evaluation of group work practice that is preoccupied with techniques and outcome and that fails to relate to the client's real need and life experience does nothing to ascertain a group worker's effectiveness in working with ethnic minorities.

By focusing on the group goal and the group process, a worker's intervention with an ethnic-minority group can be analyzed effectively by the worker. As illustrated in Table 17.1, a worker's intervention with a specific ethnic group may fall in any one of four categories:

1. Type I Error   ———   Irrelevant process, irrelevant goal
2. Type II Error   ———   Relevant process, irrelevant goal
3. Type III Error   ———   Irrelevant process, relevant goal
4. Effective Intervention ——— Relevant process, relevant goal

Table 17.1. Outcomes of Worker-Group Interaction

		Group Process	
		Irrelevant	Relevant
Group Goal	Irrelevant	I Error	II Error
	Relevant	III Error	IV Effective Intervention

The following case example illustrates the optimum effectiveness of a worker's intervention with a group of Native American female divorcees. Upon deciding that one of the group goals (outcome) was to help individual members in the group become more self-sufficient (as evidenced by decreased dependence on a male for financial support), the group worker commits a Type I error (irrelevant process, irrelevant goal) if he or she encourages the group members to transfer (irrelevant process) their original learned hostility toward males to the group worker. That ventilation in itself—irrelevant goal in terms of Native American culture's emphasis on restraint of feelings and self-control—is "curative." Type II error (relevant process, irrelevant goal) is committed if the worker engages the group members in exploring their learned dependency (relevant process) and encourages them to become totally independent (irrelevant goal in terms of Native American culture's emphasis on restraint of feelings and interdependence). A Type III error (irrelevant process, relevant goal) is committed if the worker engages the group in insight-oriented, non-verbal self-awareness-structured exercises (irrelevant process) while the group as a whole wishes to learn to become financially independent (relevant goal). Effective intervention (relevant process, relevant goal) takes place if the worker engages group members to explore (relevant process) ways by which they could obtain employment or earnings (relevant goal).

Model Application

The actual application of this model as an evaluation and treatment tool can be illustrated by the following case example involving group therapy with Native American divorcees.

This group consisted of seven Native Americans who had been divorced for a minimum of six months or more. Being divorced no less than six months was the only criterion for admission to the group. Studies have indicated that an individual is less receptive to therapy during the "shock stage"—the first three or four months after the divorce (Kreis and Patti, 1969). All the group members were trainees of a Community Health Representative (CHR) program sponsored by the United States Indian Health Service. They represented six Indian tribes: Sioux, Choctaw, Navajo, Apache, and Cherokee. Two members came from California, one from Alaska, one from Michigan, one from Florida, and two from Oklahoma. The group therapy was conducted at the Talihina Training Center, Talihina, Oklahoma, site of the CHR training program. The group worker was a Chinese male and a regular consultant to the training program. The group was contracted to meet six times on a twice-a-week basis. The average length of each session was one and one-half hours. Group sessions took place in the evening, three hours after the regular training session ended. The group worker had no previous acquaintance with the group members. One group member from California was a second cousin to one of the group members from Oklahoma. The remainder of the group had not met each other previously. The median age of this group was twenty-nine, and their median formal schooling was tenth grade. Although membership in the group was voluntary, members were contracted to attend all six group sessions. All but one member attended every session. This particular member missed the fourth session because of a legitimate physical illness.

Upon identifying the needs and wants of each group member, specific group goals were formulated at the first meeting. Three major goals were identified: (1) accomplishment of financial independence, (2) child management, and (3) remarriage. In an attempt to evaluate the effectiveness of this group therapy, behavioral anchors reflecting progress in each of these major goals (prescriptors) made by the group were established by using the Practice Outcome Inventory (see Table 17.2) (Ho, 1976).

As an evaluative instrument, the Practice Outcome Inventory is distinguished by four features: (1) it considers the clients' perceptions, subjectivity, and active involvement; (2) it considers the uniqueness of the clients' psychological and emotional state, as well as their cultural and ethnic backgrounds, environment and social conditions, current needs, and unique goals; (3) it uses terminology that is behaviorally anchored to ensure that clients are clear about their experiential definitions; and (4) it generally facilitates the practice process.

The procedure in administering the POI consists essentially of three parts: the clients' listing of descriptors—adaptive, efficiency, disabling habits and conditions, environmental circumstances—that they consider important, the clients' ranking of the relative importance of such descriptors, and the client's rating of how characteristic these descriptors are of themselves.

Table 17.2. Pre- and Postgroup Therapy Measurement of Native Amer ican Divorcees

| | | Treatment Phases | | |
| | | Pre | Post | |
Description (Goal)	Behavioral Anchor	Score*	Score	Difference
Financial Independence	More ways to obtain money	−31	+5	+36
	More ways to save money	−26	−2	+24
Child Management	More ways to discipline children	−18	+16	+34
	More ways to obtain help in caring for children	−8	+20	+28
Remarriage	More alternative life-styles	−20	−2	+18
	More knowledgeable about one's need for marriage	−26	+4	+30
	More ways to meet male companions	−22	−4	+18

*Score represents all seven members. The possible ratings are −5 (totally disatisfied with level of functioning on this dimension), −4, −3, −2, −1, 0, +1, +2, +3, +4, and +5 (completely satisfied with level of functioning on this dimension).

To protect individuals from anxiety associated with self-disclosure, only the group score of each behavioral anchor of each goal was required. Hence, each individual member was required to submit her pregroup score on each behavioral anchor anonymously. In an attempt to test the effectiveness of this goal/process-evaluative model, the meaning and the weighing (types of errors or effective intervention) of the model were explained to the group. Several examples were used to help the group assess different types of errors or effective intervention. Before each group session ended, each member was provided a rating sheet to score how productive or nonproductive that particular session had been (Table 17.3).

Table 17.3. Session Evaluation Rating Sheet

Please place a checkmark in front of *the* number (only one) that indicates how you feel about this session. Please do not write your name on this form.

Date and Number of Session _____

_____	(1)	TYPE I error _____ irrelevant process/irrelevant goal
_____	(2)	TYPE II error _____ relevant process/irrelevant goal
_____	(3)	TYPE III error _____ irrelevant process/relevant goal
_____	(4)	Effective Intervention

The group responded to the introduction of this model with confusion. Upon learning more about the value of the model and its simplicity, the group responded cooperatively. One group member volunteered, "You mean we (members) actually have so much to do with how the group progresses session by session?" The worker took this opportunity to explain to the group his knowledge and professional limitations in providing group therapy to members of different cultures and ethnic groups. Implicit in the worker's self-disclosure was his desire to elicit reciprocity from the group. To validate further the group members' ratings and perceptions of each group session, the group granted the worker's permission to audiotape each session, with the understanding that all tapes would be erased at the end of the final session to protect confidentiality. Table 17.4 indicates the sum of the group members' ratings of all six therapy sessions.

The audiotape of the first session indicated that despite a large majority of the members' expressed need for financial support, a minority expressed that financial independence was not their primary concern. In the second session, several members expressed disagreement concerning

Table 17.4. Summary Ratings for Session Evaluations

Session Number	Type I Error	Type II Error	Type III Error	Effective Intervention	Total
1			2	5	7
2	1	2	3	1	7
3			2	5	7
4			3	3	6*
5				7	7
6				7	7

*One member was absent in the fourth session.

welfare aid as a means to relieve their financial problems. These same members also expressed disapproval in placing their chidlren at child-care centers while they worked. These members' different perceptions as to how they should obtain financial and child-care assistance were reflected in their ratings: Three members assigned Type III errors (irrelevant process/relevant goal). The two members who assigned Type II errors (relevant process/irrelevant goal) perhaps felt that despite their agreement with the group's ranking financial support and child care as major problems, these were not their own primary needs or problems.

Capitalizing on the group's ratings of the second session, the worker encouraged the group to clarify further their positions at the third meeting. Two members reminded the worker that obtaining financial aid from government sources rather than from the extended family and placing children in child-care centers instead of leaving the children with trusted relatives were contrary to Native American ways of seeking help. These members' remarks were rebutted by another group member, who complained, "My nearest relative lives five hundred miles from where I live." At the end of the session, the group consensus was that individual situations might necessitate different solutions to the same problem. The group's rating to the third session was generally positive.

At the fourth session, the group dealt with the issue of remarriage. The group was relatively quiet, perhaps partly because of the absence of one member and partly because of the threatening nature of the topic. The group was silent when the technique of role-playing was introduced as a response to the group's question, "How do you talk to a man you don't know?" One member who sat next to the worker was partly coerced by the group to participate in the role-playing, but she subsequently refused to continue after the first minute. Three members' ratings of a Type III error reflected the failure of the role-playing technique with this particular group at this session.

When the worker brought up the misuse of role-playing in the fifth session, group members expressed their discomfort relating to this structured or "artificial" activity. When the worker asked what activity group members wished to employ to encounter their expressed needs and goals, one member jokingly said, "Have a good Chinese meal immediately before the next meeting starts." The worker capitalized on this member's suggestion and agreed to prepare a meal before the next meeting.

The process of engaging all group members in preparing a meal was so relaxing and therapeutic that the group volunteered to prepare a Native American meal prior to the next and the last meeting. Review of the audiotapes of the last two meetings indicated a greater degree of group cohesion. Members in general felt relaxed. There was considerable spontaneity, laughter, and serious discussion. Members freely exchanged anecdotes about ex-husbands, children, and male friends. The role of the group worker in these two sessions was limited to active listener and empathic supporter. Members of the group expressed personal satisfaction with the group therapy and a desire that the group continue after the last session. The Practice Outcome Inventory was readministered to determine members' gains through group therapy.

Summary and Conclusion

Despite the subjective nature of the Practice Outcome Inventory, this instrument did show that group members had benefited by their short-term group therapy. Since there was no control group for comparison, the effective outcome of the group therapy cannot be attributed directly to the introduction of this evaluative model. However, by carefully examining the group process recorded on audiotapes, the worker's change of technique that produced positive results was aided by the model. Perhaps one could argue that the cohesion and productivity of the last two group sessions followed the natural progression of group development. However, in view of the relatively short-term nature of the group, one wonders if group developmental theory is applicable in this case.

Judging by the group members' positive feedback and the worker's subjective experience in conducting the group, the model is a valuable tool in group therapy. This evaluative model has several significant advantages. The anonymous written evaluation in the form of a "checklist" is simple, concrete, and impersonal, so most Native American clients feel comfortable in cooperating. Such an evaluative process is congruent and consistent with Native American culture's emphasis on simplicity, concreteness, and mutual sharing. If the feedback received by the workers is negative, the worker knows immediately what type(s) of error he or she may have committed. Reviewing feedback information from the last meeting enables the group to understand fully, agree, and reaffirm the group goal(s) and the group process conducive to accomplishing that goal. Such an evaluative process involves reciprocity between the worker and the group and reduces the traditional power differential between the worker's role and the client's role (Pinderhughs, 1979). Hence, this evaluative model also can be a useful group-treatment technique in work with ethnic minorities.

References

Crompton, D. Minority Content in Social Work Education: Promise or Pitfall? *Journal of Education for Social Work,* 1976, 10, 9–18.

Ho, M. K. "Evaluation: A Means of Treatment." *Social Work*, 1976, *21*, 24–27.

Jones, D. L. "African-American Clients: Clinical Practice Issues. *Social Work*, 1979, *24*, 112–118.

Kreis, B., and Patti, A. *Up from Grief: Patterns of Recovery*. New York: Seabury Press, 1969.

Lewis, R. "Cultural Perspective on Treatment Modalities with Native Americans." In M. Bloom (ed.), *Life Span Development*. New York: Macmillan, 1980.

Pinderhughs, E. B. "Teaching Empathy in Cross-Cultural Social Work. *Social Work*, 1979, *24*, 312–416.

Queen, S. A. and Habenstein, R. *The Family in Various Cultures*. New York: Little, Brown, 1969.

18

Group Work with Chicano Youth in the School Setting

John A. Brown and Rodolfo Arevalo

This paper describes our experiences in group work with Chicano youth in the school setting. We have incorporated various features of the three models of group work identified by Papell and Rothman (1966) into a framework that has special applicability to group work with Chicanos. Chicano youths face multiple problems in American society. A major problem is their high rate of school failure. Group work practice, if it is to be effective, requires a perspective that focuses on various levels of society and how they interact to create a particular problem. Such a perspective requires an understanding of individual needs, cultural orientation, family and organization practices, and social responsibility. The perspective that best meets this need may be referred to as an integrated-models approach to group work practice.

The problems of the 1980s will be especially acute for Chicano youth who are educationally disadvantaged. Without effective intervention, the problems will become intensified. The group worker will need to possess a view of society that enables him or her to see the need for structural as well as individual change, particularly as he or she attempts to achieve constructive changes in those social systems that have an adverse effect on these youth. The eternal triangle of the individual, society, and the small group as both a buffer between these two entities and as an instrument of social change and individual growth will increasingly demand our attention in this decade. The oppressed and the powerless will need a voice—in this case, the group worker—to articulate their needs and to embrace their cause.

Chicano Youth

No question exists that Chicano youth[1] require specialized services. They face tremendous problems in attempting to gain those skills and knowledge necessary for entrance into the mainstream of American life. In attempting to maintain their cultural beliefs, they have endured considerable stress, as well as a push by social organizations to adapt American values and to assimilate into mainstream culture. Stress for Chicano youth is especially evident in their interactions with public schools. Reports have identified the school failures among Hispanics as staggering (Carter, 1970; Savage, 1984). Guerra (1972) states that in California 33 percent of the dropouts in school and about 17 percent of the juvenile delinquents are of Mexican-American descent. In addition, Guerra states that 40 percent of the inmates of penal institutions in California are of Mexican-American descent and as much as 40 to 60 percent of the total drug addicts are Mexican-Americans. Smith (1978) cites 1974 data, which reveal that while 90 percent of white youth graduated from high school and 65 percent of black youth graduated only 27 percent of Chicano youth graduated from high school. This picture has remained fairly constant (Savage, 1984) and shows no signs of improvement.

The Hispanic population, of which 7.2 million are Mexican-Americans, is projected as becoming the largest minority by 1990. Half of the Chicano population is under the age of eighteen, and the largest numbers live in the Southwestern states of California, Texas, Arizona, Colorado, and New Mexico (Arevalo and Brown, 1979). The present plight of Chicano youth in the educational system constitutes a cause for alarm. Carter (1970) suggests that many contributory causes to the school failure of Chicano youth can be located in the school. The school, in its failure to achieve its mission with Chicano youth, emerges as a primary target for change and a medium through which social change can be accomplished in the interest of these youth. As early group workers were instrumental in pushing for compulsory school laws, the group worker of today must be equally instrumental in directing his or her efforts toward achieving a more functional school environment so that Chicano youth do not emerge as educational victims. The school and its culture must be analyzed for its dysfunctional aspects.

Racism

Racism contributes greatly to the educational failure of Chicano youth. Racism is essentially a structural phenomenon; its presence can be felt throughout society. Institutional racism has cultural sanction that finds expression in societal institutions. Since racism is a structural phenomenon, group work in addressing the educational failures of Chicano youth must repeat its history and increasingly engage in social-action activities. Consequently, in the 1980s emphasis will be placed on collective action, and the small group will again become a primary instrument for achieving social and individual change.

Organizing groups for expressive and instrumental purposes has been a hallmark of American society (Tocqueville, 1945). Involvement in group efforts contributes to the well-being of society and to individual growth and helps to dispel feelings of powerlessness. The importance of the group in protecting cultural values and in advocating for social change was not lost on the early immigrants. They turned to collective actions when they discovered themselves ignored, scapegoated, exploited, victimized, and persecuted (Brown, 1975). Inasmuch as Chicanos find themselves facing similar circumstances, group efforts will be important in helping them to achieve social change. An inherent value of the small group is that it can fulfill psychological needs, strengthen cultural identification, and awaken in people a social consciousness that can lead to social action. The small group can be developed and activated for the purpose of achieving specific objectives valued by the client system being served.

Group Work Models

A model is defined as a way of conceptualizing reality. Papell and Rothman (1966) view a model as being a conceptual design to solve a problem that exists in reality. They have identified three models of group work practice: social goals, the rehabilitation/remedial, and the reciprocal. The social-goals model rests on a strong belief in democratic participation in contributing to social change. It has a focus on society that presented itself in the strivings of early group workers in the settlement houses to address the needs of immigrants and the poor. This model encapsulates the locality development and social-action models of community organization identified by Rothman (1970). Brager and Specht (1975) have identified stages of group development for community work that characterize this model and its development over time: socialization, developing affective relationships, organization building, and influencing social institutions. Clearly, it is seen that in combatting problems of a structural nature the social-goals model has much utility. The focus of this model is preventive as well as ameliorative. In history, the settlement houses best exemplified this model in action. They became the centers of change and cultural preservation for various immigrant groups. They were receptive to minorities when minorities were rejected and placed outside the mainstream of American life (Sytz, 1960). As Briar (1971) states, "Group work was conceived in the lively turmoil of progressive social reform that characterized the settlement houses in the first decade of the century" (p. 1241).

Following World War I and the period of progressive reforms, a different emphasis entered the practice of social group work. The social tenor of the times had changed. Social group work began to emphasize character building and leisure-time activities. An upsurge occurred in recreational programs and character-building agencies. These agencies were more concerned with moral standards of behavior than in pursuing advocacy in the interest of the poor. The middle class increasingly began to receive group work services, and psychoanalytic theory was making an impact on social-casework practice. The country had emerged from a war and was now more concerned with identifying its national character and destiny. The mood of the country was hopeful and enthusiastic; it had faith in its assimilative abilities. Considerable attention was placed on minorities and their place in American life. To all degrees and purposes, the place of the minority group of color in American Life had been settled. Restrictive immigration laws were passed to restrict the flow of Orientals into the country, and as Handlin (1957) states:

> By the end of the century, the pattern of racist practices and ideas seemed fully developed. The Orientals were to be totally excluded; the Negroes were to live in segregated enclaves; the Indians were to be confined to reservations as permanent wards of the nation, and all whites were to assimilate as rapidly as possible to a common standard. (p. 38)

The Supreme Court in its decision of 1896 (*Plessy* v. *Ferguson*) had validated as public policy the doctrine of "separate but equal." Fears existed about minorities and their effects on American life. Since Handlin did not mention the Mexican-American, it appears that even at that time this group was either forgotten, ignored, or viewed as an invisible minority. Paradoxically, in a period of American history in which the social-goals model was most indicated, its appeal had diminished and in its place stood a therapeutic orientation to group work practice that focused more on individuals than the problems of society. In this transition, the social science foundation that had guided group work practice was replaced with a psychological perspective, and group work practice became more function-oriented than cause-oriented.

The rehabilitation/remedial model reflects this transition. In this model the small group provides the environment and the medium for accomplishing individual change. Problems are viewed as characteristics of individuals instead of societal dysfunctioning. Group members are viewed as individuals with dysfunctional behaviors. While attention is focused on individuals, the group worker in manipulating group processes exerts three types of influence: direct, indirect and extra group (Vinter, 1974). The role of the group worker is that of an individual-change agent. This model is more likely to place responsibility for problems on the individual, and the activities of the group are directed at bringing about some modification in behavior so that the individual can adapt more favorably to societal expectations. Minorities who received group work services under this model were likely to be viewed as having individual deficits that accounted for their behavior. This model in one form or the other (behavioral, problem-solving, or group psychotherapy) characterized group work practice for many years.

The third model identified by Papell and Rothman (1966) is the reciprocal, sometimes referred to as the interactionist or mediation model. It represents a limited blending of the social-goals and remedial models. Its focus is on the individual in interaction with social systems. Its practice approach is generic in nature and it operates on a structural-functional view of society. Schwartz (1971), the developer of this model, states: "The interactionists see the social work function as one of mediating the often troubled transactions between people and various systems through which they carry on their relationships with society" (p. 1258). Some key features of this model are mutual-aid, symbiotic relationship, reciprocity, and interdependence. The group worker as a mediator assumes a neutral role in addressing systemic stress brought on by social systems in interaction. This model may be viewed as an alternative to the remedial model, which characterized group work practice at a time when the country was undergoing a period of social upheaval brought on by the civil rights struggles of the 1960s. In this struggle minorities engaged in social action to attain their rights. The Supreme Court in *Brown* v. *Topeka* (1954) had overturned the doctrine of "separate but equal." However, social progress was slow in coming. Minorities challenged existing practice approaches, which blamed them for their problems. Generic practice became the preferred approach to practice, and the reciprocal model met this need in group work practice. Whittaker (1974) identified the salient features of these three models, and Brown and Arevalo (1979) identified their utility in group work practice with Chicanos.

An Integrated Perspective on Group Work Practice

Effective group work practice with Chicanos calls for a holistic view of problem causation. This view must focus on the various levels of society (macro-mezzo-micro) and the interactions that lead to stress and systemic failures. The integration of features from the social goals model (democratic striving, social consciousness, and social responsibility), the remedial model (problematic behavior exhibited by individuals), and the reciprocal model (systemic stress, reciprocity, mutual-aid, and symbiotic relationship) provides a framework for group work practice with Chicanos. These models taken singularly present limitations for effective group work practice because of the stress acting on Chicano youth that emanate from various levels of society. The effective engagement of the problem of Chicano youth cannot be accomplished if the group worker maintains a strong allegiance to only one model. In addition, with the exception of the social-goals model, the other two models are primarily adaptive in nature. The remedial and the reciprocal models overlook the fact that the situation to which the individual is called on to adjust to may be dysfunctional, unhealthy, and perpetuate negative as well as racist practice. They do not address racism as a target of change, as expressed in Chicano youth interactions with dominant societal systems. Also, the view must be rejected that the problems faced by Chicano youth in the school system result from their culture (Heller, 1966). Certainly, questions must be raised as to the efficacy of traditional approaches in assisting Chicano youth to deal with their problems. Smith (1978) suggests that psychotherapists reflect the general culture from which they come and are not immune to cultural conditioning. Inasmuch as stereotypes about minorities are acquired through the socialization process, they are carried over into the therapeutic situation. Consequently, the group worker may engage in victim analysis instead of identifying and focusing on the foundation of the problematic behavior that results in school failure and a high dropout rate. The integrated perspective, employing salient features of each group work model, enables the group worker to focus on problems in a holistic manner as he or she observes social systems in interaction and identifies malfunctioning parts.

Practice Philosophy

Because of existing views about Chicano youth and their problems, the group worker must be prepared to focus on a number of systems simultaneously in attempting to address problems faced by these youth. These systems may include social-welfare agencies, the criminal-justice system, the school, health system, the family, the neighborhood, and gangs. The practice approach must be guided by a belief that the problems of Chicano youth result from their social encounters with dominant group institutions and not from cultural or psychological deficits. It is these primarily negative social encounters that result in psychological problems. An integrated perspective is indicated because it constitutes a holistic approach to identifying, assessing, and modifying negative interactions between Chicano youth and the school as a social system which result in the failure of the school to achieve its societal mission with these youth.

Knowledge Base of Integrated Models Perspective

The three models of group work practice identified by Papell and Rothman emphasize various knowledge bases as a way of identifying problem areas and guiding practice. Among these knowledge bases are ego psychology, group dynamics, social systems, and behavior modification. Whittaker (1974) identified the knowledge base that undergirds each model, as well as the role of the group worker. The integrated models perspective, in addition to using ego psychology, social-systems theory, and group dynamics, is also heavily dependent on symbolic interactionism and role theory as part of its knowledge foundation. These two theories are drawn from the field of social psychology. Role theory is important since it focuses on the external aspects of behavior associated with the various roles that a person carries in life. Since role expectations differ in various cultures, role theory sheds insights on expected behavior in different cultural groups. Social psychology as a discipline emphasizes group life, and role behavior is a function of group life. Since the group represents a microcosm of society, it offers an ideal setting for addressing and correcting behavior that results from the negative encounters of people in various role relationships. As Smelser and Smelser (1963) state: "The unit of analysis of a social system are not persons as such, but selected aspects of interaction among persons such as roles" (p. 1). Blumer (1969) suggests that "the discipline of social psychology must rest on the premise that the term 'psychological', however it is conceived in content, has a distinction that arises from the association of human beings with one another" (p. 101). In defining social psychology, Allport (quoted in Deutsch and Krauss, 1965) states: "Social psychology, then, is concerned with the study of actual, imagined, or anticipated person-to-person relationships in a social context as they affect the individuals involved" (p. 3).

Symbolic interactionism also provides a theoretical framework for understanding faulty interactions between various participants in a social system. As Strauss (Deutsch and Krauss, 1965) suggests, Mead's writings offers a clear alternative to the psychological theories based upon individual assumption, particularly through his insistence that individual acts are parts of larger communal acts. As stated previously, an integrated models perspective must be guided by a belief that problems for Chicano youth result from negative social encounters and not cultural or psychological deficits. Symbolic interactionism and role theory help us to understand the nature of these encounters and suggest ways of addressing them.

Blumer (1969) states that symbolic interactionism rests on three simple premises:

1. Human beings act toward things on the basis of the meanings that things have for them. Such things include everything that the individual makes note of in his physical world, including other human beings and institutions;
2. the meaning of such things is derived from or arises out of the social interactions that one has with his fellows, and
3. these meanings are handled in, and modified through an interpretative process in dealing with the things he encounters. (p. 2)

According to Blumer (1969): "The meaning that things have for human beings are central in their own right and to ignore the meanings of these things toward which people act is seen as falsifying the behavior under study" (p. 7). For example, if a Chicano youth fails in school, this may be a result of negative interactions in the school environment and should not be assessed as a result of individual deficits. In essence, symbolic interactionism involves a process of interpreting the meaning of the behavior or remarks of another person and acting on this interpretation.[2] Racism may also be viewed as an interactive process, and in many cases it contains a self-fulfilling prophecy that preordains school problems for Chicano youth. Symbolic interactionism and role theory contribute greatly to the knowledge base of group work practice and provide a sound theoretical framework for group work practice with Chicano youth.

The Roles of the Group Worker in the Integrated Models Perspective

An integrated models perspective attempts to achieve several objectives in group work with Chicano youth: (1) to develop a mutual fit between interacting systems, which includes cultural validation (reciprocal); (2) to bring about systemic changes, both structural and attitudinal, when indicated (social goals); (3) to develop, if indicated, new social systems that will advance social change (social goals); and (4) to assist students in gaining knowledge and experiences that will enhance self-image and modify their behavior so that they can more adequately cope with the negative experiences encountered in the school setting (rehabilitation/remedial). Through the small group, following an integrated models approach, these goals can be achieved.

Group involvement is not alien to Chicanos. Ramona (Burger, 1972) suggests that the Mexican-American culture offers "constant confrontation," rather than "stagnant fatalism." The small group needs to be designed to identify and address racist practices and negative interactions and their consequences. Therefore, it should be planfully designed so that these experiences can surface and be addressed within the group situation. As group members identify their experiences, the group worker gains knowledge of the importance of assuming multiple roles, focusing on multiple targets, and involving him or herself in multiple interactional systems in the interest of these youth. The group worker must also possess cultural sensitivity in understanding the unique position of these youth and the problems they face.

At various periods during the life of the group, the group worker will need to assume a variety of roles. He or she may operate as an educator, a historian of the Chicano experiences in the United States, a resource locator, a policy analyst (school policies), and an individual and family therapist. Other roles include those of facilitator, enabler, advocate, and mediator. The group worker will need to interact with group members in different settings, such as the school, the neighborhood, the home, and other social agencies. Full use is made of the five types of interviews identified by Maloney (1958). Group members will accord the worker greater validation and acceptance if he or she is present at political and neighborhood meetings which may involve them, their families, or neighborhood. Sometimes through involvement in family and neighborhood affairs, the group worker negotiates with the police, immigration authorities (in the interest of undocumented aliens), or with the juvenile court and other social systems. This approach to group work practice is similar to that described by Faris et al. (1971) and Arevalo and Brown (1979).

Group Work Practice: The Group

The school conditions that led to the development of group work with Chicano youth in the school setting have been discussed in Arevalo and Brown (1979). The original membership of the group consisted of ten teenage Chicanos, ranging in ages from thirteen to sixteen, who were referred for group services because of various school problems, such as poor attitudes, failing, authority conflicts, truancy, fighting, and suspicion of drug usage. Ethnic/racial conflicts were also evident. The school was most cooperative. In its desire to help these youths, it removed all possible obstacles to group participation.[3]

Even though these youths had serious school problems, it was important not to view them as being deviants and responsible for their problems. Rather, within the context of their total environment and racist experiences, much of their behavior was understandable and justifiable but at the same time self-defeating. Our approach to them initially was experimental. We did not want them to be resistant to group efforts, which was a strong possibility if they felt we were attributing to them the "blame" for their problems. Therefore, following a symbolic interactionist frame of reference, we acted on the assumption that their behavior resulted from the negative social interactions encountered in life, especially within the school, and their responses to these interactions. Problems were not viewed as resulting from psychological or cultural deficits. Consequently, the school itself becomes a contributing agent to the problems faced by these youth because of the interactions that occurred between them.

Group Development

All groups go through developmental stages, and various stages of group development are discussed in the literature. The stages of group development that were evident in this group paralleled the stages identified by Hartford (1971). It took considerable time for the members to develop some understanding of the purposes of the group. The positive inter-actional processes that occurred between group members and the group worker were slow in developing. While the group was not planned to be discussion-oriented, it was necessary in the beginning to focus discussion on school problems and to attempt to identify reasons for them from the viewpoints of group members. The group worker made known his values, the importance of education, and the need for Chicanos to have educated youth who could become future leaders. The group worker also discussed how school problems negatively affected them, their families, and possibly Chicanos in general. The group worker wanted the group to address this problem, and he told them that he was there to assist them.

In this approach to practice, identifying problems, seeking reasons for them, and attempting to involve group members in addressing these problems, we were reaching for a value around which the group could co-alesce. This approach was successful and provided an important distinc-tion. We were searching for *values*. Focusing on and reaching for a value can inspire hopes and dreams. It does not imply criticism or failure, but merely recognizes that something is not working the way it should. Our job is to find out why. Focusing on a problem may well be self-defeating. Anxiety may be aroused, as well as a sense of shame and a feeling of infe-riority. This approach to practice in which values become perhaps more important than problems has an existential flavor, and the focus is more on reflection than introspection. Reaching for values as a means of build-ing a group culture can be viewed as activating a curative factor within the group, which can encourage hope and a better feeling about oneself.

Group Balance

While members were not initially screened for the group and were se-lected by school personnel, a group balance emerged. Some group mem-bers wanted to improve, while others remained resigned to their situa-tions and less enthusiastic about the group. This difference in group members brought about interaction. The interaction was augmented and accelerated by the purposeful use of group activities that were employed to activate interactions and attitudes in specific situations confronting the group members. Once the dynamics of the situation became crystallized, it was possible to identify alternatives. Activities are more action-oriented and can be put to effective use with Chicano youth, who are more prone to show reactions than to discuss them. In these activities, all group mem-bers participated (part of the contract), and sometimes school personnel were invited to observe group activities as well as to interact at group meetings. Several new members were added to the group over a period of time. Some were referred and some came voluntarily. The group essentially was open-ended, and subject-focused instead of problem-focused. However, group members could freely bring problems to the group. We felt that through an increased knowledge of the problems that confronted them, identifying the reasons for them, and through improved problem-solving skills that the members would gain the "power" and skills to address their situations more constructively. Sharing ideas among members provided new approaches to previous, faulty ones.

Group Activities

Minority members may distrust professionals even if they share the same ethnicity or race. A total focus on discussion will become awkward and soon characterized by extended periods of silence and boredom. If talk was the key to improving behavior, then these students would have improved long ago. Engagement in activities bring about greater participation, both verbally and nonverbally. Also, they increase interactions among group members. Activities were selected for their educational and therapeutic values. Activities are valuable in group work with Chicanos, and the success of the group often depends on them. The activities selected for the group were bibliotherapy, sociodrama, psychodrama, auxiliary chair techniques, and group discussions, all of which involved interaction. Most of these activities called for role-playing. Luchins (1964) suggests that role-playing provides group members with the opportunity to present their expectations and achievement in social situations and to receive feedback on their previous roles and expectations. McDaniel et al. (1961) state that role-playing provides the advantage of developing a social situation in behavioral operations rather than in verbal terminology. In essence, role-playing situations focus on the social roles that people carry, the expectations of these roles, and the types of interactions that occur as they are actualized in intergroup and interpersonal relations.

Group members may be asked for examples of situations in which they feel conflicted. A situation can then be developed to duplicate this experience. The simulation of these experiences within the group provides valuable insights into how such situations can be better handled in the future. The social and psychological ramifications of racism and life experiences can be demonstrated through sociodrama and psychodrama. Sociodrama focuses on group problems, while psychodrama focuses on an individual's problems. Through reflection on these simulated experiences, group members are able to view their situations and the forces that have contributed to them. With this understanding, self-image and behavior improve.

Sociodrama is an extremely beneficial activity for addressing racism as a structural phenomenon; it can also be helpful in dispelling feelings of inferiority brought on by the dominant society's rejection of group members' culture. This activity can also be helpful in modifying racist attitudes of dominant group members when it is viewed by them. For example, a teacher who witnessed a sociodrama gained insight into how he was viewed by group members. He was unaware of his insensitivity to the plight of these youth. Another particularly revealing incident occurred in a role-playing situation. This incident highlighted the different views that existed between the older and younger generations. A Chicano youth attempted to explain to his parents the importance of studying for an examination. The parents had expected him to devote his time to another responsibility. This led to conflict. However, such conflicts are not unusual when two cultures with different expectations are involved. Ramirez (1972) states:

> Not only is this group the victim of limited education, but more often than not it is characterized by inferior educational preparation. Lack of education of the adult population has a real effect on the educational aspirations and on the educational achievement of the youth. Parents, therefore, seldom represent positive role models with regard to the requirements, restrictions, etc. of the greater society. (p. 118)

This example points up the need for the group worker to become involved with the families around resolving differences and in emphasizing the role of parents in the educational process (Brown, 1981). Bibliotherapy is a useful activity in helping Chicano youth gain an understanding of the contributions of Mexican-Americans to American society. It is equally useful in helping to dispel myths about Mexican Americans (Gaviglio, 1975).

In this integrated models approach, the group worker cannot confine activities to a specific location. He or she must be willing to go beyond the group setting and interact with group members and others in the neighborhood and in social agencies. Extragroup influence (Vinter, 1974) is critical. The worker attempts to negotiate and mediate police-youth conflict, family quarrels, and teacher-pupil estrangements. Such behavior is in keeping with the integrated models approach of intervening at various levels of society to address dysfunctional interactions that result in negative consequences.

Themes in the Group

Several themes that presented themselves in the group revolved around cultural conflict, especially powerlessness and alienation (somewhat characteristic of the feelings of minority members in a majority society), racism, anger, frustration, and feelings of inadequacy that were tied to feelings of inferiority. These themes reinforce the importance of an integrated models perspective in group work with Chicano youth, since change is indicated in a variety of systems that contribute to their problems. Because these themes are so related to racism, the group in a sense became a consciousness-raising one. Ventilation served a cathartic purpose, and it was important for the group worker to allow members to ventilate their anger and to listen to them. Helping to build a positive image or a better self-image was also important for these youth. To a degree this was accomplished through helping them to view and reflect on the Chicano past. It is in this area that the role of educator and historian of the Chicano experience becomes important. If the group worker lacks this knowledge, he or she will be unable to help in a crucial area.

Many of these youth lacked a real understanding of their past, since Chicano history is not stressed in public schools. Psychological feelings as well as cultural worth improved as members gained some awareness of their past. They also developed some awareness of how, through their behavior, they were contributing to a self-fulfilling prophecy. As these youth through various group activities reexperienced past hurts, they gained some knowledge of how to cope differently with negative encounters. They became aware that they had been negatively programmed for failure. In a sense the group was helpful in deprogramming them and their overall behavior, and their self-image improved. This is not to say that their problems were resolved, or that they did not face a constant struggle. However, they gained from the group the strength to address these problems more constructively.

Conclusion

An integrated models perspective to group work practice with Chicano youth in the school setting employs features from the three models identified by Papell and Rothman (1966) and incorporates them into a framework for guiding group work practice. This approach is indicated in group work with this population, since stress on the group members emanates from a variety of social systems at different levels of society. It attempts to address structural and individual problems that contribute to educational failure. The knowledge base of this approach is heavily dependent on symbolic interactionism and role theory. Roles as evidenced by participants in the various systems become the unit of analysis for identifying stress points and planning intervention. The emphasis of this approach is on social interactions and how these interactions, invariably consisting of power situations, negatively effect Chicano youth.

Chicano youth are not viewed as deviants, but as youth who have encountered negative situations that have influenced their perceptions of themselves and consequently of their role functioning. The group worker is called on to assume a variety of roles in mediating and modifying the social environment of these youth, as well as the perceptions held of them by others who interact with them in social encounters. Action-oriented activities constitute an important part of the group structure. Group members gain new knowledge and skills as they participate and reflect on their experiences in a dominant society with a history of racism. These reflections have positive effects in achieving behavioral change as the youth become aware of alternative ways of dealing with racist encounters. The problems presented are not viewed as a result of individual problems, but rather as a result of systemic dysfunctioning characterized by negative interactions between Chicano youth and the educational setting.

References

Arevalo, R., and Brown, J. "An Emerging Perspective on School Social Work," *School Social Work Quarterly*, Fall, 1979, 1.

Blumer, Herbert. *Symbolic Interactionism: Perspective and Method.* Englewood Cliffs, N.J.: Prentice-Hall, 1969.

Brager, George, and Specht, Harry. "The Process of Community Work." In *Readings in Community Organization Practice*, Ralph Kramer and Harry Specht, eds. Englewood Cliffs, N.J.: Prentice-Hall, 1975.

Briar, Scott. "Social Casework and Social Group Work: Historical and Social Science Foundation." *Encyclopedia of Social Work*, 16th ed. New York: National Association of Social Workers, 1971.

Brown, John A. "Voluntary Associations among Ethnic Minority Groups in Detroit, Michigan: A Comparative Analysis." Ph.D. diss. University of California, Berkeley, 1975.

_____ "Parent-Education Groups for Mexican-Americans." *Social Work in Education*, July 1981.

Brown, J., and Arevalo, R. "Chicanos and Social Group Work Models: Implications for Group Work Practice." *Social Work with Groups*, Winter 1979.

Burger, Henry. "Ethno-Lematics: Evoking 'Shy' Spanish American Pupils by Cross-Cultural Mediations." *Adolescence*, Spring 1972.

Carter, Thomas. *Mexican-Americans in School: A History of Eduational Neglect.* New York, College Entrance Examination Board, 1970.

de Tocqueville, Alexander. *Democracy in America*, vol. 2. New York: Vintage Books, 1945.

Deutsch, Morton, and Krauss, Robert. *Theories in Social Psychology.* New York: Basic Books, 1965.

Faris, B. et al. "The Neighborhood, The Settlement House: Mediator for the Poor." In *The Practice of Group Work*, William Schwartz and Serapo Zalba, eds. New York: Columbia University Press, 1971.

Gaviglio, Glen. "The Myths of the Mexican American." In *Modern Sociological Issues*, Barry Wishart and Louis Reichman, eds. New York: Macmillan, 1975.

Guerra, Manuel, H. "The Mexican-American Child: Problems or Talents." In *Pain and the Promise: The Chicano Today*, Edward Simmen, ed. New York: New American Library, 1972.

Handlin, Oscar. *Race and Nationality in American Life.* New York: Doubleday/Anchor Books, 1957.

Hartford, Margaret. *Groups in Social Work.* New York: Columbia University Press, 1971.

Heller, Celia. *Mexican-American Youth.* New York: Random House, 1966.

Luchins, Abraham. *Group Therapy: A Guide to Practice.* New York: Random House, 1964.

Maloney, Sara E. "The Interview in Group Work and Casework: A Comparison." In *Social Work with Groups.* New York: National Association of Social Work, 1958.

McDaniel, H. B., et al. *Readings in Guidance.* New York: Holt, Rinehart & Winston, 1961.

Papell, C., and Rothman, B. "Social Group Work Models: Possession and Heritage." *Journal of Education for Social Work,* Fall 1966.

Ramirez, S. "Employment Problems of Mexican-American Youth." In *Pain and the Promise: The Chicano Today,* Edward Simmen, ed., New York: New American Library, 1972.

Rothman, Jack. "Three Models of Community Organization Practice." In *Strategies of Community Organization,* Fred Cox et al., eds. Itasca, Ill., Peacock Publishers, 1970.

Savage, D. "Latino Students' Failures Staggering, Report Says," Oakland, Calif., *The Oakland Tribune,* December 13, 1984.

Schwartz, William. "Social Group Work: The Interactionist Approach." In *Encyclopedia of Social Work,* 16th ed. New York: National Association of Social Workers, 1971.

Shulman, L. *The Skills of Helping Individuals and Groups.* Itasca, Ill.: Peacock Publishers, 1979.

Smelser, Neil, and Smelser, William. "Introduction: Analyzing Personality and Social Systems." In *Personality and Social Systems,* R. Smelser and W. Smelser, eds. New York: John Wiley & Sons, 1963.

Smith, William et al. *Minority Issues in Mental Health.* Reading, Mass: Addison-Wesley, 1978.

Sytz, Florence. "Jane Addams and Social Action." *Social Work,* October, 1960.

Vinter, Robert. "The Essential Components of Social Group Work Practice." In *Individual Change Through the Small Group,* Paul Glasser et al., eds., New York: The Free Press, 1974.

Whittaker, James. "Models of Group Development: Implications for Group Work Practice." In *The Practice of Social Work,* R. Klenk and R. Ryan, eds., 2d ed., Belmont, Calif: Wadsworth, 1974.

Notes

1. In this paper Mexican-Americans and Chicanos are used interchangeably.

2. An excellent example of how the situation determines behavior is given in Stanley Elkins, *Slavery: A Problem in America's Institutional Life* (Chicago: Univer-

sity of Chicago Press, 1959) in which he compares the Jewish experience in the concentration camp with the blacks in slavery.

3. We have consistently searched for knowledge which has relevance for group work practice with Chicanos in which problem-causation is not located primarily within the individual but also in society resulting from society-individual interactions. This group afforded the chance to test such knowledge as drawn from symbolic interactionism. Essentially this was an experimental group work approach with Chicano youth. Because of its effectiveness, we plan to develop it to a greater degree in a later paper.

Part VI

Planning the Future Through Research

Part VI, "Planning the Future Research," includes three chapters, each based on findings of empirical research with small groups. Chapter 19, "Models of Group Intervention Used by Social Workers: Results of a Self-Report Survey," provides the results of a study of M.S.W.s in a midwestern community. Four areas of interest were pursued: (1) technical orientation to intervention; (2) group purposes; (3) leader activities; and (4) evaluation techniques. A standardized questionnaire was administered.

The findings suggest a proclivity toward electicism in intervention orientation among the fourteen theoretical models, but much greater concensus concerning group purposes and leader activities. Self-evaluation by the clients and goal completion were the most frequently rated modes of evaluation reported. Cross-comparisons between theoretical orientation to intervention and the other three variables do not show much consistency. In the discussion the authors raise some intriguing questions not only about the methodology of the student but also about the meaning of theoretical orientation and its relationship to actual practice.

Chapter 20, "Video Stimulus-Modeling Methodology: A format for Leadership Training in Social Work with Groups," presents an empirical training methodology for group workers. Little, if any, research exists to identify effective group behaviors. The chapter identifies modeling, behavioral rehearsal, and video feedback as essential tools in isolating and studying selected group behaviors. A classification system for categorizing twelve selected group-leadership behaviors is presented based on their import in the literature. These are used as criterion measures against which modeled videotaped behaviors of trainee/participants are evaluated. The methodology was found to be statistically significant using a one-tailed *t*-test for rating interjudge reliability and a Spearman's Rank correlation coefficient for the validity of each of the twelve behaviors selected for the stimulus/modeling videotape. Modeling through videotapes is strongly suggested for groups, since it minimizes trial-and-error learning and allows multiple chances at shaping actual behavior to modeled actions. Focus is on stimulus-modeling vignettes of desired behaviors, followed by student enactment of these, finally evaluated through video feedback. A step-by-step format for presenting the tape is delineated, and the success of an empirical study of the training efficacy of these procedures is provided. Finally, the chapter advocates that the methodology be incorporated in all facets of training for group workers.

Chapter 21, "Evaluation and Multilevel Validation of Group Services: A Brief Review of Requirements, Problems, Options, and a Proposal," focuses on the need to convince "decision makers" that group services must be given higher visibility as well as higher priority in funding. This is especially true for the status of group work since over the years it has declined in favor of individual-based interventions. However recently, the pendulum has begun once again to swing toward group work; hence, group workers must be willing to evaluate their practice to ensure proper funding. Moreover, such validation of practice needs to be marketed to planning and allocation organizations and other funding sources. The chapter proposes a multilevel-validation approach based on specific organizational services and gives examples of such studies developed through the efforts of the United Way in a few metropolitan centers. Finally, the author suggests that the research formats of these plans be modified and applied to other similar settings.

19

Models of Group Intervention Used by Social Workers: Results of a Self-Report Survey

Ronald H. Rooney, Alissa P. Herbst, Karen Rosenzweig, and Ellen Stacy

Although practice with groups of social workers antedates the use of the group modality by other professions (Wilson, 1976), the formal development of group work models is fairly recent (Roberts and Northen, 1976). There have been no published studies surveying the intervention models social workers actually employ in groups. A self-report survey of actual practice by master's-degree social workers who lead groups in one midwestern city is presented in this study. The survey was designed to answer several research questions: What models of group intervention are used and with what frequency? What group purposes, activities of the leader, and evaluation techniques are used and how often? A standardized questionnaire-interview format was used with randomly selected master's-degree social workers who lead groups. Although there is some evidence that the actual practice of group leaders may differ from their self-report of models and intervention used (Lieberman, Yalom, and Miles, 1973), in the absence of formal studies of actual practice by a wide range of social workers, a first step toward understanding their practice can be attained by studying their own reported usage of models, purposes, leader activities, and evaluation techniques.

The authors wish to express their appreciation for the conscientious, enthusiastic work done by seven social work research students who aided in the development of the questionnaire instrument and who conducted the in-person interviews. Appreciation is also given to colleagues Joan Robertson and Steve Rose for their helpful suggestions and comments on earlier drafts.

Review of the Literature

Group work theorists have been concerned that the advent of generalist core courses for social work students may result in the graduation of students to practice with groups who lack sufficient training in social group work intervention (Hartford, 1976; Hellenbrand, 1978). Lang commented that this reduction in group work skill training in graduate programs appears to have resulted in excessive eclecticism, with a great deal of borrowing from beyond the boundaries of the profession, lacking sufficient deliberation about the fit of the borrowed procedures to the ethical base and practice context of the profession (Lang, 1979). Unfortunately, there are no published studies of group work to support or dispute this assertion. Jayaratne (1978) found that more than half of a random sample of clinical social workers who were members of NASW identified themselves as eclectic (defined as the use of two or more theories informing their regular practice). Since practitioners frequently reported the combination of orientations that conflict in theory, he concluded that it is virtually impossible to develop a precise definition of clinical eclecticism beyond the simple notion that clinicians pick and choose among many different theories and techniques. While social group workers often practice in settings with professionals outside of social work, little is known about the degree to which social group work practice is eclectic, or how much social group workers are influenced by non-social-work models. The objective of this research was therefore to identify specifically what a sample of social workers believe about and do in groups. Answers to questions of this sort will fill a void in the literature and provide a base for further study.

Research Design

Sample Selection Process

A two-phase procedure of telephone calls to agencies and social workers listed in the telephone directory and referrals from other social workers was used to generate a sample of the estimated *total* population of master's-degree social workers who led groups in a medium-sized midwestern community (population: 174,000). These procedures produced a total screening pool of 138, as detailed in Table 19.1. Subsequently, half of these 138 social workers who led groups were randomly selected, controlling for sex and agency size such that the proportion of each was exactly reproduced in the actual sample. Given some margin of error in the screening process, it is important to stress that approximately three-quarters of the original sample pool was contacted. Finally, 69 (.66) of the sample contacts ($n = 102$) agreed to participate in the study. As Table 19.1 shows, 18 percent of those contacted were either not group leaders or

Table 19.1. Pool of Sample Selection

Categories of Response	Number	Percent
Total in social group worker pool	138	100
Total number of social workers screened	102	76
Social workers who agreed to participate	69	66*
Not group workers or M.S.W.s	19	18
No time available to participate	6	6
Refused to participate	3	3
Interviewed in pretest	5	5

*Percentage of those screened who agreed to participate. The 69 group workers who agreed to participate represented 54 percent of the total pool.

not master's-degree group workers, and 9 percent had no time or refused to participate.

Measurement Indexes

The instrument contained questions about models of intervention and group purposes utilized and most frequent leader activities and modes of evaluation employed. Additional questions were asked about the use of pregroup-orientation techniques and group-work training, which are reported elsewhere (Rooney, Rooney, and Herbst, 1980; Rooney and Herbst, 1980).

Group Intervention Models Utilized. Respondents were presented with a list of ten models of group interventions and the names of theorists associated with each. Four models were from the social group work literature: psychosocial (Northen); preventive-rehabilitative (Vinter); task-centered (Garvin, Reid, and Epstein); and social-work–behavioral (Rose). Six models were drawn from group-psychotherapy literature: transactional analysis (Berne); gestalt (Perls); psychoanalytic (Yalom and Slavson); Rogerian (Rogers); rational-emotive (Ellis), and psychology-based behavioral.[1] Other models might have been included, such as the functional mediating, and developmental models of social group work, but respondents could add other models to those listed. Respondents were asked to rank those models used in their practice and omit those that were not used.

Group Purposes Utilized. Ten group purposes were listed: problem-solving, communication skills, social skills, personal growth, assertiveness, support, insight, child management, parenting, and weight loss. Respondents were again asked to rank those used, to omit those not used and add any others not included on the list.

Leader Activities. Eight leader activities were listed: leading group discussion, setting up the physical structure of the meeting place, modeling desired behavior, teaching concepts or skills, setting rules, using behavioral assignments, counseling members outside the group, and using role-plays. Respondents were asked to rate whether the activities were used in all, most, few, or none of the sessions they led. As before, respondents could add other frequently used activities that were not listed.

Modes of Evaluation Employed. Respondents rated nine modes of evaluation as to whether they were always, usually, rarely, or never used. They could add other evaluation modes than those listed and could report that no formal modes of evaluation were used. The nine listed modes of evaluation were: leader assessment of client progress, client self-evaluation of progress, goal completion, contract fulfillment, behavioral measures before and after the group, behavioral measures after the group only, attitude measures, self-concept measures, and personality inventories.

Data Collection

The primary data collection instrument was a group survey questionnaire. The instrument was pretested on twenty-five respondents who fit the criteria of the sample of master's-degree social workers who lead groups but were not randomly sampled. Some questions were asked in an open-ended format in the pretest and then were changed to close-ended questions in the actual survey, with categories developed from analysis of the pretest. Additional response categories were added to close-ended questions from analysis of the "other" responses to the pretest. The instrument was administered by trained student research interviewers.

Description of the Sample

More than 60 percent of the respondents were female. The average group worker in the sample had been working with groups for five years since graduation and had run about twenty groups. Three-quarters worked all or most of the time in public settings, and about half worked at least occasionally with involuntary clients. Groups usually ran to twelve sessions or fewer. Three-quarters worked in educational or preventive settings, while only 19 percent were in private counseling; 40 percent worked in small agencies employing three or fewer M.S.W.s, while 36 percent worked in larger agencies employing ten or more M.S.W.s. Group work tasks took an average of eight hours of paid work time each week, or less than 20 percent of the work week. Pregroup interviews were frequently used by 70 percent of the sample, and a written description was used by more than half as part of pregroup orientation. Modes of pregroup orientation that have the primary purpose of aiding the prospective member to make an informed choice were less frequently used than those that aid the leader in assessing the appropriateness of the member for the group (Rooney and Herbst, 1980). Respondents listed their own experience in leading groups and interaction with co-workers as greater influences on practice than workshops, formal courses, books, articles, and research (Rooney, Rooney, and Herbst, 1980).

Since comparable data are not available for social-work practice with groups in other communities or, in fact, for group practice by other professionals, such as psychologists and psychiatrists it is not known whether this sample is typical of group work practice or distinctive from the group practice by other professions. The finding that the group practice of these respondents was largely part-time, often carried out in public settings and frequently working with involuntary clients, may be distinctive from the practice of more traditional group psychotherapy. (see Table 19.2).

Table 19.2. **Demographic Characteristics**

	n	Percentage of Sample
Sex		
Male	27	39
Female	42	61
Number of years in the field		
1–3	26	38
4–6	18	26
7–10	8	12
11–39	17	25
Number of groups led		
1–5	14	20
6–10	9	13
11–20	14	20
21–100	21	30
100+	11	16
Proportion of time in private practice		
0	38	55
1–49	11	16
50–99	8	12
100	12	17
Agency size		
1–3 MSWs	28	41
4–9 MSWs	16	23
10+ MSWs	25	36

Research Findings

The Use of Group Intervention Models

Respondents listed a mean of five of the listed models as influencing their practice, with none reporting influence by only one model. Only four models (task-centered, social-work–behavioral, gestalt, and Rogerian) were listed by more than half of the respondents (See Table 19.3), and almost half added another model to those listed. In fact, the "other" models had a higher mean rank than any of the ten listed models. Fourteen additional models were listed by respondents, only one of which was based in social work (problem-solving generalist). Among those models added that are not based in social work were body therapies, rational behavior (Maltzlox), national training labs (NTL), provocative, existential, and radical therapy, but none of these was listed by more than one respondent.

When another model was added, respondents were consistent in ranking it as a high influence. The models of social group work were on the whole less frequently listed and ranked lower than those models developed outside social work. If one considers the Rose model as allied with a behavioral model developed outside work, the influence of social group work models appears to be even more limited. The social-work–behavioral model had a higher mean rank than any of the other nine models and was listed as influencing more than half of the respondents. Frequency of listing and mean rank did not always correspond, as in the case of the task-centered model; the model was listed more frequently than any others, yet the mean rank was fifth of the ten. One interpretation might be that the task-centered model was frequently used but of relatively low influence. Of interest is the fact that the psychoanalytic model was least frequently listed and the lowest influence of the ten models.

Table 19.3. **Influence of Group Intervention Models**

	Percentage*	Mean Rank**	Standard Deviation
Other model (not categorized)	44	2.07	2.07
Social work–behavioral (Rose)	54	2.70	1.71
Gestalt (Perls)	52	2.86	1.98
Psychology-based behavioral	28	3.00	2.08
Task-centered (Garvin, Reid, Epstein)	58	3.08	1.87
Rogerian (Rogers)	52	3.28	1.78
Psychosocial (Northen)	33	3.35	1.90
Preventive rehabilitative (Vinter)	46	3.50	2.21
Transactional analysis (Berne)	42	3.79	2.06
Rational emotive (Ellis)	44	4.13	2.08
Psychoanalytic (Yalom, Slavson)	26	4.67	2.54

*The percent of the sample ($n = 69$) ranking the model as an influence.

**The mean rank given the model by those respondents reporting use of it.

In order to examine the combinations of models used, a frequency distribution was developed of models listed among the top three influences (see Table 19.4). Every *possible* combination of models was listed within the top three influences by at least one group leader. The most frequent combinations were gestalt and Rogerian and behavioral and task-centered, with about a quarter of the sample listing each combination. Seemingly conflicting orientations, such as a combination of a behavioral orientation and Rogerian or gestalt, were listed by almost 20 percent of the sample, and three respondents listed both behavioral and psychoanalytic orientations.

The highly eclectic use of models appears to characterize this sample of group workers. By Jayaratne's definition of eclecticism, *all* of the respondents would be considered eclectic. Since the survey was not designed to study eclecticism, data are not available to determine whether workes practice different models with different groups or blend them within a single group. Nine respondents commented that their practice was characterized by an eclectic combination of models. One group leader commented that "I use many models together, based on the need to serve. I don't think in terms of a model." A second noted, "No experienced therapist uses any of these models to the letter; they incorporate it into their practice. It is more important to understand and use the concepts and theory rather than a model per se." Since the question did not specify current influences, it is possible that conflicting orientations might represent changes over time; one respondent noted that his present frame of reference differed from the past, making the question difficult to answer.

While there was low consensus on model use and theoretical eclecticism of some form, consensus was high on the purposes for groups.

Most Frequent Group Purposes

Respondents selected a mean of 5.8 purposes for groups per person, with seven of the ten listed purposes selected by more than half. Three of the more generic purposes (problem-solving, communication skills and support) were included as purposes by more than three-quarters of the sample, with problem-solving and communication skills achieving the highest mean rank of listed purposes. More specialized purposes such as weight loss and parenting were less frequently selected. Of the twenty-one write-in responses added by respondents, eleven could be categorized as "training, education" with specialized purposes, such as imparting information about health, adoption, foster care, and stress management. The high ranking of skill-teaching purposes (problem-solving, commmunication skills, and social skills) might also be explained by the high number of workers in an educational-preventive setting.

Table 19.4. Frequency Distribution of Group Intervention Models

Models of Group Intervention	PS	R	G	TC	TA	PR	Psych	SWB	RET	Psybeh
Psychosocial (PS)	17(.25)*	12**	10	9	7	9	7	9	4	7
Rogerian (R)		28(.41)	23	13	14	10	9	19	9	12
Gestalt (G)			29(.42)	16	17	10	11	19	14	9
Task-Centered (TC)				33(.48)	7	20	6	22	15	10
Transactional Analysis (TA)					19(.28)	14	4	10	6	7
Preventive-Rehabilitative (PR)						23(.33)	3	4	7	6
Psychoanalytic (Psych)							9(.13)	4	3	4
Social-Work–Behavioral (SWB)								32(.46)	20	16
Rational Emotive (RET)									19(.28)	7
Psychology-based Behavioral (Psybeh)										15(.22)

*The diagonal represents the number and percent of all group leaders reporting the use of the group model within their top three influences.
**The number of group leaders reporting this combination of group models within their top three influences.

Table 19.5. Group Purposes

	Percentage*	Mean Rank**	Standard Deviation
Other	30	2.67	1.53
Problem-solving	77	2.76	1.81
Communication skills	83	2.97	1.50
Social skills	59	3.12	1.57
Personal growth	70	3.42	2.07
Assertiveness	54	3.73	2.18
Support	78	3.80	1.94
Insight	32	4.59	2.22
Child management	52	4.11	2.52
Parenting	36	4.72	1.86
Weight loss	6	4.75	3.50

*The percent of the sample who reported leading groups with this purpose.
**The mean rank given by those respondents who lead groups with this purpose.

A frequency distribution was developed (see Table 19.6) with the top four choices of intervention models and top six group purposes selected (the mean number of choices for each). As in the frequency distribution of group intervention models reported above, every possible combination of group purposes and group intervention model was selected by at least one person. The most frequently occurring combinations, with about 40 percent each, were communication skills as a purpose and a social-work–behavioral, gestalt, or task-centered intervention mode. In addition to the percentage of the total sample selecting each combination, the percentage of those who had selected a model within their top four who also selected a given purpose within the top six was also calculated. In this way, the distribution of purposes could be better examined with the less frequently selected intervention models. The same range of percentages appears for each model; there were only slight tendencies for certain models to be associated with certain purposes. All three persons who frequently work with weight loss as a purpose noted task-centered, rational-emotive, and social-work–behavioral orientations. Yet within the total of those selecting these models as influences, relatively few worked with weight loss.

Chi-square tables were developed between purposes selected and number of years of postgraduate practice. Assertiveness was the only purpose significantly associated with years in the field; fifteen (.48) workers with four or fewer years of experience ranked assertiveness among their top six group purposes, whereas only seven workers (.18) with more than four years' experience did.

It appears that there was more consensus among respondents about group purposes than there was on using models of intervention, with three purposes ranked by more than 70 percent of the sample, while only

Table 19.6. Frequency Distribution of Group Purposes by Group Intervention Models

					Models of Group Intervention					
Group Purposes	Group Purposes (n = 69)	Psychosocial (n = 17)*	Rogerian (n = 28)**	Gestalt (n = 29)	Task-centered (n = 33)	Transactional analysis (n = 19)	Preventive-rehabilitative (n = 23)	Psychoanalytic (n = 9)	Social-work-behavior (n = 32)	Rational emotive (n = 19)	Psychology-based behavioral (n = 15)
Social skills	41	65(16)*	61(25)**	57(25)	66(32)	42(12)	65(22)	44(6)	69(32)	63(17)	67(14)
Assertiveness	31	41(10)	54(22)	57(25)	33(16)	53(14)	39(13)	55(7)	53(25)	63(17)	73(16)
Communication skills	56	76(19)	89(36)	93(39)	82(39)	84(23)	83(28)	55(7)	84(39)	68(19)	87(19)
Parenting	21	24(6)	36(14)	38(16)	27(13)	42(12)	30(10)	44(5)	44(20)	21(6)	40(9)
Child management	17	18(4)	18(7)	31(13)	21(10)	37(10)	26(9)	33(4)	28(13)	26(7)	27(6)
Personal growth	43	55(13)	71(29)	69(29)	61(29)	63(17)	57(19)	66(9)	59(28)	58(16)	67(14)
Insight	30	59(14)	46(19)	41(17)	27(13)	42(12)	39(13)	66(7)	38(17)	47(13)	47(10)
Weight loss	3	6(1)	4(1)	3(1)	9(4)	5(1)	4(1)	11(1)	9(4)	16(4)	13(3)
Support	49	88(22)	71(29)	72(30)	79(38)	68(19)	74(25)	66(9)	66(30)	68(19)	73(16)
Problem-solving	51	88(20)	71(29)	66(28)	82(39)	63(17)	78(26)	55(7)	78(36)	68(19)	80(17)

*The percent of those respondents ranking the model among their four influences who rank this group purpose among their top six. This is the first number in each vertical column or horizontal row.

**The percent of the total sample (n = 69) who ranked both the model among the top four and the group purpose among the top six. This is the second number, in parentheses, in each vertical column or horizontal row.

four intervention models were ranked by more than half. The impression of considerable eclecticism in the sample is maintained, however, since at least one respondent selected every possible combination of intervention model and group purpose. Although it might be assumed that certain models of intervention might fit more readily with particular group purposes, percentages within those selecting each intervention model were generally similar across group purposes. The fact that a model of intervention and a group purpose were both highly ranked by a respondent does not necessarily mean that they were used together in the same group.

Usage of Group-Leader Activities

Group leaders reported usage of a mean of each of the eight leader activities that were recorded as at least sometimes used by more than 80 percent of the sample. Three activities were reported by respondents as used in all or most sessions: leading group discussion, setting up the physical structure of the meeting place, and modeling desired behavior. Use of behavioral assignments, counseling members outside the group, and role-plays were used more rarely (see Table 19.7).

Since certain models specify particular techniques, it was anticipated that the distribution of intervention models and leader activities would not be random. As in the case of the other frequency distribution, there were at least two group leaders who reported each possible combination of activity and intervention model (see Table 19.8).

Since the behavioral and task-centered models frequently call for use of behavioral assignments, it was anticipated that those respondents who listed these models as high influences would also report frequent usage of behavioral assignments. Although a higher proportion of the behaviorally influenced practitioners reported frequent usage of behavioral as-

Table 19.7.   Leader Activities

	Percentage*	Mean Rating**	Standard Deviation
Leading group discussion	99	1.57	.63
Setting up physical structure of meeting place	93	1.80	.92
Leader models desired behavior	96	1.81	.83
Leader sets rules	96	2.13	.82
Leader uses behavioral assignments	83	2.59	.91
Leader counsels members outside the group	88	2.61	.84
Leader uses role-plays	87	2.65	.82

*The percentage of responsents (n = 69) who use this leadership activity at least occasionally.

**Rating scale was 1 = always, 2 = usually, 3 = rarely, 4 = never in all sessions.

Table 19.8. Frequency Distribution of Group Intervention Models by Leader Activities

					Models of Group Intervention					
Leader Activities	Leader Activities (n = 69)	Psychosocial (n = 17)	Rogerian (n = 28)	Gestalt (n = 29)	Task-centered (n = 33)	Transactional analysis (n = 19)	Preventive-rehabilitative (n = 23)	Psychoanalytic (n = 9)	Social-work-behavior (n = 32)	Rational emotive (n = 19)	Psychology-based behavioral (n = 15)
Model	57	*82(20)**	89(36)	83(35)	82(39)	89(25)	83(28)	66(9)	84(39)	84(23)	93(20)
Teach	48	53(13)	71(29)	79(33)	64(30)	79(22)	70(30)	44(6)	75(35)	74(20)	80(17)
Role-play	27	24(6)	43(17)	59(25)	36(17)	42(11)	26(9)	33(4)	50(23)	47(13)	60(13)
Setup	56	88(22)	79(32)	76(32)	79(38)	95(26)	91(30)	78(10)	88(40)	79(22)	93(20)
Counsel outside group	27	29(7)	21(9)	34(14)	42(20)	21(6)	61(20)	22(3)	31(14)	32(9)	20(4)
Rules	47	65(16)	68(28)	72(30)	70(33)	68(19)	57(19)	66(9)	69(32)	74(20)	66(14)
Assignments	32	24(6)	46(19)	45(19)	36(17)	42(11)	35(11)	44(6)	56(26)	47(13)	60(13)
Discuss	66	100(25)	93(38)	97(40)	94(45)	100(28)	96(32)	89(12)	94(43)	100(28)	100(22)

*The percentage of the high users of the group intervention model who frequently use this activity. This is the first number in each vertical column or horizontal row.

**This is the second number, in parentheses, in each vertical column or horizontal row.

signments than was true of those influenced by other models, use by more than slightly over half of those workers might have been anticipated. Since the task-centered model specifically calls for use of tasks completed by clients outside sessions, the low reported usage by those identifying themselves with that model is particularly mystifying. The responsibility to lead discussion, to set up the physical structure of the meeting rooms, and to set rules was frequently reported across users of all models. The leader modeling desired behavior was frequently used by more than 80 percent of the users of all models but psychoanalytic. Similarly, the psychoanalytic respondents were lowest of the ten in usage of the role of the leader as teacher of concepts and skills. This might fit the image of the psychoanalytically influenced practitioners in groups as playing a less active role than practitioners influenced by other models.

There was considerable range in the use of role-plays, with high usage reported by more than half the behavioral (both psychology and social-work-based) and the gestalt practitioners. Lowest usage was reported by psychosocial and preventive-rehabilitative practitioners. Counseling members individually outside the group session was used frequently by more than half of the preventive-rehabilitative practitioners, with most others using it infrequently.

Chi-square tables were developed between high usage of each leader activity and the number of years of experience in the field. Practitioners with four or fewer years of experience were more likely (p = .04) to teach concepts and skills than those with five or more years of experience.

While eighteen responses were added in the "other" category for leader activities, only four activities were mentioned more than once. Five workers commented that the leader role includes encouraging group participation, and three added that the worker role includes understanding the communication and power system of the group. Three workers mentioned the role of the leader as the facilitator of group exercises, such as the "empty chair" technique, fantasy, and body work, and two mentioned bringing in outside resources.

The ten listed leader activities were at least occasionally used by 80 percent of the sample, and five activities were used in all or most sessions. Although there were slight tendencies for practitioners from particular orientations to report a bit more or less than others of some activities, on the whole the pattern of usage appeared similar across the models. One explanation might be that the activities were cast at such a global level that all practitioners, regardless of orientation, could report high usage, while their actual use and understanding of each might differ. Another explanation might be that these activities form a core of group work practice regardless of theoretical orientation. There might be a similarity of function that surpasses theoretical differences.

Use of Evaluation Techniques

More than half of the respondents reported at least occasional use of eight of the nine listed evaluation techniques, with a mean of four techniques reported as used in all or most groups (see Table 19.9). Leader assessment of client progress, client self-evaluation of progress, and goal completion were reported by more than 90 percent of the sample as used in all or most groups. Formal modes of evaluation, such as behavioral, attitude change, self-concept, and personality measures, were reported as rarely used.

Frequency distributions were tabulated between use of group intervention models and frequent use of evaluation modes (see Table 19.10). Three-quarters of the practitioners of each intervention model reported high usage of leader assessment and all but the psychoanalytic practitioners for client self-evaluation. Two-thirds of the practitioners of all models reported high usage of goal completion measures, with the exception again of psychoanalytic practitioners. More than half of the practitioners of five of the nine models reported high usage of contract completion. Less than a third of the practitioners of all nine models reported frequent usage of attitude-change measures and personality inventories, and less than half of each for self-concept measures. More than half of the behavioral and rational-emotive practitioners reported high usage of behavioral measures before and after the group, as though even higher percentages might have been expected. Less than a quarter of the psychoanalytic and transactional-analysis practitioners reported such high usage of behavioral measures.

Use of evaluation instruments and formal measures of behavioral change were found to be less frequently used by workers in the sample than less formal modes, such as assessment by the leader, client self-evaluation, and goal completion.

Table 19.9.   Use of Evaluation Techniques

	Percentage*	Mean Rating**	Standard Deviation
Leader assessment of client progress	93	1.81	.86
Client self-evaluation of progress	90	1.94	.91
Goal completion	90	2.04	.95
Contract fulfillment	70	2.75	1.02
Behavior measures before and after the group	64	2.83	1.10
Behavioral measures after the group	51	3.06	1.01
Attitude measures	62	3.07	.91
Self-concept measures	52	3.12	1.01
No formal evaluation	48	3.29	.89
Personality inventories	28	3.65	.64
Other forms of evaluation	70		

*Percentage of respondents (*n* = 69) who ever use this method of evaluation.
**Rating scale was 1 = always, 2 = usually, 3 = rarely, 4 = never.

Table 19.10. Frequency Distribution of Models of Group Interventions by Methods of Evaluation

Methods of Evaluation	Group Purposes (n = 69)	Psychosocial (n = 17)	Rogerian (n = 28)	Gestalt (n = 29)	Task-centered (n = 33)	Transactional analysis (n = 19)	Preventive-rehabilitative (n = 23)	Psychoanalytic (n = 9)	Social-work-behavior (n = 32)	Rational emotive (n = 19)	Psychology-based behavioral (n = 15)
Attitude-change measure	16	6(1)*	25(10)**	24(20)	27(13)	16(4)	26(9)	00(00)	31(14)	32(9)	20(4)
Self-concept	19	29(7)	29(12)	31(13)	36(17)	32(9)	39(13)	11(1)	28(13)	37(10)	33(7)
Goal achievement	51	71(17)	68(28)	72(30)	82(39)	74(20)	83(28)	44(6)	78(36)	79(22)	73(7)
Behavioral measure before and after group	26	35(9)	46(19)	34(14)	33(16)	26(7)	43(14)	22(3)	56(26)	53(14)	66(14)
Behavioral measure after a group	21	29(7)	29(12)	28(12)	33(16)	32(9)	43(14)	11(1)	34(16)	37(10)	33(14)
Personality inventories	4	6(1)	11(4)	7(3)	6(3)	00(00)	4(1)	00(00)	6(3)	00(00)	13(3)
Contract completion	30	53(13)	43(17)	55(23)	39(19)	63(17)	39(13)	44(6)	44(20)	53(14)	60(13)
Leader assessment	59	88(22)	86(35)	90(38)	85(40)	74(20)	91(30)	78(10)	81(38)	79(22)	80(17)
Client evaluation	57	82(20)	86(35)	86(36)	85(41)	91(30)	66(9)	78(36)	95(26)	87(19)	80(17)

*Percentage of those ranking the group intervention model within their top three who frequently used this method of evaluation. This is the first number in each vertical column or horizontal row.

**The percentage of the total sample (n = 69) who frequently used both the group intervention model and the method of evaluation. This is the second number, in parentheses, in each vertical column or horizontal row.

Summary

Before moving to a discussion of the possible implications of the findings, a brief review of the data may clarify the results.

1. Sixty-nine social workers who lead groups in a medium-sized midwestern city were randomly selected and interviewed about their practice with groups. Two-thirds of the sample were female, and most had worked for four or more years, leading twenty or more groups. Workers devoted eight hours, or less than 25 percent of their paid work week, to group work activities, and most were employed in public or educational-preventive settings.

2. The sixty-nine respondents reported usage of fourteen models of group intervention *in addition* to the list of ten provided in the instrument. There appeared to be little consensus in the models of intervention influencing practice. Seemingly diverse models were combined by workers, since every possible combination of models was reported as high influences by at least one worker, with most reporting the use of four group intervention models. Social group work models were less frequently ranked as high influences on practice than models of group work developed outside the profession.

3. Higher consensus was found around the purposes for groups, since support, problem-solving, and communication skills were ranked highly by 75 percent of the sample. Few discernible patterns could be found in the combination of intervention models and group purpose.

4. High consensus across the sample was found for the use of three leader activities: leading group discussions, setting up the physical structure of the meeting place, and modeling of desired behavior by the leader. There appeared to be less random association of intervention models with leader activities, since in six of the nine activities patterns of usage appeared consistent across theoretical orientations.

5. Assessment of client progress by the leader, self-evaluation by the client, and goal completion were the most frequently occurring modes of evaluation reported. Formal evaluation techniques using standardized instruments or behavioral measures were reported as rarely used in the sample, with only a slight tendency for the behavioral and rational-emotive practitioners to use behavioral measures.

Discussion

Retrospective awareness of problems in the design and implementation of a study is often the product of the process of analyzing data. Issues in reliability and internal and external validity will be considered before discussing the findings and exploring tentative directions for further work.

Reliability Issues

A measure is said to be reliable if the same data would have been collected in repeated observation of the same phenomena (Babbie, 1979). Social workers in this sample were asked to reflect over their entire postgraduate practice with groups. Clearly, this was a simpler task for those respondents who graduated most recently, since they were comparing experiences with relatively few groups, while those at the other extreme of experience were in some cases trying to recall more than a hundred groups. One respondent noted, as reported above, that a listing of models influencing practice was complicated by the fact that those influences have changed over time. Specifying current practice or putting a time limit of perhaps two years on that recollection might have aided in the specificity and reliability of the data gathered.

Validity Issues

Validity refers to the degree to which a measure accurately describes the concept it is intended to measure (Babbie, 1979). Internal validity, then, refers to the degree to which conclusions drawn accurately reflect the phenomena studied. Questions have been raised earlier about the validity of self-report data as an accurate measure of the data that might have been collected by another method, such as observation. The data in this study do not permit the conclusion that because a social group worker reports high influence by, for instance, a psychosocial model of practice, a trained observer would necessarily note the influence of that model on practice. The seeming diversity of the reports about the use of intervention models may reflect a pervasive unfamiliarity and lack of use of those models as defined. For example, although a high proportion of the respondents (.58) reported influence by the task-centered model, other reports indicating infrequent usage of behavioral assignments or tasks and the lack of association with a brief course of treatment could mean that the practitioners are familiar with the model but do not practice it as described by the developers (Garvin, Reid, and Epstein, 1976). More possibly, they indicate influence of the model based on the fact that much of their work is task-related—associating with the name as a description of part of their practice, rather than a full-fledged model. The data might also have been strengthened if respondents had been asked to report the specific models, activities, and evaluation modes they have used with a particular group.

The degree to which the findings can be generalized to other communities or areas (external validity) is also in question because the sample was drawn from one midwestern community. The fact that a well-known social-work behavioral theorist of group practice teaches in the community may also account for the relatively high influence of behavioral modes of group practice reported. Questions were not asked in the sample about the graduate school of social work attended, whether respondents had chosen a group work concentration, or the number of group-theory and intervention courses completed. Hence, inferences about the influence of graduate group work training cannot be drawn. The study can best be seen as a descriptive analysis of practice as reported by social workers who lead groups in one midwestern city. Similar studies need to be carried out with social group workers in varied employment settings and locales. Broader studies of group practice by bachelor's-degree level workers and those trained in other professions would also be useful. Also, controlled studies of actual observations of group workers in practice will be useful in describing more specifically the common intervention strategies actually employed.

Discussion of Findings

With these caveats, the findings of the study can be cautiously explored to aid in the generation of hypotheses about group work practice that might be tested using a less exploratory methodology.

1. Social workers leading groups in this sample reported many and diverse theoretical orientations to practice. This might reflect theoretical eclecticism, although the authors are inclined to agree with Jayaratne (1978) that the sense is rather one of *technique* eclecticism, with workers combining techniques based on what seems to work with their client group without major concerns about the underlying theoretical justification for the technique. More refined study is needed of the phenomenon of eclecticism. In one term, we lump together those who use complete models selectively with different client groups and problems, those who blend them in a personal mode of practice, and those who are simply eclectic in terms of their choice of techniques. In any case, "pure" association of those leader activities and evaluation modes one would expect to accompany high influence of models that exemplify their use was not found. When high usage of behavioral-change measures was not reported by self-described behaviorists, a few alternative hypotheses are suggested. Perhaps few practitioners trained in formal models actually followed their prescriptions to the degree expected by the model. It may also be that the realities and pressures of the practice situation may impede usage of techniques and activities even if the practitioner wished to do so. Thus, more study is required about the degree to which practitioners are guided by intervention models: Under what conditions and at what stages do practitioners appear to use formal models, and does this vary with the specificity of the model?

2. Higher consensus was found in the sample on the purpose of groups, leader activities, and evaluation modes used. This might simply

reflect that these activities were more concretely within the daily experience of the respondents than the issue of models influencing practice. Problem-solving, communication skills, and support were ranked as frequent purposes in the practice of three-quarters of the respondents. This relative consensus on purpose may not indicate that similar approaches are used to attain these purposes. They may also be indicative of the high numbers of practitioners in the sample employed in educational-preventive settings, in which teaching functions in groups are frequent. To the degree that social workers in other areas are heavily involved in skill-teaching functions with groups, group psychotherapy and social group work models focused on individual change may be less relevant than educational models of group practice.

All eight leader activities were reported to be used at least occasionally by more than 90 percent of the sample, with leading discussion, setting up the physical structure of the meeting room, and modeling desired behaviors ranked as employed in all sessions by most workers. Again, the activities may have been cast at such an abstract level that very real differences in the ways in which these activities might be performed might be hidden. It should be noted, however, that those respondents reporting high influence of psychoanalytic practice also reported considerably less frequent levels of these three highly active leader functions. These functions may be similar across most models or simply describe similarities in aproach to groups that are not influenced by models.

Leader assessment of progress, client self-evaluation, and goal completion were reported as used in all groups by 90 percent of the sample. Formalized modes of evaluation involving standardized instruments or measures of behavioral change were rarely used by respondents, regardless of reported theoretical influences. Data are not available from other fields as to whether such formalized evaluation modes are used more frequently than reported here. Lack of training in their usage, or a judgment that their value is not worth the expenditure of time and energy required, might explain their low usage here.

3. Among theoretical influences reported, social work models were ranked as less influential than models of group psychotherapy. Data from this sample might indicate that social workers are little influenced by formal models of group intervention, regardless of the source inside or out of the profession in the day-to-day choices of group purposes, leader activities in the group, and modes of evaluation.

In another study (Rooney, Rooney, and Herbst, 1980), group workers sampled were near consensus that both continuing-education materials for group workers and graduate group work curricula should concentrate on the teaching of specific technologies for work with specialized client groups and settings combined with a general understanding of the group as a functioning communications and power system. The teaching of theory was recommended primarily as an aid in understanding the rationale for techniques rather than as comprehensive guides to practice. There is evidence that the indiscriminate use of groups may be dangerous to group memmbers as well as helpful (Levinson, 1973; Galinsky and Schopler, 1977). Trainers and group work educators might well protest (and have) that such highly specialized concentration on particular techniques and specific groups can be counterproductive if not based in a firm understanding of a broader approach to practice. Whether desirable or not, results of this study would indicate that group workers want the kind of immediate "hands-on" training that they can directly apply when working with groups.

The burden is on continuing-education trainers, group work educators, and the group work theorists who influence them to demonstrate the integration of theoretical rationales for intervention, with guidance in selective use of appropriate techniques and modes of evaluation. Lang (1979) called on group work theorists to take this step in developing more specific guides to practice. Without such development, group workers, like the one in this sample, might be expected to be more highly influenced by non-social-work models or continue to develop highly personal models, selecting techniques to fit situations without the influence of formal guiding models.

References

Babbie, Earl R. *Survey Research Methods*. Belmont, Calif.: Wadsworth, 1973.
_____ *The Practice of Social Research*. Belmont, Calif.: Wadsworth, 1979.
Galinsky, Maeda J., and Schopler, Janice H. "Warning: Groups May Be Dangerous." *Social Work*, 1977, 22 (2), 89–94.
Garvin, Charles D.; Reid, Williams; and Epstein, Laura. "A Task-Centered Approach," in Roberts and Northen (eds.), *Theories of Social Work with Groups*. New York: Columbia University Press, 1976.
Hartford, Margaret E. "Group Methods and Generic Practice." In Roberts and Northen (eds.), *Theories of Social Work with Groups*. New York: Columbia University Press, 1976, pp. 45–74.
Hellenbrand, Shirley C. "Integration Takes Time." *Social Service Review*, 1978, 52 (3), 456–67.
Jayarantne, Srinika. "A Study of Clinical Eclecticism." *Social Service Review*, 1978, 52, 621–31.
Lang, Norma C. "A Comparative Examination of Therapeutic Use of Groups in Social Work and Adjacent Human Service Professions: Part 2—The Literature from 1969–1978." *Social Work with Groups*, 2 (3) (1979) 197–220.
Levinson, Helen. "Use and Misuse of Groups." *Social Work*, 1973, 18, 11–73,.
Lieberman, Morton A.; Yalom, Irvin D.; and Miles, Matthew B. *Encounter Groups: First Facts*. New York: Basic Books, 1973.

Roberts, Robert W., and Northen, Helen (eds.). *Theories of Social Work with Groups.* New York: Columbia University Press, 1976.

Rooney, Ronald H.; Rooney, Glenda D.; and Herbst, Alissa P. "Continuing Education and Graduate Training Needs for Group Work: Results of a Survey of Social Workers Who Lead Groups." Unpublished manuscript, School of Social Work, University of Wisconsin, Madison, 1980.

Rooney, Ronald H. and Herbst, Alissa P. "Use of Pre-Group Orientation by Social Workers Who Lead Groups." Unpublished manuscript, School of Social Work, University of Wisconsin, Madison, 1980.

Rose, Sheldon D. *Group Therapy: A Behavioral Approach.* Englewood Cliffs, N.J.: Prentice-Hall, 1977.

Wilson, Gertrude. "From Practice to Theory: A Personalized History" in Roberts and Northen (eds.), *Theories of Social Work with Groups.* New York: Columbia University Press, 1976, pp. 1–44.

Notes

1. Social-work–behavioral was differentiated from a psychology-based behavioral model to separate Sheldon Rose's model for social-work practice (Rose, 1977) from those developed outside the profession. Apparently the respondents also made this distinction, since only 16 percent (see Table 19.4) ranked both highly.

20

Video Stimulus-Modeling Methodology: A Format for Leadership Training in Social Work with Groups

Nazneen S. Mayadas and Wayne D. Duehn

This chapter presents a training methodology for group workers. Based on a review of the literature, it appears that the efficacy of social groups is far from conclusive. Galinsky and Schopler (1977) suggest that group intervention should be viewed with caution, since there is evidence that group experiences may be as detrimental to some individuals as they are beneficial to others. Similarly, Bednar and Kaul (1978) state that group therapy should be viewed as a two-edged sword, which can both hinder and help clients. Statements such as these suggest that components that impede or facilitate various group outcomes remain unspecified, and little, if any, attempt is made to define their operational measures in the ongoing context of practice.

Among the problems encountered in addressing this issue are inability to develop individualized outcome measures (Galinsky and Schopler, 1977; Hartford, 1971; Klein, 1972; anad Yalom, 1975) and replicable research designs (Bednar and Kaul, 1978). Furthermore, the theoretical and empirical literature uses "group work" both in education and practice evaluation as an undifferentiated, independent variable so that the

This chapter is an abridged version of the chapter "Leadership Skills in Treatment Groups" in Marshall and Kurtz, eds., *Interpersonal Helping Skills*, San Francisco: Jossey-Bass, 1982, originally presented at the Second Annual Symposium on Social Work with Groups, November, 1980, Arlington, Texas. The authors wish to acknowledge Mr. Edward Collier for his efforts in developing and testing the videotape "Selected Therapeutic Behaviors by a Group Therapist."

contributing factors to deterioration are as uncertain as are many of the factors attributed to constructive change. Thus, few educational models exist for imparting clinical skills for group treatment. Of those that do exist, none has been empirically tested. Casper (1970) presents a conceptual framework for the comparative analysis of one approach for ongoing group processes. His primary vehicle for teaching group processes is an experiential model within the classroom situation. Implicit in this approach is the assumption that group experiential learning is either equated with clinical-skill acquisition, or that skill competencies per se are deemed outside the purview of group work practice courses. Schwartz's (1964) contention that we cannot teach the skills of practice in the classroom, that we can only teach behaviors associated with the analysis of skills and with modes of theorizing about the nature of the helping process, typifies the latter stance. Competent group work demands practitioners who not only analyze or theorize but also *"do."* This is consistent with Truax and Carkhuff's (1967) criticisms that clinical training programs have taught theory and client dynamics rather than how to interact with a client within the therapeutic process. In an effort to redress this need, this paper presents a typology of group leadership skills, together with an educational video-modeling format by which these skills can be acquired.

Modeling and Group Leadership Behavior

Recent clinical and empirical evidence suggests that modeling can be an effective and efficient method for teaching and modifying complex social behaviors (Bandura, 1969; 1971; Bandura, Jeffery, and Wright, 1974; Blanchard, 1970; Doster, 1972; Friedman, 1972; Gutride, Goldstein, and Hunter, 1973; Green and Marlatt, 1972; Hersen, Eisler, Johnson, and Pinkston, 1973; Ivey and Authier, 1978; Marlatt, 1970; McFall and Lillesand, 1971; McFall and Twentyman, 1973; Muzekari, 1973; O'Conner, 1972; Rathus, 1973; and Young, Rimm, and Kennedy, 1973). When modeling is combined with video feedback and behavioral rehearsals, the rate of learning is accelerated (Ivey and Authier, 1978). In modeling, a person views the most appropriate interactional behaviors vis-à-vis the demands of the situation under examination. Such social learning is fostered by exposure to designed, simulated models, where performance is intentionally patterned in terms of clearly delineated behaviors that can be emulated. Once a learner has developed an adequate behavioral repertoire, increased reliance is placed on the use of verbal or pictorial symbolic models. A modeled performance provides substantially more relevant cues with greater clarity than can be conveyed by verbal description. A combination of both verbal and demonstrational procedures is most effective in transmitting new behavior patterns. The establishment of complex social repertoires is generally achieved through a graduated process wherein individuals pass through an orderly learning sequence that guides them in progressive steps toward the desired behavior. Consequently, the efficacy of modeling procedures will depend to a large extent on the care with which the modeled performance is programmed (Mayadas and Duehn, 1977a; Ullman and Krasner, 1965). In clinical group work and education of group work practitioners, few such programmed modeled performances exist.

While social-work practice and education are challenged to give increasing attention to quality control (Bloom, 1978; Duehn and Mayadas, 1977), it is regrettable that group work is virtually void of research directed toward examining the comparative effectiveness of varied means of instruction. Despite existing methodologies for differential decision making relative to teaching techniques (Kirkpatrick, 1969), education for social group work has relied on bland statements of instructor preference unsupported by empirical data. Thus, the problem is not only to determine the most effective means for imparting clinical group work skills but also to identify those factors contributing to actual skill acquisition.

Based on the above discussion, together with the authors' continuing attempt to move forward an empirically oriented competency-based curriculum (Duehn and Mayadas, 1977; Mayadas and Duehn, 1977b), this paper outlines performance criteria for the clinical group worker. Described here is the development of a classification system for categorizing selected group leadership behaviors using videotaped stimulus/ modeling procedures. Specifically, twelve essential clinical group work behaviors were operationalized. Further, through the use of video simulations, a tape was developed for use in training group leaders. The videotape provided stimulus cues for trainee reactions, as well as modeled responses to the stimulus cues. This format was used in the demonstration of the twelve leadership behaviors.

Selection of Leadership Behaviors

The twelve verbal leadership behaviors were selected on the basis of their existing import in empirical and theoretical literature, as well as the authors' clinical experience. The behaviors were:

1. *Reinforcement of Groups' Verbal Interaction:* Those leader statements that give recognition, support, and encouragement to member-member verbal exchanges (as opposed to leader-member communication).

Research indicates that an open, group-centered communication network has positive effects on member morale (Shaw, 1976) and interpersonal attraction (Cartwright and Zander, 1968), leading to goal achievement. Social group work literature similarly emphasizes the import of mutuality in group communication. Klein (1972) notes that group cohesion is a function of communication efficacy and influences goal-attainment activities. Hartford (1971) underscores the importance of "total communication" in that it both facilitates and symbolizes group cohesion. Further, through this interaction people act, react, and arrive at some coalescence that produces the groupness. Konopka (1963) provides numerous examples where worker's reinforcement of an open communication network is seen as the *central* principle of group work practice. While the literature is resplendent in anecdotal testimonials of how group learning serves as a "rehearsal stage" for subsequent group work practice, both this isomorphism and the extent to which actual clinical skills are transmitted remain untested.

2. *Reinforcement of Individual Responsibility:* Those leader statements that demonstrate, request, or emphasize members' responsibilities to the group.

Yalom (1975) identifies the importance of each group member being accountable for his or her own actions within the group process. Likewise, Northen (1969) notes that positive change is facilitated when members recognize their respective responsibilities for the group's process and outcome. Konopka (1963) indicates that a primary skill of any group leader is to extablish the importance of member participation and responsibility. She views these two components as essential for hastening the interactional process and for giving special status and encouragement to group members. More operationally, Klein (1972) advises that the leader is under a mandate to emphasize individual responsibility by explicating procedures whereby members are held responsible for their actions, and ultimately for group processes and outcomes.

3. *Establishment of Leader/Member Co-Evaluation Functions:* Those leader comments that make explicit reference to conjoint evaluative and monitoring tasks of all participants.

That all members take part in the evaluative and monitoring processes is an important ingredient for Northen (1969) and operationalizes the group as a model of democratic processes. For Yalom (1975), group passivity and dependency are antitherapeutic and more likely to occur when this self-evaluative norm fails to develop. The importance of involving members in evaluative function is also underscored by Gottlieb and Stanley (1967); Levine (1967); Phillips (1957); and Schopler and Galinsky (1974). Co-evaluation comprises a complex range of ongoing activities that are directed toward monitoring progress, assessing impediments to goal attainment, and reconciling group goals with individual preferences.

4. *Reinforcement of Group Importance:* Those leader responses that give the group a higher priority than other simultaneous activities and competing demands on members. Specifically, it refers to statements regarding group attendancem continuity, punctuality, completion of

between-session tasks, and reinforcement of group members' statements pertaining to the usefulness and value of the group experience. Yalom (1975) suggests that the ideal therapeutic posture is created when members place a high priority on the group experience. This notion is strengthened when the leader uses statements that explicitly model the group's importance. Likewise, Hartford (1971) speaks of the necessity for members to be anchored in the group, particularly during the formation phases, in that it serves as a prerequisite in building interpersonal trust and facilitating treatment outcomes. Rose (1972) notes that a primary means for increasing group attraction is the worker's reinforcement of regular attendance and group task completion.

5. *Negotiation and Enforcement of Treatment Contract:* Those leader statements that specifically refer to the reciprocal obligations of leader and members. In these statements the leader discusses and clarifies definitions of roles, mutual expectations, and the steps involved in the treatment process. So central to treatment are these contracting skills that Croxton (1974) maintains that they provide the platform on which the entire therapeutic process is built and by which members' accountability is measured. Northen (1969) notes that the worker's actions are crucial in determining group purpose. The establishment of a contract with individual members regarding the service to be provided is essential. Additional rationale for skilled performance in this area is provided by Garvin and Glasser (1974), who emphasize that contracting has both ethical and practical roots, with the former resting on social work's commitment to self-determination of the client and the latter based on increasing the likelihood of goal attainment and client continuance in treatment. Bernstein (1964), Frey and Meyer (1975), and Konopka (1963) have written extensively on the "working alliance," stressing both the importance of distinguishing this agreement from other relationships and advocating the importance of clear and precise messages concerning treatment goals, reciprocal obligations relating means to ultimate expectations. According to Hartford (1971), "setting a contract" is a crucial aspect of group formation and is essential in establishing criteria for alternative courses of action.

6. *Reinforcement of Intragroup Focus:* Those leader comments that indicate that immediate interactions within the group take precedence over those experiences that are or have been external to the group. Rose (1972) suggests that leader's verbal reinforcement of positive evaluative statements about persons in the group, group usefulness, and group activities result in: (1) the increased frequency of such statements, and (2) greater attraction to the group in which intragroup activities take precedence over other activities. Similarly, Yalom (1975) stresses the import of an inside focus by emphasizing that the immediate interactions within the group take precedence over external events and the distant past of its

members. The group leader for Klein (1972) plays a major role in constructing a therapeutic milieu by deliberately excluding those extra system inputs that interfere with the group's interpersonal processes. The immediacy of the events and the fact that they are "for real" make it possible for positive learning to take place. Events that occurred in the past or outside of the group are relevant only insofar as they are manifested in current group interaction. Giving credence to this skill is both explicit and implicit acknowledgement of limiting interventions to behaviors that are directly observable and amenable to change.

7. *Reflections of Affect:* Those leader verbal behaviors that selectively reflect observed affective states of individual group members. In Rogerian (1951) literature this concept is viewed as related to empathy, or being able to view the world from the client's subjective emotional stance. Such statements are considered important in the development of empathetic understanding. Pernell (1962) identifies empathy as an essential skill component for developing group cohesion. More operationally, Klein (1972) states that workers should actively invite, accept, and reinforce expressions of feelings and affect. "He operates on the level of feelings instead of intellectualization . . . and he reflects the feeling messages as well as being responsive to them" (pp. 193–94). Vinter (1967) describes the worker as one who relates to feelings, is responsive, and in so doing provides rewards or reinforcements to such expressions. While recognizing the importance of affect reflection for therapeutically oriented groups, Hartford (1971) suggests that it be used differently and with caution when applied to task groups. Through case illustrations, Konopka (1963), in a variety of settings, provides examples where workers reflect specific affective states of members.

8. *Reflection of Content:* Those leader statements that provide group members with information that the content of their preceding verbal statement has been heard. Consistent with literature on verbal conditioning, client content to a large extent is governed by worker's verbal behavior. Similarly, the group leader directs content foci by selectively reinforcing member verbalizations, thus maintaining the balance between group process and task achievement. Thus, an effective group leader seeks to help individual members improve their communication through active listening and modeling. Klein (1972) suggests that the worker restate in his own words what individual members have expressed. Likewise, Northen (1969) outlines procedures for improving the transmission of content among group members: "The worker is helpful if he knows the power of words to help or to hurt" (p. 179). Restatement, a therapeutic process suggested by Phillips (1966), is useful when ideas being presented are exceedingly complicated or are distorted by perceptual biases.

9. *Appreciation of Self-Disclosure:* Those leader statements that provide

information to members on cognitive and affective states of the leader and are facilitative of treatment goals. Expression of worker's feeling and cognitions in group sessions are powerful tools for modeling interpersonal openness (Jourard, 1964). Hartford (1971) implies that modeling procedures are a means by which the skilled leader creates a permissive atmosphere, frees informational exchange, and promotes acceptance of cognitive and affective diversity. An important skill for Klein (1972) is the worker's use of self. This is translated into verbal behaviors whereby the group leader actively shares his own feelings and cognitions rather than assume an impassive practice stance.

10. *Confrontation of Interactional Discrepancies:* Those leader comments that point out discrepancies between attitudes, thoughts, or behaviors of individual members. Confrontative skills, regardless of theoretical orientations are employed by social work practitioners to make clients more aware of behavioral and verbal incongruities. Its relevance to group work is of special significance in that perceptual distortions and behavioral discrepancies are less likely to be denied when subjected to the conjoint scrutiny of leader and members. This is consistent with Sundel and Lawrence's (1964) approach, where confrontation is employed only for observable behavioral discrepancies. Klein (1972) operationalizes worker confrontation techniques by listing a series of questions designed to help members assess the group situation, their behavior in the group, and the appropriateness of behavior in the context of contracted treatment goals. In this process, members become aware of what the situation is, what they actually do, and what they can accomplish. Vinter (1974) also speaks of the worker's task of confronting group members with inconsistencies between their behaviors and the long-term consequences of such actions. From a behavioral perspective, Rose (1972) suggests that confrontation be used as a punishment procedure to bring deviant behavior into conformity with group norms and goals.

11. *Modification of Negative Labeling:* Those worker statements that shift members' interpersonal negative evaluations of each other to situation-specific descriptions of undesirable behaviors. Such statements provide members safety from fears of unrestrained attack and hostility, create a group norm that distinguishes behaviors from innate personality characteristics, and provide specific information on only those interactional behaviors that are directly amenable to modification. Yalom (1975) contends that the very act of attaching a negative label to a group member constitutes an attack. It is the worker's responsibility to convert this attack into descriptive feedback. Klein (1972) states that workers provide a poor example if they are unable or unwilling to handle statements of hostility and anger. Through their verbal and nonverbal behaviors the workers must model not only their comfort with these feelings but also shift the focus from an attack to a constructive confrontation.

Sundel and Lawrence (1974) note that a requisite rule to be established by workers in group treatment is that members must refrain from hostile confrontation with each other. Thus, members are reinforced when they limit comments to observed behaviors without interpreting unobserved motives for behaviors. Hartford (1971) indicates that the innate effects of labeling must be controlled in that they are primarily designed to discredit individual group members. Leadership skills are needed to separate facts from inferences and distortions. Likewise, Konopka (1963) decries the group worker's support of labeling and indicates that it is more profitable to examine the specifics of what individuals do, rather than engage in fanciful guesswork of how personalities can be interpreted through behaviors.

12. *Reinforcement of Noncompetitive Member Attributes:* Those leader statements that explicitly acknowledge and enhance unique attributes and contributions without fostering competition. This skill operationalizes a central underpinning value of the profession—the uniqueness of the individual. Hare (1976) provides ample evidence to support the need for individual recognition in both socio-emotional and task-oriented groups. Implicit is the worker's responsibility to create a climate of mutuality where individuality is recognized and respected. Konopka (1963) identifies individualization in the group as one of the five basic key values of social group work methodology. Similarly, Northen (1969) states that the social worker must individualize persons within groups. Such individualization occurs when a person's needs, capacities, and environment are understood and taken into consideration by the worker.

Development of the Stimulus-Modeling Videotapes

Bandura's (1974, 1971, 1969) extensive research highlights factors that increase the efficacy of vicarious learning. Behavioral performances are more likely to occur when there is full, accurate, discriminative attention directed at the intended modeled behaviors: when modeled behavior is vivid, novel, and multiple; when the model is perceived as having high prestige, expertise, and demographic similarity to observer; when the model is rewarded for engaging in the depicted behavior; when the model is seen as having interpersonal attractiveness; when the observer has received a specific instructional set; when conflicting, competing, or nonrelevant stimuli are minimized; and when the observer is given feedback and is rewarded for modeling.

Given the above discussion, vicarious learning or modeling, as well as its procedural implementations, is easily achieved through the use of videotapes. Modeling through videotapes has great potential for training group therapists in that the array of complex interpersonal and social skills requisite for leadership can be identified, portrayed, systematically presented, and subsequently imitated, thus eliminating trial-and-error learning inefficiencies so characteristic of many training modalities. Thelen, Fry, Fehrenbach, and Frautschi (1979) suggest that incorporation of video modeling promotes educational control, convenient use of multiple models, repeated observations of the same model, use of the modeling tape in numerous training situations, and the potential for self-administered learning.

In designing the videotapes the authors presented a stimulus situation as the cortex within which the leadership was to be enacted. Each leader response was paired with a contrasting nontherapeutic response based on recent research findings that suggest that portrayal of antithetical behaviors increase acquisition of desired skills (Ivey and Authier, 1978). The time frame for each paired episode was approximately three minutes. The therapeutic vignettes and their antithetical counterparts were enacted by individuals specifically trained through extemporaneous role-playing to portray explicitly the skills described above without the context of group interaction.

Rating and Reliability of Stimulus-Modeling Tape

Informal rating procedures were used as pretest measures to improve the quality of the stimulus-modeling tape. Judges taking part in this process were various faculty members and students at the University of Texas at Arlington. Feedback from this review led to several script revisions. The raters were also requested to note ambiguous and problematic content and technical flaws. Changes made at this point resulted in the deletion of extraneous script, so that the vignettes portrayed only those stimulus cues that elicited responses operationalized in the leadership typology. All twelve behaviors were approved for inclusion in the final tape. Interjudge reliability was established by using a one-tailed t-test, significant to the .005 level of probability. Interbehavior reliability was established through computing a Spearman's Rank Correlation Coefficient for each behavior, significant at the .01 level of probability.

Stimulus-Modeling Videotape Format for Leadership Training

In skill acquisition, learners first react to the stimulus cues and then are exposed to the modeled response. The format is presented sequentially.

1. *Verbal Instructions.* Verbal instructions are more likely to facilitate modeling when they both activate a person to respond and describe the relevance and ordering of responses. In order to ensure attention to instructional sets, verbal instructions are provided relevant to the specific skill practiced, concurrent with the stimulus cueing and various modeled presentations. Further, Bandura's (1969) research provides consistent

and decisive evidence that the subject's attention is a necessary precondition for learning. For example, the rationale for a specific skill is presented prior to exposure to the video model.

2. *Stimulus Cueing*. The stimulus protion of the vignette is presented to elicit trainee reactions and generate discussion.

3. *Modeling Videotape Presentations*. The video-modeled leadership skill and its antithesis are presented to the learner and subsequently discussed. It is essential that the learner be taught to recognize appropriate stimuli that elicited the video model's response. This is achieved through a series of questions where the learner is asked to identify the skills and their apropriateness to a variety of group therapeutic interactions. The modeling tape may be stopped at predetermined, selected intervals in order to emphasize specific cueing and behavioral components.

4. *Behavioral Rehearsals and Simulations*. The learner practices or rehearses the specific skill in a variety of therapeutic group simulations. These behavioral rehearsals are videotaped for playback, critique, and subsequent practice.

5. *Performance Feedback*. After these behavioral rehearsals are taped, specific feedback procedures are employed to provide learners with information on the quality of their performance. (Learning theory suggests that reinforcement is given for achievement before making suggestions for improvement.) During replay, the tape is stopped frequently to focus on selected aspects of predetermined behaviors of concern. Learners in the group are asked to comment on skill performance.

This unique combination of verbal instruction, viewing the modeling tape, and the immediate playback of enacted leadership skill for critique provides learners with a mechanism for verification of skill acquisition. Use of videotape feedback not only aids in correcting nontherapeutic behaviors, but it acts as a potent reinforcer for other desired behaviors already in the therapeutic repertoire. The steps are repeated until the leadership skill reaches the criterion level of mutual satisfaction for both instructor and learner (Mayadas and Duehn, 1981).

6. *Clinical Critiques*. Finally, videotapes of actual group-treatment sessions are submitted for clinical critique of leadership skills.

Preliminary Findings and Discussion

The preliminary findings reported here undertook to examine the results of the video-modeled procedures in the acquisition of leadership skills. The sample consisted of thirty second-year students in the Graduate School of Social Work. Data were collected over three semesters on three groups of ten students each from a seminar on group therapy.

The dependent variables reported here are five behaviors selected from the twelve-item leadership typology: (1) establishment of leader-member coevaluation function, (2) reinforcement of group importance, (3) negotiation and enforcement of treatment contract, (4) reinforcement of intragroup focus, and (5) confrontation of interaction discrepancies. The presentation of data on these five skills is arbitrary, based on practical time-cost contraints. Data on the remaining seven skills in the typology are currently under investigation.

The pre- and posttraining measures for the five leadership skills are displayed in Table 20.1. These data collected from videotapes on each student demonstrating the five leadership skills in simulated group sessions at the beginning and end of the semester. To control for effects, such as stage of group formation and problem focus, the same group vignette was used as stimulus material in both pre- and postmeasures. Percentage of behavioral occurrences were computed from ratings of independent judges and compared by t-tests.

Table 20.1.   Mean and Standard Deviations for Pre- and Posttraining Measures

Measures	Preprogram		Postprogram		
	Mean	SD	Mean	SD	$t(df = 27)$
Establishment of leader/member coevaluation function	4.18	1.91	6.76	1.46	2.57**
Reinforcement of group function	5.46	2.36	9.72	3.14	1.96*
Negotiation and enforcement of treatment contract	7.12	1.23	9.36	1.41	2.69**
Reinforcement of intragroup focus	10.63	3.16	15.28	2.39	3.63***
Confrontation of interactional discrepancies	3.76	1.79	6.91	1.62	4. 89***

*$p < .05$
**$p < .01$
***$p < .001$

As indicated by the results, subjects increased their use of all five leadership skills. It must be kept in mind, however, that these are quantitative rather than qualitative measures of leadership. While the data suggest that video-modeling formats increase leadership behaviors, it leaves unaddressed the question of their appropriateness and relevancy within the context of ongoing group process. Put another way, it only answers the simple question, "Are the behaviors there, and to what extent?" The latter concern rests on critique through verbal and video feedback.

The results of the present study indicate that not only is it possible to develop a reliable modeling videotape demonstrating leadership skills but also that such a technology can be effectively applied to ongoing training situations. Although this is a first step in determining the specific microcomponents of leadership behaviors, it is a prerequisite to determining behavioral relevance and assessment of effective leadership styles. The present study leaves these areas unaddressed as heuristic suggestions for future, more elaborate investigations.

While the acquisition of leadership skills has been satisfactorily demonstrated by the findings reported in this paper, establishing the effectiveness of these skills in various group situations still remains a function of clinical judgment. At this point, subjective impressions from clinical critique (step 5) suggest not only generalization effects from simulation to actual practice but also serve as a measure of goal attainment. Further, subjective ratings of group member satisfaction indicate relevancy and contextual appropriateness of leadership behaviors.

The advantage of developing such a system for training group therapists is that it reduces a set of complex behaviors into their discreet microcomponents. In addition, this typology may be profitably applied in studies related to client outcomes, leadership profiles of group therapists, minimum requisites for professional practice and the relationship of these leadership behaviors to content structuring, stage of group development, member characteristics, and group composition.

The presentation of discreet leadership skills via video-modeling formats provides a systematic and structured methodology by which knowledge of group worker behaviors can be acquired and, through practice, mastered at identified criterion levels. This is a departure from the more traditional educational approaches where didactic content and experiential learning are frequently isolated from each other and the onus of integration placed on the learner. Further, rarely within traditional approaches are competency levels explicitly identified. The educational model explicated here is only a first step in the direction of an explicit competency-skill-based program for group workers. This methodology needs to be tested within a variety of group work contexts with different theoretical orientations. The differential effects of verbal instruction, videomodeling, behavioral practice, and feedback need to be examined further through more controlled experimental procedures. More specifically, research is needed to determine optimal number and length of video presentations consistent with group leaders' information-processing capacity. Likewise, hierarchical ordering of skills, timing of exposure to model behaviors, practice performance, and other format components need to be specified in order to ensure maximum learning.

In conclusion the video-modeling methodology explicated here needs to be incorporated into training for group workers. Specifically needed are technological skills for developing modeling tapes, the employment of these materials in explicitly designed treatment formats, and assessment of their effects on clinical outcomes.

References

Bandura, A. *Principles of Behavior Modification*. New York: Holt, Rinehart & Winston, 1969.

———— Psychotherapy Based upon Modeling Principles. In A. E. Bergin and S. L. Garfield (eds.), *Handbook of Psychotherapy and Behavior Change: An Empirical Analysis*. New York: John Wiley & Sons, 1971.

Bandura, A.; Jeffery, R. W.; and Wright, C. L. "Efficacy of Participant Modeling as a Function of Response Induction Aids." *Journal of Abnormal Psychology*, 1974, *83*, 56–64.

Bednar, R. L., and Kaul, T. J. "Experimental Group Research: Current Perspectives." In S. L. Garfield and A. E. Bergin (eds.), *Handbook of Psychotherapy and Behavior Change: An Empirical Analysis*, (2d ed.) New York: John Wiley & Sons, 1978.

Bernstein, S. *Youth in the Streets*. New York: Association Press, 1964.

Blanchard, E. B. "Relative Contributions of Modeling, Informational Influences, and Physical Contact in Extinction of Phobic Behavior." *Journal of Abnormal Psychology*, 1970, *76*, 55–61.

Bloom, M. "Challenges to the Helping Professions and the Responses of Scientific Practice." *Social Service Review*, 1978, *52*, 584–95.

Cartwright, D., and Zander, A. *Group Dynamics: Research and Theory*. New York: Harper & Row, 1968.

Casper, M. "The Use of the Class as a Group to Teach Group Process." In *Teaching and Learning in Social Work Education*. New York: Council on Social Work Education, 1970.

Croxton, T. A. "The Therapeutic Contract in Social Treatment." In P. Glasser, R. Sarri, and R. Vinter (eds.), *Individual Change Through Small Groups*. New York: The Free Press, 1974.

Doster, J. A. "Effects of Instructions, Modeling, and Role Rehearsal on Interview Verbal Behavior." *Journal of Consulting and Clinical Psychology*, 1972, *39*, 202–9.

Duehn, W. D., and Mayadas, N. S. "Entrance and Exit Requirements of Professional Social Work Education." *Journal of Education for Social Work*, 1977, *13*, 22–29.

Frey, L. A., and Meyer, M. "Exploration and Working Agreement in Two Social Work Methods." In S. Bernstein (ed.), *Exploration in Group Work*. Boston: Boston University School of Social Work, 1975, 1–11.

Friedman, P. H. "The Effects of Modeling, Role Playing, and Participation on Behavior Change." *Progress in Experimental Personality Research*, 1972, *6*, 41–81.

Galinsky, M. J., and Schopler, J. H. "Warning: Groups May Be Dangerous." *Social Work*, 1977, *22*, 89–93.

Garvin, C. D., and Glasser, P. H. "Social Group Work: The Preventive and Rehabilitative Approach." In P. Glasser, R. Sarri, and R. Vinter (eds.), *Individual Change Through Small Groups*. New York: The Free Press, 1974.

Gottlieb, W., and Stanley, J. H. "Mutual Goals and Goal Setting in Casework." *Social Casework*, 1967, *48*, 417–77.

Green, A. H., and Marlatt, G. A. "Effects of Instructions and Modeling upon Affective and Descriptive Verbalization." *Journal of Abnormal Psychology*, 1972, *80*, 189–96.

Gutride, M. E.; Goldstein, A. P.; and Hunter, G. P. "The Use of Modeling and Role Playing to Increase Social Interaction among Asocial Psychiatric Patients." *Journal of Consulting and Clinical Psychology*, 1973, 40, 408–15.

Hare, A. P. *Handbook of Small Group Research*, 2d ed. New York: The Free Press, 1976.

Hartford, M. *Groups in Social Work*. New York: Columbia University Press, 1971.

Hersen, M.; Eisler, R. M.; Miller, P. M.; Johnson, M. B.; and Pinkston, S. G. "Effects of Practice, Instructions, and Modeling on Components of Assertive Behavior." *Behavior Research and Therapy*, 1973, 11, 443–51.

Ivey, H. E., and Authier, J. *Microcounseling: Innovations in Interviewing, Counseling, Psychotherapy and Psychoeducation*. Springfield: Charles C. Thomas, 1978.

Jourard, S. *The Transparent Self*. Princeton: Van Nostrand, 1964.

Kirkpatrick, F. H. "Techniques for Evaluating Training Programs." *Journal of the American Society of Training Directors*, 1959, 13, 3–9.

Klein, A. F. *Effective Groupwork: An Introduction to Principle and Method*. New York: Association Press, 1972.

Konopka, G. *Social Group Work: A Helping Process*. Englewood Cliffs, N.J.: Prentice-Hall, 1963.

Levine, B. *Fundamentals of Group Treatment*. Chicago: Whitehall, 1967.

McFall, R. M., and Lillesand, D. B. "Behavior Rehearsal with Modeling and Coaching in Assertion Training." *Journal of Abnromal Psychology*, 1971, 77, 313–23.

McFall, R. M., and Marston, A. R. "An Experimental Investigation of Behavior Rehearsal in Assertive Training." *Journal of Abnormal Psychology*, 1970, **76,** 295–303.

McFall, R. M., and Twentymen, C. T. "Four Experiments on the Relative Contributions of Rehearsal, Modeling, and Coaching to Assertion Training." *Journal of Abnromal Psychology*, 1973, 81, 199–218.

Marlett, G. A. "A Comparison of Vicarious and Direct Reinforcement Control of Verbal Behavior in an Interview Setting." *Journal of Psychology*, 1970, 16, 695–703.

Mayadas, N. S., and Duehn, W. D. "Stimulus-Modeling Videotape Formats in Clinical Practice and Research." In J. L. Fryrear and R. Fleshman (eds.), *Videotherapy in Mental Health*. Springfield, Ill.: Charles C. Thomas; 1981.

_____ "Stimulus-Modeling Videotape for Marital Counseling." *Journal of Marriage and Family Counseling*, 1977a, 3, 35–42.

_____ "The Effects of Training Formats and Interpersonal Discriminations in the Education for Clinical Social Work Practice." *Journal of Social Service Research*, 1977b, 1, 147–61.

Muzekari, L. H., and Kamis, E. "The Effects of Videotape Feedback and Modeling in the Behavior of Chronic Schizophrenics." *Journal of Clinical Psychology*, 1973, 29, 313–16.

Northen, H. *Social Work with Groups*. New York: Columbia University Press, 1969.

O'Connor, R. D. "Relative Efficacy of Modeling, Shaping, and the Combined Procedures for Modification of Social Withdrawal." *Journal of Abnormal Psychology*, 1972, 79, 327–34.

Pernell, R. B. "Identifying and Teaching the Skill Components of Social Group Work." In *Education Developments in Social Group Work*. New York: Council on Social Work Education, 1962.

Phillips, G. M. *Communication and the Small Group*. Indianapolis: Bobbs-Merrill, 1966.

Phillips, H. *Essentials of Social Group Work Skill*. New York: Association Press, 1957.

Rathus, S. A. "Instigation of Assertive Behavior Through Videotape-mediated Assertive Models and Directed Practice." *Behavior Research and Therapy*, 1973, 11, 57–65.

Rogers, C. R. *Client-Centered Therapy*. Boston: Houghton Mifflin, 1951.

Rose, S. D. *Treating Children in Groups*. San Francisco: Jossey-Bass, 1972.

Schopler, J. H., and Galinsky, M. J. "Goals in Social Group Work Practice: Formulation, Implementation and Evaluation." In P. Glasser, R. Sarri, and R. Vinter (eds.), *Individual Change Through Small Groups*. New York: The Free Press, 1974.

Schwartz, W. "The Classroom Teaching of Social Work with Gropus." In *A Conceptual Framework for the Teaching of the Social Group Work Method in the Classroom*. New York: Council on Social Work Education, 1964.

Shaw, M. E. *Group Dynamics: The Psychology of Small Group Behavior*. New York: McGraw-Hill, 1976.

Sundel, M., and Lawrence, H. "Behavioral Group Treatment with Adults in a Family Service Agency." In P. Glasser, R. Sarri, and R. D. Vinter (eds.), *Individual Change Through Small Groups*. New York: The Free Press, 1974.

Thelen, M. H.; Fry, R. A.; Fehrenbach, P. A.; and Frautschi, N. M. "Therapeutic Videotape and Film Modeling: A Review." *Psychological Bulletin*, 1979, 86, 701–20.

Truax, C. G., and Carkhuff, R. R. *Toward Effective Counseling and Psychotherapy: Training and Practice*. Chicago: Aldine, 1967.

Ullman, L. P., and Krasner, L. "Behavior Modification Through Research Modeling Procedures." In L. P. Ullman and L. Krasner (eds.), *Research in Behavior Modification*. New York: Holt, Rinehart & Winston, 1965.

Vinter, R. D. "Problems and Processes in Developing Social Work Practice Principles." In E. J. Thomas (ed.), *Behavioral Science for Social Workers*. New York: The Free Press, 1967.

———— "The Essential Components of Social Group Work Practice." In P. Glasser, R. Sarri, and R. D. Vinter (eds.), *Individual Change Through Small Groups*. New York: The Free Press, 1974.

Yalom, I. D. *The Theory and Practice of Group Psychotherapy*, 2d ed. New York: Basic Books, 1975.

Young, E. R.; Rimm, D. C.; and Kennedy, T. D. "An Experimental Investigation of Modeling and Verbal Reinforcement in the Modification of Assertive Behavior." *Behavior Research and Therapy*, 1973, 11, 317–19.

21

Evaluation and Multilevel Validation of Group Services: A Brief Review of Requirements, Problems, Options, and a Proposal

John H. Ramey

No amount of discussion of the values of social group work or social work with groups is of any vaalue unless we reformulate and reconfirm its importance and are able to convince the decision makers that services utilizing groups are of high enough priority and demonstrated validity to merit funding at a significant level of visibility.

Given group work's early and continuing identification and development at the heart of some of the largest and most important institutions shaping our concepts of welfare and our society, this is in turn surprising, regrettable, and unfortunate. On the other hand, it is understandable. Our society has changed drastically in this century. The great pioneers of these institutions, who were also among the recognized leaders of our cities and nation, have departed. The technically, highly competent professionals who have replaced them have for the most part focused on the organization and provision of the services rather than on their contribution to social development and their political support.

Groupwork contributed much more than its 5 percent share of members to the devlopment of the National Association of Social Workers (NASW) and more than its share to the Council on Social Work Education (CSWE) and to deanships of schools of social work. But, until recently, group work has been outvoted in the politics of professional methodological decision making right from the start. An increasingly conservative public, administration, judiciary, and social-work profession, particularly since the early Nixon days, have together made it much more acceptable to identify the individual as the source of personal and social problems and to focus resources on people-changing intervention activities. Social science and social work research has focused on validating these strategies. The demands of both public and voluntary funding sources in all areas of social services has been for more immediate, more specific, and more prioritized accountability for accomplishments and for productivity.

Group work has of course developed and adapted to an even wider variety of settings and problems. Integrated methodological approaches have focused on understanding the various social systems impacting a problem with an eye on strategies for intervention at those points in the systems appearing most amenable to effective and efficient change. These approaches have absorbed group work into the whole fabric of generalist social work practice negating its separate identity. Nevertheless, institutions focusing on service to and through groups persist. Further, there arppear to be significant differences in worker-intervention strategies, modes and activities that significantly differentiate work with groups from individual counseling and that require separate service structures, personnel, and evaluation systems.

Wide variations in purpose and the size of the intervention unit have made the measurement and validation of specific accomplishments in social work with groups itself a complex, often inconclusive, and infrequent object of rigorous investigation. Until recently, *Social Work Research and Abstracts* (hereafter referred to as *Abstracts*) reported only three to six articles per issue under the primary heading "Group Work." Contrast this with twelve to twenty-six per issue for "Casework" and six to thirty-five for "Administration." Only one doctoral dissertation in 1978 and 1979 focused on social work with groups. With the appearance of the new journal *Social Work With Groups*, the number of articles on group work in *Abstracts* has increased considerably. Most group work research has focused on the outcome of individual therapy or developmental change, often within the farmework of a remedial treatment model (in such fields of practice as mental health, mental retardation, counseling, physical health, or juvenile justice), or on the study of a single institutional program or on a particular concept. Inasmuch as the validation of group work appears to yield to research and funding much as other individual treatment activities by measuring the achievement of individual goals, it would appear to be on fiscally safe ground with public, business (insurance and other third-party payors), and voluntary funding sources.

In a continuing attempt to answer Tropp's question, "Whatever happened to group work?" (Tropp, 1978), this presentation proposes to focus on all the problems and strategies for validation of that larger group of more traditional agencies and services whose programs and purposes relate to the continuing development of healthy, socially concerned, responsible, and involved groups in a socially conscious populace and to working with specialized groups who are having particular difficulty with socialization or resocialization into successful roles in our society. These are the social group services of the settlements and neighborhood centers, Jewish community centers, Catholic youth organizations, YMCAs, YMHAs, YWCAs, YWHAs, boys' and girls' clubs, Urban Leagues, International Centers, camps, and similar organizations. Scouting programs (Boy and Girl Scouts, Campfire Girls) and 4-H Clubs are similar but present special problems through the extensive use of volunteer leadership, which must also be considered. In general, such services and programs, except 4-H, are funded through voluntary contributions, primarily through the United Way.

For several decades, voluntary contributions for such services and programs have not increased at the rate of population increase or economic inflation and have not expanded to be able to meet new needs in an increasingly complex and troubled society. The administrative perception is that priority use of funds should be to help people currently in trouble, and that increasingly sophisticated accounting of the benefits of services in relation to costs must be made to justify continuing and expanded fundings. The priorities planning systems used by some United Way's (UWs) have resulted in lower priorities for group than individual services (Creviston, 1979). Not only have these highly computerized, sophisticated political decision-making processes resulted in relatively and absolutely reduced funding, but these same computers have been used by researchers and administrators to provide "hard" data about the quality and quantity of other services. (We do recognize the challenge presented from similar sources by the "casework is dead" research movement.)

Government and foundation funding from various sources has also been available. In the past this has often been program-grant-oriented, as with the New York City Youth Board, Juvenile Delinquency prevention programs, the Haryou Act, Mobilization for Youth, and the Hard-to-Reach Youth Project. Increasingly, sources such as Title XX also have asked for effectiveness and cost-benefit evaluations, but these are primarily in terms of the achievement of individual-change goals. The usual responses to UW, government, and foundation demands have been to plead inability to provide such information, to provide inadequate information, to continue to provide older philosophical justifications (shades of Dewey, Lindeman, Addams, Coyle, et al.), to get on the political muscle to maintain funding, to give up or get pushed out, or to be subject to outside attempts to impose individual service evaluation procedures on group services.

The thesis here is that group workers must move away from a stance of resistance toward one of initiating the ongoing program evaluation in their own terms. They must be able to design and carry out those investigative procedures that will document the ongoing importance, value, and productivity of such services and programs in terms of recognized social goals. Perhaps then the social developmental and adjustmental goals (socialization and resocialization) and maintenance of the social fabric may be given a new vitality, a renewal of social validity and support. To say that this process will not be easy is an understatement. In a time of decreasing support for all social programs, increased support for group services will appear to come at the expense of other, more "worthy" social-welfare service constituencies.

In our own situation with a "priorities" planning and allocation process, "group social development" services are in "priority group five," lowest in a five-category scale, and they are fifth out of six within that category—next to last. "Youth Development—Troop Services" is fourth out of seven in priority group four, and "group social adjustment" is third in the same priority category. Projected United Way fund allocations are for a 3.5 percent decrease in priority-five services and a 2.8 percent decrease for priority four in 1981. Grant that in a poor fund-raising year, priority-one services will receive a 0.7 percent decrease, over a period of years group services have and will continue to receive less, while other higher-priority services receive more or are cut less. (Alternative proposals considered but rejected would have reduced category five by as high as 11.68 percent while incrasing category one by as high as 3.82 percent!) Since these allocations are constant-dollar figures that do not account for high inflation, it is obvious that it is almost just a question of who goes down the tube first and fastest. At the moment, group services seem to be among those headed for funding oblivion.

My inquiries into the allocations processes in other cities have indicated similar directions throughout the country. The decline appears to start with the American Association of Group Workers' (AAGW) merger into NASW. It was not purposefully done, but it is not incidental. The symposia on social work with groups are a major step in reversing the trend, as is the publication of the journal *Social Work with Groups* and the consequent enlargement of references in *Abstracts*. The most important part of our work is yet to come and has only been started, tentatively in a few places: that is, reestablishing group services as a number-one priority with the planning and allocations organizations, with the contributing publics, and with the social-work profession. This requires adequate documentation that what is done is of significance and quality and is successful. It requires the knowledge and acceptance of such outcome statements by decision makers. As one United Way planning staff member remarked to me, "What you may really need is a marketing plan" (see Lovelock, 1979). There is some truth to that, but the requirements go much beyond.

A search of the "Research" and "Doctoral Dissertation" listings in *Ab-*

stracts from 1977 through 1980 revealed only one listing (Doucet) related to general validation of group services. Interestingly, there is a significant reduction in references to studies in the three succeeding summaries of research edited by Henry S. Maas for NASW. In the 1966 summaries, William Schwartz reported studies of "Evaluations and Outcomes" in three classifications: "movement studies," "program evaluation," and "agency impact" (Maas 1966, p. 178–82). In 1971 Schwartz reported that "the picture is that of a few rigorous efforts in a fairly unproductive field" (Maas, 1971, p. 175). In 1978 Norman P. Polansky and Marilyn L. Kent reported (in a section on services, "Troubled People,") that interest in and research related to group dynamics has dwindled in all the social sciences" (Maas, 1978, p. 170).

Although in 1971 Schwartz had summarized 255 items of research literature under "Neighborhood Centers and Group work" (Maas, 1971, pp. 130–91), he was forced to report "the study of agency effectiveness has never been an area of considerable activity among neighborhood centers, and now that the classic self-study device has fallen into relative disuse, the output is close to nil" (ibid, p. 180). This was foreboding and should have been instructive.

In the area of practice research there has been a continuing if modest flow of increasingly sophisticated studies on the understanding and uses of groups in a wide variety of settings and in relation to a wide variety of clientele and problems. There have likewise been the few but significant theoretical contributions and summary works. But practice research validation does not constitute agency or service validation, whether specific or general, although it certainly provides the underpinnings. The abstract of a doctoral dissertation I have not yet seen, "Organizational Effectiveness in Voluntary Service Organization: A Study of Quebec Regional Council of Leisure," by Laval Doucet (D.S.W., University of Toronto, June 1978), appears to sum up the research problem as well as we have seen in its application to group service agencies. There is "no evidence that a general measure can replace a set of specific measures of effectiveness. It was concluded that there are serious methodological problems in dealing with overall effectiveness in small and changing voluntary service organizations" (*Abstracts*: 14(3) p. 50, no. 746). In addition, there was no evidence of a statistically significant relationship between the goal structures of organizations as perceived by decision makers and by professional staff.

What we propose is a multilevel validation approach. It would take into account the necessity for selecting optimum measures of effectiveness and efficiency in specific organizational service provision in relation to (1) practice research literature, (2) measures of specific agency service, and (3) measures to support public and planning/allocating agency acceptance of data. Just as the model of society held by a practitioner will determine the definition of the problem and the social intervention (Segalman, 1976), so will the models held by the planning/allocation agency determine the acceptability of the evaluation procedures and outcomes. By taking the initiative, an agency or group of agencies may at least be able to influence and negotiate the evaluation model and procedures. In this context one must realize that all evaluation is political. One must secure in writing the agreement to the most favorable terms available.

Two other notes before proceeding. The day of evaluating agencies as such is gone. Specific services are funded and evaluated. Likewise, the day of long intervals between evaluation and validation processes is over; it must be an ongoing demonstrable process. It will no doubt involve the use of computers to tabulate and analyze large quantities of continuing information.

For large agencies one could suggest an extension of Scott Briar's "clinical scientist" suggestion: A staff member should be free to experiment, measure, and analyze various approaches to work with groups of various purposes and designs within the agency as well as develop overall, ongoing measures of service effectiveness. It would be expensive at first, but it would probably pay off in the long run in effectiveness and support. YMCAs, Jewish centers, Scouts, and some neighborhood centers might be well able to afford this approach. It has some precedent in the type of research done in evaluation of a five-year MIMH-funded delinquency-prevention program at the Seattle Atlantic Street Center in the 1960s.

There are problems in bringing outsiders on the research staff that result in action-research tensions (Maas, 1971, p. 179): "the general frustrations of defining criteria of success, using researchers who are unfamiliar with the programs and hence unable to establish proper categories for data collection, the scientific interest in 'basic' research that often obscures the curiosity about specific program data and statistics, and the problems involved in generating reasonable conclusions from specific events" (ibid., p. 175).

One recently developing alternative is to bring onto one's staff an "applied sociologist," although this generally narrows the theoretical and methodological perspective, as does bringing on a reserach psychologist or other discipline-oriented researchers. Our preference is for the development of high-level social work practice research competence independent of any other discipline. We would of course expect a competence in group work also. With the developing surplus of Ph.D.s and researchers in the various disciplines in academia, this may not be a far-off impossibility, even if one cannot locate such competence at the M.S.W. level. These general in-house approaches can of course generate documents and news to secure recognition and support, although one must carefully avoid the kind of publicity once generated by a large agency under a headline to the effect: "Street Workers Create Fifth Column in Gangs."

A second approach is illustrated by the January 1978 report prepared by the Research Department of the Health and Welfare Planning Association of Pittsburgh, "The Role of the Voluntary Sector in Children and Youth Services in Allegheny County." Backed up by a nineteen-member "panel of representatives of the youth serving field" (public and private) including a faculty member from the University of Pittsburgh School of Social Work, the research staff examined "the changes which have taken place in services, clientele, funding, and scope (of youth services) since 1960. Included in this field are all of the major recreation and character-building agencies—the Ys, Scouts, Boys Clubs—as well as general casework agencies, multipurpose centers and the more specialized casework and service agencies serving children and youth up to the age of 24" (p. i). After exploration of agency data, professional service changes, and demographic data, the study concluded: "After much deliberation and debate, the Committee decided essentially that voluntary youth serving agencies should continue to do what they have been doing, perhaps more vigorously" (p. 23). The principal roles identified were (1) innovator, (2) advocate, and (3) standard setter. The impact and agency service response to several trends were explored: declining youth population, pervasive segretation, teen unemployment, teen pregnancies, decreasing presence of adults in many homes, and crises in public education. Changes in service organizations, definition, and funding support were explored. The impact of two basic movements was noted: stress on community-based noninstitutional services and "the struggle for equality, which has meant emphasis on the legal rights of children." (p. iii, 23). Several areas were defined for further exploration: the impacts of (1) pluralism (mergers), (2) centralization, (3) dependency, and (4) effectiveness (pp. vi, 24). Overall it was a reasonable, broad-brush, issue-oriented unifying report and process, and it appeared to strengthen the base for continued high-level support for group services in Pittsburgh as part of an overall plan for services to youth. As part of the Planning Council's overall strategy for validating services, it was a most appropriate approach. Earlier studies had focused on aging and housing, and later studies would pick up other service areas.

Another, more innovative approach is represented by the goal-formulation comparative-evaluation approach to "quantitative measurements in Group Services—Social Developments" prepared by the research staff of United Way of Metropolitan Chicago over a four-year period under the auspices of first a task force and then a special seven-person committee of agency personnel. Russell Hoegrefe was the chairman and Jean E. Bedger was Director of Evaluation Research.

Using the 1948 American Association of Group Workers' (AAGW) definition of group work as its base, service objectives were defined:

> a. To provide opportunities for the development of satisfying social experiences, relationships and skills.
> b. To provide opportunities for the development and expression of artistic or other talents.
> c. To develop leadership skills.
> d. To enhance capabilities for democratic group participation and decision making.
> e. To provide new educational, cultural and environmental experiences.

In conformance with the Community Fund, now United Way's purpose to develop evaluation systems for all funded services, the purposes of this effort were further delineated by the special committee.

Initial Purposes

1. The purpose was to develop indicators of effectiveness of group services.
2. To distinguish between effective and less satisfactory service as perceived by the consumer-participants.
3. To look at satisfactory and less satisfactory service as perceived by the providers of the service.
4. To ultimately evaluate levels of effectiveness of service among agencies.
5. To have a system flexible enough to cover a variety of activities and members.

The goal of the field test was to analyze the information and to identify factors that can be used to evaluate the service. (pp. 2–3)

Two goal-oriented, copyrighted questionnaires were developed: "The members' questionnaire included thirteen questions with forty-five choices. The group leaders' questionnaire related to the same goals and activities using twenty-eight questions and seventy-two choices. In addition, a method for ranking groups and leaders by supervisors was developed. The questionnaires contained both forced choice and open ended items" (p. 6). Two consultants were hired to process and analyze the more than 10,000 responses expected in the project following a rigorous methodology. Twenty agencies nominated 3,864 groups, which, through random sampling and technical editing, became 707 groups in the final analysis. Full correlations of all data were completed. As a result of the field trial, the questionnaires were revised for the next-round study. Specific outcomes are interesting but not the focus of this presentation. Nevertheless, it is significant that the conclusions state: "The descriptive data provide new information about groups and agencies, but do not evaluate the quality of those services," and "the person-centered goals arose as the significant input and outcome of group services" (p. 56).

My investigation of the literature of the United Way of America and the files of its local affiliate, as well as a call to the national office, have failed to turn up any current, similar efforts. This is in spite of several excellent program-evaluation texts, several new journals, and articles as far back as Zalba and Stein's efforts, which Schwartz hoped (in Maas, 1971) would have applicability to group services.

Another important alternative is the use of the "true experimental" and other rigorous designs. (See Kushler and Davidson, (1979); Ross, Freeman, and Wright, (1979). The application of the clinical-scientist concept might enhance its possibilities, however. Still, there are legal, ethical, political, and practical considerations that limit the use of true experimental and other rigorous designs even in casework, let alone in group work (Koss and VanHouten, 1978).

In both instances—Pittsburgh and Chicago—it is obvious that the study design matches the expectations of the decision-making/planning body as well as the agencies whose services are being studied. The constituency was well understood by both sides and an agreed-upon, appropriate rationality was applied. Undoubtedly, both cities will change the investigations in the future, perhaps radically, but probably incrementally. Whichever approach an agency, group of agencies, United Way, or other planning organization takes, it is important that we choose and proceed with the business of the scientific and political validation of group services. Otherwise, group work may be at risk, if it is not already. Joel Fischer's admonition to casework is applicable to group work as well when he suggests that without a focus on the validity of casework, there is the probability of the outside imposition of change on the profession. Our job is to validate what Frankel and Sundel have described as the more traditional and important uses of groups that have been neglected in the face of the use of groups for clinical purposes.

Our own plan and hope is to proceed with the dual focus modified from both of the studies described and to encourage agencies to develop more research-oriented practice. In the face of other demands, diminishing resources, the probable challenge to the current resource-distribution ratings, and the probable costs of such an effort, in spite of some halting efforts, we have not begun the larger study.

What we perceive as necessary in the near future is the development of multilevel validation processes consisting of the following:

1. Related studies from the research literature
2. Demographic analysis of population and related incidence of problems and need
3. Goal-achievement studies of types of services in specified agencies, communities, and groups
4. "Clinical" investigation of improvements in group service provision
5. Quantitative investigation of continuing group services

We hope to move on it soon and hope other agencies and professionals can too. In the meantime, we hope to gather the experiences of others and to share theirs.

References

Bedger, Jean E. "Group Services—Social Development: A Study of 707 Groups and Leaders," Chicago, Ill.: United Way of Metropolitan Chicago, January 1979 (mimeographed).

Creviston, Richard, L. "Setting Priorities in Akron," *Community Focus*, October 1979, 3 (8), 2–4.

Doucet, Laval. "Organizational Effectiveness in Voluntary Service Organization: A Study of Quebec Regional Council of Leisure." Toronto, D.S.W., June 1978.

Fischer, J. "Does Anything Work?" *Journal of Social Service Research*, 1978.

Frankel, A. J., and Sundel, M. The Grope for Group: Initiating Individual and Community Change, *Social Work with Groups*, 1 (4), (1978), 399–405.

Health and Welfare Planning Association. "The Role of the Voluntary Sector in Children and Youth Services in Allegheny County." Pittsburgh: Health and Welfare Planning Association, January 1978 (mimeographed).

Koss, Margo Percival, and VanHouten, Therese A. "Measuring the Effects of Human Services on the Lives of Clients." *Community Focus*, March 1978, 2 (2), 27–30.

Kushler, M. G., and Davidson, W. S. Using Experimental Designs to Evaluate Social Programs. *S. W. Research and Abstracts*, 1979, 15 (1), 27–32.

Lovelock, Christopher H. "Marketing for Nonprofits." *Community Focus*, July 1979, 3 (4), 19–22.

Maas, Henry S. (ed.), *Five Fields of Social Service: Reviews of Research*. New York: National Association of Social Workers, 1966.

_____ *Research in the Social Services: A Five-Year Review*. New York: National Association of Social Workers, 1971.

_____ *Social Service Research: A Review of Studies*. Washington, D.C.: National Association of Social Workers, 1978.

Rossi, Peter H.; Freeman, Howard E.: and Wright, Sonia R. *Evaluation: A Systematic Approach*. Beverly Hills: Sage Publications, 1979.

Segalman, R. "Theoretical Models of Social Structure and the Practice of Social Work." *Arete*, 1976, 4 (1), 37–50.

Tropp, E. "Whatever Happend to Group Work?" *Social Work with Groups*, 1978, 1 (1), 85–94.

Index

275

Contributors

Paul H. Glasser, Ph.D., is Professor and Dean of the Graduate School of Social Work at The University of Texas at Arlington, having served on the faculty at the University of Michigan for 20 years, much of that time as Head of the Social Group Work Program. He has had extensive social work practice and research experience and has been a Fulbright-Hays Scholar in the Philippines, Italy, and Australia. In addition to being author and co-author of many journal articles, his publications include *Individual Change Through Small Groups* with Sundel, Sarri, and Vinter, and *Families in Crisis*, completed with his wife Lois N. Glasser. He has been the editor of several social work and social science journals including *Social Work With Groups* and was senior editor, responsible for all of the articles on social work practice of the 1971 edition of the *Encyclopedia of Social Work*. He continues to be interested in social work practice, the family, poverty, and, most recently, ethical and moral issues of the profession.

Nazneen Sada Mayadas, D.S.W., is Professor of Social Work at The University of Texas at Arlington. She has considerable experience, and has published widely, on the integration of videotape technology with social work practice, training, and research, specifically as it applies to individuals and small groups. She has developed a number of stimulus/modeling videotapes for the training of clinicians and research in the field of interpersonal behaviors. Dr. Mayadas served for four years in the United Nations in Geneva, as Chief of Social Services in the Office of the High Commissioner for Refugees. In this capacity she had worldwide responsibilities for supervising and coordinating the social services aspects of the refugee program. Her interest in refugees and transcultural social work is ongoing and she continues to present papers and publish articles in this area of social work practice.

Rodolfo Arevalo, M.S.W., Ph.D., Associate Vice-President for Academic Affairs and Professor, Social Work, California State University, Los Angeles.

John A. Brown, Ph.D., Professor, Social Work, San Jose State University.

Catherine Cobb, M.S.W., Private Practitioner, Edmonds, Washington. Cofounder, Divorce Lifeline's Children's Program, Seattle, Washington.

Louis A. Colca, Associate Professor, Social Work, State University of New York at Buffalo. Consultant/Trainer, New York State Child Welfare Institute.

Wayne D. Duehn, Ph.D., Professor, Social Work, The University of Texas at Arlington.

Paul H. Ephross, Ph.D., Professor, Social Work, University of Maryland, Baltimore.

Roland Etcheverry, M.S.W., Ph.D., Assistant Professor, Social Work, University of New York at Albany.

Maeda J. Galinsky, M.S.W., Ph.D., Professor, Social Work, University of North Carolina at Chapel Hill.

James A. Garland, M.S.S.W., Professor, Social Work, Boston University.

Charles Garvin, Ph.D., Professor, Social Work, The University of Michigan.

Martha E. Gentry, Ph.D., Associate Professor, Social Work, University of Kentucky.

Margaret E. Hartford, Ph.D., Professor Emeritus, Gerontology and Social Work, University of Southern California.

Alissa Herbst, M.S.S.W., University of Wisconsin.

Hisashi Hirayama, D.S.W., Professor, Social Work, University of Tennessee, Memphis.

Man Keung Ho, Ph.D., Professor, Social Work, University of Oklahoma. Director, Moore Transcultural Family Study Center.

Rebecca Parsons McCoy, L.C.S.W., M.S.G., Caseworker and Volunteer Coordinator, Jewish Family Services, Valley Storefront, North Hollywood, California.

Henry W. Maier, Ph.D., Professor Emeritus, Social Work, University of Washington.

Francis J. Peirce, Ph.D., Professor, Social Work, University of Oklahoma; Private Practitioner, Shawnee, Oklahoma.

Ruby B. Pernell, Ph.D., Professor Emeritus, Social Work, Case Western Reserve University.

John H. Ramey, M.A.S.A., Associate Professor, Social Work, University of Akron.

Ronald H. Rooney, Ph.D., Associate Professor, Social Work, University of Minnesota.

Karen Rosenzweig, M.S.S.W., University of Wisconsin.

Emily Tiktin Schoenfelder, M.S.W., Associate Professor, Social Work, University of North Carolina at Chapel Hill.

Janice H. Schopler, M.S.W., Associate Professor, Social Work, University of North Carolina at Chapel Hill.

Max Siporin, Ph.D., Professor Emeritus, Social Work, State University of New York at Albany.

Ellen Stacy, M.S.S.W., University of Wisconsin.

Martin Sundel, Ph.D., Professor, Social Work, University of Texas at Arlington.

Sandra Stone Sundel, M.S.S.W., Private Practitioner, Dallas, Texas.

Ronald W. Toseland, Ph.D., Associate Professor, Social Work, State University of New York at Albany.

Hugh Vaughn, Ed.D., Associate Professor, Social Work, University of Tennessee, Memphis.